D0754408

A FUTURE
FOR THE
HISTORICAL
JESUS

A FUTURE FOR THE HISTORICAL JESUS

THE PLACE OF JESUS
in PREACHING AND THEOLOGY

Leander E. Keck

ABINGDON PRESS/Nashville and New York

A FUTURE FOR THE HISTORICAL JESUS

Copyright © 1971 by Abingdon Press

ISBN 0-687-13883-3
Library of Congress Catalog Card Number: 70-148073

SET UP, PRINTED, AND BOUND BY THE
PARTHENON PRESS, AT NASHVILLE,
TENNESSEE, UNITED STATES OF AMERICA

for my sons
Stephen and David

CONTENTS

Foreword 9

List of Abbreviations 15

1 Jesus in the Hands of Determined Critics 17

    I. Who Is the "Historical Jesus"?
    II. The Validity of Our Question
    III. The Road Ahead

2 The Historical Jesus and the Character of Faith 47

    I. The Contour of a Debate
    II. The Proposed Mode: Trust
    III. The Potential of Trust

3   The Historical Jesus and the Gospel 100

    I.   What Is "Gospel"?
    II. Gospel in the Early Church
    III. The Historical Jesus as a Question

4   The Historical Jesus and Salvation 154

    I.   Toward a Rehabilitation of the Issue
    II. Models of Salvation Through Jesus
    III. Salvation by Trust in Jesus

5   The Historical Jesus and the Character of God 208

    I.   The Legitimacy of the Question
    II. The God of Jesus
    III. Jesus, the Parable of God

Epilogue 261

Index 267

FOREWORD

CAVEAT LECTOR

"The theologian's passion is more easily devoted to talking than to hearing, and expends itself in the impatience in which we talk past each other rather than in the patience with which we must listen to each other."

GERHARD EBELING

[Penemue, one of the angels] "instructed mankind in writing with ink and paper, and thereby many sinned from eternity to eternity and until this day. For men were not created for such a purpose, to give confirmation to their good faith with pen and ink."

BOOK OF ENOCH 69:9-10

Odd as it may seem, it is by no means certain that the historical Jesus has a future in preaching and theology. Despite the steady stream of books and articles about Jesus, many reflecting the rejuvenated and reformulated "Quest," it is far from clear that preaching is being vitalized by the work of historians or that theology is being reshaped by it. Not even the so-called radical theology, which retained Jesus as its North Star, succeeded in providing a future for Jesus *post mortem dei*. So it may readily appear foolhardy to propose that the future lies with the historical Jesus, for it is widely assumed that "the search for the real Jesus" (to use title of C. C. McCown's book) is a dead-end street. How can the historical Jesus occupy a central role in sermon and theology if the historians cannot set before us the authentic Jesus himself?

9

Besides, why preach the historical Jesus from ancient rural Galilee to secularized megalopolitan men preoccupied with making a future for themselves? What has he to do with urban planning, population control, air pollution, and thermonuclear war? As if that were not objection enough, is it not the case that the root problem today is the possibility of valid "God talk" at all? Under these conditions, talk of the historical Jesus might imply either a diversionary move, or a retreat to views long since shown to be untenable, or worse still, sheer pietism or traditionalism in sophisticated garb. Or are these impressions premature?

There is a sense, of course, in which the theme needs no justification, for whatever else one may accuse Christians of, their (our) preoccupation with Jesus appears endemic and irradicable. But that is just the point! Is this penchant for appealing repeatedly to Jesus warranted? Is *all* Christian talk of Jesus responsible?

But even the givenness of Christian concern for Jesus is not able to dispel suspicions, especially in light of recent theological history. Consequently, we must not only think through the place of Jesus but evaluate the place that has been assigned to him already. Accordingly, a critical, and, at times, polemical, tone cannot be eschewed.

It cannot be claimed that this book embodies permanent certitudes or non-negotiable positions throughout. It is, rather, a proposal and an exploration that gathers into itself reflections and analyses that have been mulled over for more than five years. Bringing them into something of a coherent form is partly a way of ascertaining where my own thoughts have been tending, and partly a way of inviting others—preachers and theologians as well as fellows in the New Testament guild —to think through again a perennial matter. These chapters represent more a progress report than a finished product, as those who read and heard earlier drafts will quickly note.

By inviting a wide range of readers to participate, I hope to expand their responsibility. In this country, far too many preachers and pastors see themselves primarily as consumers in the theological and academic market, led willy-nilly by what is hawked this year as new theology; repeatedly they are are reminded that they must "keep up"—that is, buy the latest books (including this one, of course)—as if they were not participants in the theological process but only its beneficiaries, as if the life of the church had nothing to contribute to theological work. Not many physicians would view their practice this way. Still, the longer the preacher thinks of himself in this mode, the more true it will become. But the pastor needs to be a working theologian in order to be an effective preacher. This conviction explains, in part, why I have borne down so heavily on Chapter 3. The professional theologian—and I use the word in its widest sense—is not in a totally dissimilar situation, for despite satisfactions one may derive from his disdain for the church (given the character of today's church, this is the cheapest of sports), it is questionable whether he can avoid giving an accounting to the Christian community (not merely contemporaries!) for the import of his work. Or is the theological task and labor legitimated only by "the world out there"; is the theologian accountable only to the academic fraternity? Whatever be the prospects for the historical Jesus, I suspect that neither the church (in the sense of the Christian community) nor the theological peer group will have a future in isolation from the other. Who heeds a preacher if what he says lacks cogency and power? Who heeds a theologian if he speaks only for himself to anyone in earshot? When this situation obtains, both are expendable; they exist only so long as cultural momentum permits them to legitimate themselves.

I am not unaware that whoever undertakes to elicit conversation on so wide a front makes himself exceedingly vulnerable, for experts in the several disciplines touched here can easily fill the margins with references to unattended literature and considerations. Apart from the fact that I do not claim to record all thoughts that have passed through my mind or to note all that I have read (this may relieve reviewers of the need to call the matter to the attention of *their* readers!), I

11

assume that the difference between a learned quibbler and a serious student needs no explanation. Moreover, since despite numerous revisions something of the public lecture style should remain, directness and simplicity were considered essential even on a printed page. Still, the legitimating paraphernalia of the scholar's guild are not wanting—the footnotes. Nowadays, unfortunately, they appear to confer not only authority but status, so that frequently they suspend from each phrase like so many scalps dangling from a Sioux belt. Still, despite the many matters not noted, they may allow the reader to sense the variety of colleagues whose work has contributed to these reflections. Above all, their location should not be taken as a sign of unimportance.

I have alluded to the morphology of these chapters. The book had its actual genesis in a single lecture given at Wake Forest University in October, 1965. Shortly thereafter, this was developed into two lectures delivered at Oberlin Graduate School of Theology (since merged with Vanderbilt) as the Kepler Lectures. By March, 1967, they were completely recast and offered as the Hayward Lectures at Acadia University (Wolfville, Nova Scotia). Among the suggestions received then was one stressing the need for a discussion of what the phrase "the historical Jesus" is taken to mean; Chapter 1 is a response to that observation. As the text later underwent revisions for publication it was shared again with clergy and laymen at Meredith College (1967), Methodist ministers in Indiana (1967), and with clergy and laymen in Knoxville, Tennessee, in 1969. How can one give public notice of the multiple contributions that were made on such occasions, as well as those which have come from students?

I am pleased, however, to record my sincere appreciation for the gracious hospitality extended to me at Acadia University. Its President, Dr. James Beveridge, and the Dean of the Theological Faculty, Dr. M. R. Cherry, and their colleagues together with the donor of the lectureship, Mrs. Hayward, provided a delightful occasion. That week in March, on the snow-laden campus in a picturesque setting, was an occasion whose memory I cherish. My sole regret is that it has taken so long to bring those lectures into their present form for the wider public. On the other hand, comparing what was said then with what is published now shows that there have been some gains!

LEANDER E. KECK
THE DIVINITY SCHOOL
VANDERBILT UNIVERSITY

LIST OF
ABBREVIATIONS

AGSU	Arbeiten zur Geschichte des Spätjudentums und Urchristentums
BhTh	Beiträge zur historischen Theologie
BJRL	Bulletin of the John Rylands Library
EvTheol	Evangelische Theologie
FRLANT	Forschungen zur Religion und Literatur des alten und Neuen Testaments
FsöT	Forschungen zur systematischen und ökumenischen Theologie
HTR	Harvard Theological Review
ICC	International Critical Commentary
JBL	Journal of Biblical Literature
JThC	Journal for Theology and the Church

JR	*Journal of Religion*
NovTest	*Novum Testamentum*
NTS	*New Testament Studies*
NTTS	*New Testament Tools and Studies*
RGG [3]	*Die Religion in Geschichte und Gegenwart, 3. Auflage*
SBT	*Studies in Biblical Theology*
SJTh	*Scottish Journal of Theology*
ThWB	*Theologisches Wörterbuch zum Neuen Testament*
TR	*Theologishe Rundschau*
WMANT	*Wissenschaftliche Monographien zum Alten und Neuen Testament*
ZNW	*Zeitschrift für die neutestamentliche Wissenschaft und die Kunde des Unchristentums*
ZThK	*Zeitschrift für Theologie und Kirche*

1

JESUS IN THE HANDS OF DETERMINED CRITICS

> "The greatest achievement of German theology is the critical investigation of the life of Jesus. What it has accomplished here has laid down the conditions and determined the course of the religious thinking of the future."
> ALBERT SCHWEITZER

> "There is nothing more negative than the result of the critical study of the Life of Jesus."
> ALBERT SCHWEITZER

If Jonathan Edwards' sinners had cause to worry about their fate in the hands of an angry God, the historical Jesus might well have been uneasy about his destiny among critics and theologians. Still, he has remarkable resilience and endurance. Ironically, today it is the critic who is insecure, for two centuries of work have not made it safe to speak of the place of the historical Jesus in preaching and in theology.

Today's discussion-situation is a theological Vietnam in which one is not sure from what direction the next salvo may come, or with what weapons or for what reasons,[1] despite the present lull in the fighting. Neither the course of individual battles nor the outcome of this war is predictable. However, this essay is not a series of war dispatches informing the home folks how the battle fares for or against the sons and grandsons

17

of Bultmann. Rather, it is an attempt to stake out central matters, to ascertain afresh where the battles are to be fought. The first ground to be gained concerns clarity with respect to the phrase, "the historical Jesus." Not until this is in hand, even tentatively, can we move to the next objective—his place in the sermon and in theological discourse.

I. Who Is the "Historical Jesus"?

Obviously, the adjective "historical" qualifies the noun "Jesus." Before the rise of historical criticism and scientific historiography, such a restriction would have been meaningless. Moreover, the phrase "the historical Jesus" has itself undergone historical changes that are not to be overlooked.

A. *A Changing Concept.* A century ago, when Friedrich Schleiermacher's lectures on the life of Jesus were published,[2] David F. Strauss, that scarred veteran of theological battles, wrote a rebuttal that he titled *The Christ of Faith and the Jesus of History*.[3] This way of putting the matter caught on and survived long after both giants were castigated by the lesser men who were their successors. Consequently, today in common parlance, "the historical Jesus" means Jesus "as he actually was" before Christians began to interpret him in ways he had not foreseen and which he may not have understood or tolerated if he had. In a word, "the historical Jesus" often has an anti-dogmatic, anti-theological, even anti-Christian ring. But this meaning was not invented by Strauss. In a real measure, it is the legacy of Hermann S. Reimarus, the eighteenth-century Semitist at Hamburg whose work was published posthumously by Lessing.[4] Reimarus contended that we must draw an absolute distinction between what Jesus said and did and what the apostles (Evangelists) reported him to have said and done. It is not overstating the case to claim that all historical study of Jesus is a critical appropriation of this view or a debate with it.[5]

Liberal theology, in its various forms, turned this negative meaning in a positive direction. For liberalism, if one is per-

18

mitted a generalization here, the Jesus of history offered a way of reformulating Christian religion without being bound to the classic Christian dogmas, such as atonement or Chalcedonian Christology. Jesus was the man whose religion of the fatherhood of God and the infinite value of the individual soul,[6] symbolized in the kingdom of God as a moral task or inward state, was made the basis of our own religion. Inevitably Paul was disparaged, and often played off against Jesus.

Yet all was not well. Near the end of the nineteenth there appeared two[7] attacks on the liberal appropriation of such a historical Jesus. Both contended that such a Jesus was not really historical and that those current efforts to reconstruct him were a lost cause. The first came from Martin Kähler,[8] who argued that the Jesus constructed by nineteenth-century lives of Jesus was an abstraction without foundation in history; moreover, he maintained that the real Christ was the one proclaimed from (Protestant) pulpits and appropriated in the believer's heart. Besides, the "historical Jesus" was nothing less than an illicit Christology bootlegged into the theology under the guise of history, since it reduced the biblical, preached Christ to the dimensions of a historical person to whom the laws of historical causation and psychological development apply as to any other person, whereas the Gospels present us with the sinless Son of God. In other words, he rebuffed Reimarus' claim that we are *justified* in distinguishing a factual, historical Jesus from the Gospel Jesus. More famous is Albert Schweitzer's repudiation of the liberal Jesus. After surveying the sweep of historical research, he showed that commonly the reconstructed Jesus was a retrojection of the scholar's own paradigm.[9] But in contradistinction to Kähler, Schweitzer insisted that Jesus himself could be recovered and that he was an apocalyptic preacher who was quite different from what both the orthodox and the liberals thought he was. In this way, Schweitzer's work renewed the tension between the historical Jesus and the Christ of Christian faith. But how did the Christ of faith emerge? Later, Bultmann formulated the pressing question: How did the Proclaimer (of the kingdom) become the Proclaimed (in the church's gospel)? [10]

The so-called new quest of the historical Jesus,[11] launched to overcome precisely this hiatus between the Jesus of history and the Christ of faith, emphasized the continuity between Jesus and the Christian message about him. Existentialism made this line of attack possible because it sees in Jesus' message an understanding of man's existence before God which is also found in the Christian gospel about Jesus, even though Jesus' own ideas were different from those of Paul, John, or other parts of early Christianity. The continuity between Jesus and the gospel, then, lies not in the claim that the church believed what Jesus believed but in the fact that common to both is the same grasp of man's existence, however this be conceptualized.[12] Making Jesus himself central to Christian preaching simply brought to the surface what was latent in Jesus' own message, even if the church did so with a mythological outlook that was strange to Jesus and to us as well.

What the course of historical study of Jesus has made evident, then, is that "the historical Jesus" is an ambiguous phrase and that its meanings depend largely on the actual setting in which it is used. It can mean (a) "Jesus as he actually was," someone quite different from the whole range of Christian interpretations. (b) This factual Jesus may be viewed as incompatible with true religion as well as with Christianity, as Reimarus in fact saw him; or (c) he might be viewed as the bulwark of true religion as the liberals did; or (d) he might be seen as bringing to expression in his own idiom an understanding of man's existence which is continued in a variety of Christian interpretations, including Paul's. Moreover, the very multiplicty of portraits of Jesus suggests that (e) the historical Jesus is not really an uninterpreted Jesus but Jesus as the historian is able to recover and reconstruct him,[13] that is, the historical Jesus is the historian's Jesus, not a Kantian *Ding an sich*. Our question, therefore, is sharpened: Is the historian's Jesus, the Jesus reconstructed by critical methods, centrally significant for Christian faith and thought, or is such a Jesus irrelevant or even inimical to it? If the historically recovered Jesus is significant, what sort of significance is appropriate to the historian's labor and result, as well as to the believer's commitment? This is the central theme we shall explore.

In doing so, it is absolutely essential to understand that we are not speaking of any particular historian's Jesus. What is under discussion is the generic enterprise of historical study and reconstruction. For the theological issue at hand, what matters is that Jesus be recovered and reconstructed by rigorous historical method, by a discipline that has widely accepted norms and principles of inquiry and reasoning. This is why we must get a clearer picture of how a historian studies Jesus and of the sort of results he can obtain.

B. *The Historian's Art and the Gospels.* Far too many discussions of our problem have gone askew because the nature of the historian's work has not been seen with sufficient clarity. It is one of the merits of Van A. Harvey's recent book, *The Historian and the Believer,*[14] that it shows forcefully the character of historiography and applies it to Jesus. Harvey rightly insists that there are no special rules for the study of Jesus, and that the historian's craft requires a characteristic morality of knowledge: he must provide adequate warrants for his conclusions. For our inquiry, three elements of the historian's task are of paramount importance.

The first is the need to maintain a skeptical attitude toward the sources, the Gospels, requiring them to establish their trustworthiness under careful scrutiny.[15] This skepticism in method is not to be confused with sheer hostility, of course, just as it in no way minimizes the need to be open to new ways of approaching the material. A skeptical attitude is to be not merely tolerated but nurtured because it is essential to historical work. Accordingly, the historian of Jesus measures the reliability of the Gospels as bearers of historical data about Jesus.

The second element is the need to answer historical questions with historical considerations rather than logical ones. For example, if we ask, Did Jesus think he was the incarnate Word? our answer must be subject to historical criteria alone. One cannot argue that since Jesus was the incarnate Word, it is

21

inconceivable that he knew less about himself than did the church. Rather, the only way the question can be answered is by sifting the evidence critically and consistently according to the accepted norms of historical study. And this, in turn, means building one's case by the same canons of accuracy and probability which apply to any historical figure (*pace* Kähler!). To return to the illustration, a person whose language and thought-world are thoroughly that of Aramaic-speaking Galilean Judaism does not use categories drawn from Greek philosophy or mythology to think about himself.

The third element is the obligation to account for the sources as they are, not merely to sift them for hard-core facts. Accordingly, it is not enough to discount Matthew's portrait of the Pharisees and Jesus; one must explain why he treats the subject as he does, namely, that he throws back into Jesus' own situation the sorts of tensions his own church has with the synagogue. Seeing this allows one to ask further, subtler questions—though difficult to answer: was there something about Jesus which led the church to develop such tensions? What is the significance, on the other hand, of the church's effort to deal with its problems by appealing to Jesus' precedent? Not until such questions are pursued has the historian done his duty to the sources, and not until they are understood can one speak reliably about Jesus. One of the major gains since World War II has been a clearer understanding of the Evangelists as theological interpreters of Jesus. Thus Wrede (see note 7) has been vindicated methodologically, whatever one might think of his actual conclusions. Redaction criticism,[16] the technical name for this enterprise, distinguishes the Evangelists' own use of the material from the traditions themselves and thus allows one to see the Gospels' place in the development of early history as a whole. Thereby the work of form criticism, which tended to regard the Evangelists as collectors and editors rather than theologians in their own right, has been corrected.

Now all this seems too self-evident, thus pedantic, when we have in view the historical quest of Socrates, Constantine, or Bismarck. Yet despite more than fifteen decades of historical work on Jesus, many Christians shrink from applying historical criteria across the board to Jesus. Two reasons lie behind this: one is that absolute claims are made about this man as the Word and Deed of God. The other is that it has been assumed that historical study will, and must, support these claims. Combined, these assumptions form an unstated but powerful syllogism:

    a) What Christians believed about Jesus is the truth.
    b) Jesus was a historical person.
    c) Therefore historical study will confirm what Christians believe.

This has been the traditional attitude against which all critical historical study of the Bible has struggled ever since the Enlightenment. Today's thunderstorms over the historical Jesus merely mark where the cold front has now moved since it first appeared over the Old Testament long ago.

In principle, then, what *sort* of Jesus will be reconstructed from the Gospels? Fundamentally, the historian's Jesus will not be simply a paraphrase of the Gospels, supported by learned notes. Inescapably, the historian's Jesus will be reduced in size precisely because he used the tools of his trade as we have sketched them.[17]

At this point, if not before, a characteristic objection is registered: "But the Gospels are works of faith! They cannot be treated like any other document." The first point is a correct fact, but the second is a wrong conclusion. The Gospels are indeed impregnated throughout by Christian faith; neither the Gospels as a whole nor the individual items in them would exist at all were it not for the faith of the Christian community, which transmitted the traditions about Jesus and for the sake of which the texts were written. But by no means does this prevent the historian from going about his task according to the rules. No historian works only with neutral, "objective" materials unaffected by the values, convictions, and conceptual horizons of those who provide them, be these materials diaries, eye-witness accounts, quotations, or nonliterary remains. In fact, it is precisely this limited, biased, partially inaccurate character of all sources of information about any person which

23

makes historiography necessary in the first place. The Gospels do contain solid information about Jesus, though the present form of the material may not be historically accurate.

For example, in Mk. 1:16-20 the stories of Jesus calling the disciples are so saturated by Christian faith that it is very difficult to work with them historically. They compress the account in such a way as to highlight what Christian preachers used them for: models of the call and response to Jesus.[18] (This is how speakers normally tell illustrations; they pare away everything but what is essential to the point.) The historian does not simply discard these stories just because they do not report the actual process by which Jesus acquired disciples, especially in view of a quite different report in John 1. Rather, he admits that we cannot reconstruct what happened but affirms, in conjunction with other data, that Jesus did summon followers to be in special relation to his mission, that they were drawn from a variety of backgrounds among the working class, that several may have been John's disciples previously, and so forth. While these conclusions are less than all four Gospels report, they are also more because they are critically ascertained and can therefore be used to draw inferences about Jesus (e.g., he did see the founding of a community as part of his task). Consequently, one ought not to be shocked, as Kähler was, to discover that the historian's narrative diverges from that of the Gospels at important points. It is precisely the ethos of the historian's art that requires him to follow the canons of historiography and not the canons of the Gospels. That, in fact, is exactly what "historical reconstruction" means.

But have we taken account sufficiently of the inconvenient fact that historians working with the same methods on the same texts produce widely divergent results? We shall see how frequently the multiplicity and tentativeness of results have fed the widespread rejection of the historian's Jesus for theology and preaching. At this junction, it suffices to say that this phenomenon of multiple results is nothing other than the historicity of historical work; that is, the shifting and conflicting conclusions manifest ways in which all historians and their labors are affected by the historical situation in which they work. However—and this must not be overlooked—in this regard the historian is not one hair's breadth worse off than the philosopher, theologian, or preacher, for historicity affects us all. Historians of Jesus carry no heavier handicap than anyone else. Just as the theologian's God-talk has no fixed Archimedean point but reflects his own historicity without diminishing his intent to talk about God as accurately as possible, so the historian intends his reconstruction to be an accurate comprehension of Jesus, and both the theologian and the historian are open to self-correction by means of the critical method itself. We should no longer be intimidated by the theologian's taunt, "But whose historical Jesus shall I interpret?" as if that made refusing to deal seriously with any historically recovered Jesus legitimate! This sort of objection has been around long enough; it is time to send it packing.

Preliminary observations such as ours might be regarded, in some quarters at least, as a return to an abandoned positivism in historiography which was dominated by a quest for "facts." In anticipation of such disdain, it must be said that those who advocate the so-called new understanding of history and of historiography (an existentialist view) themselves admit that the "new" does not displace the "old" but rests squarely on it. The allegedly new historiography intends to penetrate the facts, not merely to ascertain them and explain them. Such an approach seeks to understand the past by questioning it and thereby to come to terms with its inner logic, and with oneself.[19] The concern for the "new quest of the historical Jesus" rests precisely on the use of the old quest for facts, especially on the recovery of the words of Jesus, for without them the self-understanding of Jesus (or, Jesus' understanding of existence) could not be located in order to be compared with that of the kerygma. To check this point, one needs but note how frequently Ernst Fuchs, who presses the existentialist interpretation, relies on the work of Joachim Jeremias, who is by no means an existentialist, for the recovered words of Jesus' parables.

C. *Through the Gospels to Jesus.* It is not necessary to rehearse the procedures that are followed step by step in the study of Jesus.[20] We will, instead, comment on certain aspects of the process which are sometimes overlooked. This may also indicate my relation to the enterprise and to its unfinished tasks.

That the place to begin is with a critical understanding of the Gospels is clear. Nor is it necessary to emphasize the importance of text, literary, redaction and form (or tradition) criticism in doing so. They are assumed throughout. More important here is seeing clearly how attending to these tasks affects our knowledge of Jesus. For the sake of being clear, as well as provocative, five theses will be formulated and explicated in brief.

1. He who studies only the canonical Gospels does not understand them.
2. He who studies only the Synoptics and ignores John understands neither.
3. He who still makes Mark and Q paramount misunderstands everything.
4. He who relies only on Jesus' own words misunderstands him.
5. He who isolates Jesus cannot understand him at all.

First, he who studies only the canonical Gospels does not understand them. Three considerations, at least, justify this thesis.

(a) Since the canonical Gospels are but part of the Jesus-tradition literature, they must be read in light of the whole. Since 1947, we must add certain texts found in Egypt (Nag Hammadi Gospels)[21] to the previously known texts lumped together as "the apocryphal gospels," [22] as well as stories about Jesus and sayings attributed to him which are scattered throughout early Christian literature.[23] But why attend to extrabiblical sources when already canonical ones contain more material than the historian is willing to trust? It is not so much a matter of sleuthing for new facts or new authentic sayings, though this is not to be neglected, as it is the need to see the

Jesus tradition as a whole. Not until we do can we understand why our canonical Gospels exist at all and why they read as they do. For example, when one sees the whole range of texts that are called "gospels," it becomes essential to ask, Just what makes a text a gospel? How does the author understand this classification? Does he see it as a literary form of the good news (Mark), or has the word "'gospel" become the title for any kind of text about Jesus (e.g., the Gospel of Truth or the Gospel of Thomas [both!] [24])? In addition, we need to seek the tendencies that mark the transmission of the many traditions about Jesus. Form criticism called attention to the tendency of the tradition in its early stages to contract into essentials and in its later stages to expand again.[25] The clearer our knowledge of the overall trends in the transmission and use of the Jesus traditions, the sharper is the profile of any given story and of entire texts, including canonical ones. Just as the archeologist excavates carefully so that each find can be plotted in relation to the entire excavation, and to other digs as well, so the student of Jesus must relate each piece of Jesus-material to the whole Jesus tradition. Because virtually no one can do this by himself any longer, much more collaboration, and perhaps less competition, is called for.

(b) Since all our texts about Jesus were produced after Paul, and were contemporaneous with the rest of early Christian literature, the Jesus-materials cannot be read in isolation from the reconstructed history of the entire early church. Already Reimarus sensed that he could not portray a nationalistic Jesus without asking how such a person became the basis for a quietistic church. There has never been a reconstruction of Jesus which does not imply a reconstruction of early Christianity as well, for the simple reason that it is the church's texts which are being scrutinized and assessed. It is at this point that the third aspect of the historian's work exacts its toll (see above), for if one must not only sift the sources but account for them as well, he cannot evade the question of the development of the church in which the Gospels and their antecedents were used. Thus, for example, one must investigate further the implications of the fact that the same decade pro-

27

duced Matthew, John, Revelation, and I Clement shortly after Hebrews, Ephesians, and Luke-Acts appeared.

(c) In addition to the internal history of the church (not restricted to the history of ideas either!) we must reckon also with the cultural milieu in which the church transmitted the traditions of Jesus. Once again, it was form criticism which pioneered in this effort by using Hellenistic and Jewish forms of oral tradition to illumine the way the Jesus materials were transmitted. But what we have only begun to explore is how the conceptual milieu, the underlying suppositions of the several kinds of Judaism, and the diverse theologies of the Hellenistic world affected what the church believed necessary to say about Jesus and how it must be said. What matters is not merely how to talk about Jesus to those not yet Christian, though it includes this; it is also, and perhaps chiefly, a question of how Christians with these backgrounds will themselves think about Jesus.[26] After all, they did not deposit their Hellenistic or Jewish presuppositions at the door when they entered the church. But above all, it is time to study the Synoptic Gospels in this regard, for John is not the only one that responds to its environment. (Chapter 3 will venture several observations in this area.)

In short, it is increasingly evident that whoever undertakes to study Jesus historically finds himself pondering texts and motifs that cut across the whole range of antiquity. That is why whoever studies only the canonical Gospels does not understand what he reads.

Second, he who studies only the Synoptics and ignores John understands neither. Since the work of Strauss, John has been set aside because it is "too theological," and the historical Jesus has been recovered from the Synoptics.[27] But redaction criticism demonstrates that each of the Gospels is a theological work in its own way. It will undoubtedly remain the case that the Synoptics will provide the bulk of the materials for studing Jesus; still, today we jeopardize our understanding of the Synoptics if we ignore John.

Various test-holes indicate that although the present Fourth Gospel comes from the end of the first century, some of its materials come from the earliest days of the church; consequently, our Fourth Gospel is really the end product of a long tradition.[28] This requires us to ask how the oldest discernible layers are related to Jesus himself, and how this tradition-stream was related to the Synoptic one. If John did not know our Synpotics but knew some of the materials now in them (as is generally conceded), can it also be said that the Synoptic stream was cognizant of John's? Did they merely wave at each other across the street, or did they affect each other? In any case, one cannot ignore John completely if he wants to understand the Synoptics or reconstruct Jesus. By no means is this a call to return to the pre-Strauss era when John and the Synoptics were harmonized. Rather it is to say that we must pursue two questions: What are the historically reliable data embedded in John? [29] And, What is the relation of the Synoptic mode to the Johannine mode of presenting Jesus? In other words, just as we must see the entire sweep of the Jesus-traditions, so we must study the canonical Gospels together because what distinguishes John is not the dominance of theology but solely the kind of theology which shapes the narrative of Jesus.

Third, he who still makes Mark and Q paramount misunderstands everything. Despite William Farmer's arguments,[30] the priority of Mark has not been overturned. Nevertheless, our reliance on Mark's outline has been eroded completely. Again, it was form criticism which compelled us to gauge the historical accuracy of each item on its own merits and not to give presumptive weight to something just because it is found in Mark. Since Mark's outline is more theologically shaped than historically accurate, we can no longer use Mark to outline Jesus' career.[31] Since both Matthew and Luke use Mark's outline, more or less, and since John's is clearly not historical when taken as a whole, we have no way of tracing cause and effect in Jesus' career, nor of sketching his inner development.

Similarly, our refusal to make Q paramount does not reflect the fact that its existence is denied from time to time.[32] Far more important is remembering that we can no longer use Q to argue that Jesus was a teacher of moral ideals because certain of the more perplexing theological and eschatological materials are not found in it. One of the things to be investigated further is the underlying theological stance of Q and the relation of this to that of similar collections of sayings, such as the Gospel of Thomas (which has 114 sayings but no narrative) and its sources, and to the traditions of Jesus' teaching which lie behind the Fourth Gospel.[33] Since it is highly unlikely that any of these cycles of teaching material took shape without a christological base of some kind, explicit or tacit, there is no reason to think that in dealing with a Q saying we have a Jesus not yet Christianized. Rather, we may have a piece of Jesus tradition which a particular Christian theology could adopt with but minor changes in wording.

Be that as it may, what is at stake is whether one relies on documents or on individual traditions in whatever document they may appear. The whole direction of twentieth-century study has been away from the former and toward the latter. Though it is difficult to prove, one suspects that the old primacy of documents over individual traditions reflects the aftermath of the church's custom of associating the Gospels with apostles (Matthew and John) or with their associates (Mark with Peter, Luke with Paul). Now that it is evident that no apostle can be linked so closely with any of our Gospel texts, and that all of them are the work of unknown authors drawing on the traditions of the churches, we can no longer depend on any document as the presumed historical norm by which to measure the others or to reconstruct Jesus' career. To do so would be to misunderstand the entire nature of the Jesus tradition and to ignore the course of Gospel criticism. What makes a datum reliable is not the document in which it is found but its intrinsic authenticity as established by careful testing.

Fourth, he who relies only on Jesus' words misunderstands him. This ought to be self-evident, yet especially since Bultmann's *Jesus and the Word* critics have slipped into supposing that it is the words of Jesus which are truly important,[34] largely because they are easiest to ascertain critically. But this preoccupation with his words is quite inadequate.

(a) Ernst Fuchs has rightly insisted that Jesus was his own interpreter. By this he does not mean that Jesus explained himself, made himself the subject of discourses in which he justified what he said. Rather, he reminds us the Jesus' deeds are the context of his word,[35] that word and deed interpret each other. This is why Fuchs makes so much of Jesus' eating with outcast publicans and sinners. Moreover, an earlier book by R. H. Fuller [36] scored Bultmann for restricting his interpretation of Jesus to materials found only in the first parts of the Synoptics. The point is that the entire lifework of Jesus is the context of his words, that no interpretation of Jesus which restricts itself to an exposition of his teaching grasps the whole man. Unfortunately, for theological reasons rather than truly critical ones, Fuchs himself ignores the healing and exorcist aspect of Jesus' deeds.[37]

(b) Despite the new hermeneutic's penchant for emphasizing the event-fullness of word and the word-character of deeds, and despite its service in overcoming a positivistic attitude toward historical data, the fact remains that this entire discussion is set in motion by the need to relate Jesus phenomenologically to a Word of God theology, albeit a chastened one. Moreover, this theological mode appears to be incapable of penetrating what seems essential to that mode of theology in which Jesus himself moved—apocalyptic. I hope to show elsewhere that apocalyptic must be understood not as arithmetic speculation and visionary compensation for depraved religion but as a serious and significant effort to think theologically about God, created world, and chosen people. Whatever its limitations—and they are serious—it nevertheless moves away from the individualistic reading of Jesus and of faith which marks existentialism and its fondness for "word." In any case, it is unlikely that any mode of theology does justice to Jesus the Jew which has no place for a theological understanding of God the redeeming creator of things as well as of selves and for God the faithful keeper of his word to Israel. As we shall see, such matters are essential not only for an accurate delineation of Jesus; they belong theologically to the center of his significance. Unwelcome as they may be,

31

these motifs can no more be decreed to be marginalia in Jesus than unwanted results of medication can be dismissed as side effects.

(c) Given the momentum and direction of critical study, inevitably a premium was placed on ascertaining the very words of Jesus—the *ipsissima verba*.[38] After all, it was essential that we determine hard-core data that would not crack under scholarly pressure. Only in this way could one be reasonably sure that when he claimed, "Jesus said . . ." it was really Jesus who was being quoted and not the secondary tradition or Evangelist. But having made this point, we must also see that in the last analysis it is too restrictive. Is it not also possible for a reporter to formulate Jesus' point into a sentence that embraces what he said at greater length? One example is Mk. 1:14-15: "Jesus came into Galilee preaching the gospel of the Kingdom of God, saying 'Repent and believe [in the gospel] for the kingdom of God is at hand.' " This is almost universally acknowledged to be at the same time a formulation by the church and an accurate summary of what Jesus had to say. But is this the only instance? In other words, we need to pay renewed and continual attention to the non-genuine words that may nonetheless transmit sound tradition. Here, of course, one must be guided by the *ipsissima verba* if one is not to rehabilitate sayings without due warrant, but we need not remain restricted to them. A second dimension of of this necessity to loosen the tyranny of the *ipsissima verba* comes from the character of the church itself. Schleiermacher and his modern counterpart, John Knox, insisted that the effect of Jesus belongs with the man himself,[39] that to the event belongs its future, that which it brings into existence. What is called for is not obliteration of the difference between Jesus and the church, but release from the bondage of supposing that at every point the church and Jesus are incommensurate or of thinking that Jesus became the victim of the church as if from the first it did not consider itself also accountable to Jesus and to its tradition of him.[40] Here, too, great caution is required, but this aspect of our knowledge of Jesus ought not be ignored.

Fifth, he who isolates Jesus cannot understand him at all. What is in view here is not just isolating Jesus from the church but especially isolating him from Judaism, not only from what he produced but from what produced him. Both the fourth and fifth theses have in view the tyranny of the negative criteria. We have already laid the basis for our observations. The negative criteria have been used throughout the life of Jesus research, but have reached a certain prominence recently.[41] According to this method, that material is genuinely from Jesus which cannot be attributed to the early church on the one side or to Judaism on the other. Thus, sayings in which Jesus explicitly interprets his death are subtracted from the data because here the church formulated its theology and attributed it to Jesus. As noted, this was an absolutely essential step for criticism to take at the time. The same thing was done with materials that appeared to be "typically Jewish" or in which Jesus appears to reason as a rabbi. What was left, then, was that material which was explicitly or implicitly eschatological, and the resultant Jesus was inevitably either a consistent apocalyptic preacher or a non-apocalyptic preacher of eschatological parables but without a "Christology." Inevitably, the quest for distinctive materials led to a distinctive Jesus. And here my reservations begin.

(a) It is pure assumption to regard the historical Jesus as the distinctive Jesus, partly because this definition subtly erodes what we normally mean by historical. Instead of the distinctive Jesus we ought rather to seek the characteristic Jesus, not merely a Jesus rigorously consistent with elements peculiar to him. That is, we need to ascertain what was characteristic of him, and this may include a capacity to hold diverse motifs in tension. After all, what appears consistent to a Western university professor may not have been consistent to a first-century Aramaic-speaking preacher of the Kingdom who was at home in a different kind of logic.[42] Again, it is not possible or necessary to abandon the negative criteria, but it is possible and necessary to emancipate oneself from their tyranny. In doing so, it is again mandatory to

33

proceed with care. Yet it is only in this direction that the truly historical Jesus can be found.

(b) The negative criteria have produced not only a non-Christian Jesus, but an unJewish one as well, for repeatedly Jesus is separated from Judaism at every significant point. Judaism can, apparently, be affirmed safely as part of Jesus' background but not as part of his substance. But who will openly declare, since Renan, that Jesus was not really and not centrally a Jew? Far more needs to be done to rehabilitate the Jewishness of Jesus, not simply because good Jewish-Christian relations commend it but because the integrity of our picture of Jesus requires it. In any case, I see no reason why the Jewishness of Jesus needs to be overcome before he can be the object of gentile Christian faith, just as I find it odd, if not impossible, to be told on one page that Jesus lived and worked as a rabbi and on another to read that a given saying cannot come from Jesus because it is typically rabbinic! Certain consequences of these observations will prove important in the final chapter.

In formulating these five theses somewhat polemically, we have sought to indicate something of the present state of the discussion and to suggest more the *character* of our knowledge of Jesus than its actual content. Essentially, we have a body of hard-core data arrived at by use of the negative criteria, surrounded by a penumbra of "softer" materials that must not be ignored.

If the Jesus who is recovered must be discerned in independent items of tradition individually judged on their own merits, then it is the historian who combines the pieces into a larger structure, whether it is a logical order designed to make it easier to work with a theme (e.g., kingdom of God) or a formal one designed to facilitate analysis of similar kinds of material (e.g., miracle stories or parables). This is why both Bultmann's *Jesus and the Word* and Bornkamm's *Jesus of Nazareth* are organized as they are [43] and why no critical history of Jesus has been written for a generation. This situation also explains why liberals have been so reserved about form criticism, for they suddenly found themselves conservatively clinging to the Markan outline because this was needed to talk about the development of the life of Jesus.[44]

Yet few historians are content to merely ascertain the authentic materials and to cluster them in order to explain them; today, most want also to probe their internal coherence and to explicate this vital center as best they can with reference to the man from whom they come. That is, the critic of the traditions becomes the critical historian and interpreter of the man. In this process, one's conception of Jesus as a whole, and what the data suggest about him, clearly reflects his own sense of what is important and his stance toward the things Jesus stood for. This is the historicity of the historian to which we referred earlier. It will become evident in due course that this step is crucial to the argument of the book, since the delineation of Jesus implicates the historian himself. As we said before, the historical Jesus, precisely because he is the historian's Jesus, is no Kantian *Ding an sich*.

These paragraphs constitute no adequate description of the multiple dimensions of critical study of Jesus, just as they do not outline a theoretical defense of that effort—a methodology. They do not even express an optimistic claim that now at last we can solve the problem of the historical Jesus and evolve a reconstruction that is permanent. Rather, they suggest that the historical study of Jesus *can* be pursued today and that limited results can be attained. That is, we can reliably ascertain Jesus, though only in part. While we cannot know Jesus as completely as we once may have thought, we can know important things solidly. The fact that historians are loathe to claim more than probability for their results does not mean that those results are unimportant, as if only permanent conclusions are worthy of use in theology. This modest result is sufficient to tell us what Jesus was like and ample enough to work with fruitfully in theology. That is the underlying thesis we are exploring and testing.

II. The Validity of Our Question

Our problem is to determine whether and how the historian's Jesus, the probable Jesus reconstructed by critical methods applied by historians with histories of their own, is pivotal or peripheral for preaching and theology, faith and thought. The scope of the question at hand is wider than it may first appear, and its validity not to be assumed.

A. *A Theological Issue.* Given the importance of Jesus for history not only in the West but through it for the entire globe, there is no more need to defend the historical study of Jesus and of Christian origins than for justifying the study of Socrates for the history of thought. While it would be fruitful to explore the impact of Jesus on world history, and while one should not overlook the theological issues raised by that impact, neither question is our concern here. Rather, we deliberately focus the problem as it appears in the concerns of faith and theology because it is the Christian community that has most at stake. Does every believer, every preacher of the gospel, every theologian, have central matters on stage here, or is the historical Jesus of concern only as a research area for persons interested in that sort of thing?

The answer is not as evident as one might surmise; in fact, the scope of the question is not immediately evident either. Since it is the aim of the entire book to respond affirmatively to the issue that has been posed, we simply note three dimensions of its theological character.

(1) Sermons repeatedly cite Jesus and draw inferences from him to the life of the hearers. The focus may be on what Jesus said, or what he did, or how he lived, or what he was all about. The legitimacy of doing this is beyond dispute within the Christian community. What must be ascertained, however, is whether there are any historical warrants for the content of such appeals, whether one can say justifiably that Jesus did, said, or thought what is claimed for him. Clearly, any use of Jesus to sanction an appeal to the congregation collapses if it becomes evident that Jesus did not, in fact, do what he is alleged to have done. In other words, it is the integrity of preaching which is at stake in the historical Jesus— unlesss the name "Jesus" merely refers to a Christ-figure who need not have been a concrete person. The integrity of the

36

preacher himself is also involved, especially if he suspects that his claims for Jesus are not really supportable but only useful in persuasion. How does the preacher's critical understanding affect what he says about Jesus and how he sets him before the congregation? In a word, it is a question of whether Jesus is an expendable commodity to be used at will by the preacher. The accountability and responsibility of the preacher for his preaching is, I assume, a matter of some theological, not merely professional, significance, because Christian preaching coordinates Jesus with God.

(2) Interestingly, it is precisely because some interpreters of Christianity take their theological responsibility seriously that they are relatively uninterested in the historical Jesus. They develop this stance lest they compromise the Christian faith, that is, a Protestant understanding of faith. Many have become sufficiently mesmerized by kerygma theology [45] to regard the entire matter with disdain. Frequently, he who is concerned about the historical Jesus appears to be under a cloud of suspicion lest he be guilty of heresy—the heresy of wanting a historical peg on which to hang his faith, of seeking a prop that makes radical faith so easy that it is no longer pure faith. We will deal extensively with this theme in the next chapter. Suffice it here to say that the entire book is a running debate with this view and its implications. In debating the issue, of course, we grant that a theological question of paramount importance is under review: the character and content of one's faith.

(3) Many persons today appeal to Jesus as a model for action and belief, persons not necessarily members of Christian congregations at all but commonly found outside the identifiable church altogether. Students disenchanted with the establishment, especially with the ecclesiastical one, readily identify with Jesus as the Great Protester, the Nonconformist, etc. Here, too, the question of the justification of doing so arises. But our purpose in raising this point is not to say "Tut, tut" to nonconformists who appeal to Jesus or to quibble with them over particulars. Because such appeals (We might think of the "poor" Jesus of Francis of Assisi or Tolstoi, or of Cleage's

Black Messiah) call the presumed understanding of him into question, we must reckon with the ideological distortion of Jesus, whether by the Establishment or by its critics. Whatever its limits, careful historical study is a major bulwark against ideology (a theme taken up in Chapter 3).

B. *The Christological Center.* What is the relation of the historical Jesus to Christology as a whole? In brief, we restrict ourselves to a segment of the total entity called "Jesus Christ," to a part of the subject matter of Christology. To miss this point would be tantamount to limiting faith and theology in a way that has no precedent. Conversely, overlooking this limiting of the subject matter would lead to a fatal inflation of the historical Jesus as a self-disclosing, self-evident, self-validating object of Christian faith, as if one had merely to perceive accurately what was "there" in Jesus in order to have the content of Christology. Popular piety has, ironically enough, often taken such a posture, despite the fact that the church has never sanctioned such Docetism and the fact that self-validation is something no historical person enjoys.

A full-orbed statement of who Jesus is and what he is for faith would require us to deal with matters implicit in the role of the historical Jesus in faith, such as the relation of the Godhead to revelation in history generally, the relation of the pre-incarnate Word to God the Creator (to speak in traditional categories), the Christ of Christian experience and devotion, and the relation of the Lord to the church in history and at its end. Nevertheless, though the historical Jesus is but a part of the whole of Christology, it is the crucial part without which nothing else has validity or significance in the long run. In a word, thinking theologically about the historian's Jesus leads to the whole christological task and affects the whole scope of Christian faith. This is why Pannenberg is justified in treating the historical Jesus in terms of a "christology from below" [46]—a theme to which we will return in Chapter 5.

Just as we do not contend that the historical Jesus is all one must have in order to believe Christianly, so we do not assume that every believer must be a critical historian in order to believe at all, or to do so rightly. That would be absurd.[47] What is maintained, however, is that every believer and every theologian has central things at stake in the historical study of Jesus, just as citizens of all sorts have their lives at stake in the work of scientists, economists, and politicians whose work they may not comprehend or even know about.

C. *The Historicity of Theology.* This third element of the legitimacy of our question does not need to be defended but incorporated. We have in view not simply the historicity of the historical Jesus (that the reconstructed Jesus varies from period to period and from scholar to scholar) but also the historicity of faith and the theology as a whole. Since later chapters will deal with these matters, suffice it now to suggest that the demise of Christendom means that faith will be found and Christian theology be developed in the pluralistic marketplace of ideas where they were, in fact, born originally. To argue in this setting that the historian's Jesus is irrelevant to faith and theology is possible only for him who does not perceive where he stands. Precisely because the name "Jesus" refers to a historical figure of the public past and not to a private myth or meaning-syndrome, the door is open to inquiry concerning him to whom Christians give allegiance. Today, historical understanding is as basic to our world view as was myth to the ancient one. What sort of faith is it that prohibits investigation of its object? But with these matters, we are already deeper into the argument than an introductory chapter calls for.

III. The Road Ahead

The theme to engage our attention in the next chapter is the place of the historian's Jesus in Christian faith. This will allow us to develop more carefully what has been asserted somewhat brusquely in the preceding paragraphs. Chapter 3 will then take up the question, How shall we present the historical Jesus in the sermon so that men can trust him? Chapter 4 will carry this forward by exploring the results of

39

trusting Jesus; specifically it will discuss the relation of trust to salvation. Finally, Chapter 5 will take up the explicit *theo*logical question—the significance of the historical Jesus for the understanding of God.

Clearly, this order is not an inevitable one, though I believe it to be intelligible. By putting the discussion of faith and preaching ahead of that concerning theology, we do not imply that preaching is untheological or independent of theological reflection, just as we do not suggest that theology is controlled by what is preachable. Rather, the order reflects the fact that in recent times it has been the act of preaching which precipitated lively theological work. Moreover, witnessing to faith and inviting to faith are acts that forge questions that make theological work inescapable. In any case, we cannot deal with this matter until we clarify the place of the historical Jesus in the act of believing, and to this we now turn.

NOTES TO CHAPTER ONE

1. Ernst Käsemann observed that New Testament study as a whole has gradually become a "world-wide jungle war" and that he cannot, therefore, be as optimistic about its results as Joachim Jeremias. "Blind Alleys in the 'Jesus of History' Controversy" in *New Testament Questions of Today*, trans. W. J. Montague (Philadelphia: Fortress Press, 1969; German ed., 1965) p. 29.
2. Schleiermacher's *Das Leben Jesu* (Berlin: G. Reimer, 1864) was reconstructed from student notes (a horrible fate to contemplate!). Translated by S. MacLean Gilmour, it will be published by Fortress Press in a series of "The Lives of Jesus." It will be introduced and edited by J. C. Verheyden.
3. This book is to be translated and published in "The Lives of Jesus" (see foregoing note); the translator and editor is L. E. Keck.
4. Though Lessing knew the identity of the author, he published parts of the manuscript as "Fragments of an Unknown Writer." This, coupled with heretofore untranslated sections dealing with the resurrection, is included in "The Lives of Jesus" (see note 2). Introduced and annotated by Charles Talbert, it was published in 1970.
5. One may see this most readily in Robert Eisler's controversial *The Messiah Jesus and John the Baptist*, trans. A. H. Krappe (New York: Dial Press, 1931) in which he not only says the whole quest of the historical Jesus is a story from Reimarus to Reimarus (playing on the German title of Schweitzer's survey, *Von Reimarus zu Wrede*) but attempts to prove that Jesus was indeed a

political insurrectionist as Reimarus had argued. S. G. F. Brandon's recent book, *Jesus and the Zealots* (Manchester: Manchester University Press, 1967; New York: Scribner's, 1968) reopens the question, though without the hostility toward traditional Christianity evinced by Reimarus, and without insisting that Jesus too was a Zealot. A similar position was taken by Paul Winter, *On the Trial of Jesus* (Berlin: de Gruyter, 1961).

6. It was Harnack, commonly regarded as the ablest spokesman for Continental liberalism (along with Albrecht Ritschl), who formulated the heart of Jesus' message in these terms. *What Is Christianity?* trans. T. B. Saunders (Torchbook; New York: Harper, 1957), pp. 51, 63.

7. Actually, there was also a third attack, launched by Wilhelm Wrede. He showed that Mark, the foundation of the liberal lives of Jesus, was not a historical account of Jesus but a theological document whose picture of Jesus was governed by Mark's own theory of the "Messianic secret." Thus while Kähler launched a theological offensive, Schweitzer (and Johannes Weiss) mounted a historical one based on the apocalyptic meaning of the kingdom God, and Wrede launched a truly critical one based on a careful reading of Mark. *Das Messiasgeheimnis in den Evangelien* (Göttingen: Vandenhoeck & Ruprecht, 1901; 3rd printing, 1963). Wrede was not discussed in the body of the text because he did not really modify the conception of the phrase "historical Jesus" though he did modify its content; he implied that one could not know anything about Jesus' "Messianic self-consciousness" since Messiahship was predicated of Jesus only by the later church.

8. In 1953 Kähler's *Der sogenannte historische Jesus und der geschichtliche biblische Christus* (ed. Ernst Wolf) was republished by Chr. Kaiser Verlag in Munich. This reprint of the first edition of 1892 included divergent passages from the second edition of 1896. In 1964 Fortress Press published Carl Braaten's translation of Wolf's edition as *The So-Called Historical Jesus and the Biblical Christ.* It includes Braaten's extensive introductory essay.

9. *The Quest of the Historical Jesus,* trans. W. Montgomery (London: A. & C. Black, 1910; reprinted by Macmillan, 1968).

10. See, e.g., *Theology of the New Testament,* trans. Kendrick Grobel (New York: Scribner's, 1951), I, 33.

11. The phrase comes, of course, from James M. Robinson's survey and interpretation, *A New Quest of the Historical Jesus,* SBT 25 (Naperville, Ill.: Allenson, 1959). A revised edition was published in German under the title, *Kerygma und historischer Jesus* (Zurich: Zwingli-Verlag, 1960). In 1967 this was modified again. Van Harvey's and Schubert Ogden's critique takes account of the English and the first German edition. "How New Is the 'New Quest of the Historical Jesus'?" in *The Historical Jesus and the Kerygmatic Christ,* ed. Carl Braaten and Roy Harrisville (Nashville: Abingdon Press, 1964), pp. 197-242.

12. In this way already Bultmann overcame the alleged gulf between

41

Jesus and Paul. See "The Significance of the Historical Jesus for the Theology of Paul" (1929), in *Faith and Understanding* I, 220 ff., as well as "Jesus and Paul" (1936) in *Existence and Faith*, trans. and ed. Schubert Ogden (Meridian Books: Cleveland: World, 1960), pp. 183 ff. This line is developed farther in the important article by Herbert Braun, "The Meaning of New Testament Christology" in *JThC* 5 (1968), 89-127 (Torchbook; New York: Harper). James M. Robinson has explored the possibility that an essential element of Jesus' understanding of existence is expressed even in Christian Gnostic texts from the second century. "The Formal Structure of Jesus' Message," in *Current Issues in New Testament Interpretation* (Piper Festschrift), ed. William Klassen and Grayson Snyder (New York: Harper, 1962), pp. 104ff.

13. See Robinson, *A New Quest* . . . , Chap. II.
14. (New York: Macmillan, 1966; paperback ed., 1969.)
15. The difference between a radical and a conservative critic concerns primarily not their answers to historical questions, but the way they approach the material. The radical critic throws the burden of proof on the material, accepting nothing as hard-core data which cannot be shown to merit reliance, while the conservative trusts the material until evidence prevents him from continuing to do so.
16. Redaction criticism (a loose rendering of *Redaktionsgeschichte*, a word coined by Willi Marxsen) moves beyond Henry J. Cadbury's concerns with stylistic and thematic interests of the Evangelists, as represented in his *Making of Luke-Acts* (New York: Macmillan, 1927; republished in London by S.P.C.K. in 1958). For *Luke*, Hans Conzelmann's *Theology of St. Luke*, trans. Geoffrey Buswell (New York: Harper, 1960; 1st German ed., 1954) has achieved "classical" status. For *Mark*, the pioneering work was done by Willi Marxsen, *Der Evangelist Markus*, FRLANT 67 (Göttingen: Vandenhoeck & Ruprecht, 1956); a translation was published by Abingdon Press as *Mark the Evangelist* in 1969. Eduard Schweizer's commentary on Mark applies this method throughout: *The Good News According to Mark*, trans. Donald H. Madvig (Richmond: John Knox, 1970). For *Matthew*, Günther Bornkamm and two students have published basic studies available in English: *Tradition and Interpretation in Matthew*, trans. Percy Scott (Philadelphia: Westminster Press, 1963). For a survey of redaction criticism of the Gospels, see Joachim Rhode, *Recovering the Teaching of the Evangelists*, trans. Dorothea Barton (Philadelphia: Westminster Press, 1968; German ed., 1966). A brief, but eminently usable, introduction is provided by Norman Perrin, *What Is Redaction-Criticism?* (Philadelphia: Fortress Press, 1969). Because to date most work has been done by doctoral students working on manageable problems, many analyses either concentrate on a particular block of material or trace selected themes in a given book.
17. Günther Bornkamm's important *Jesus of Nazareth*, trans. Irene and Fraser McLuskey (New York: Harper, 1960; 1st German ed.,

1956) misses this point, as I have pointed out in my "Bornkamm's *Jesus of Nazareth* Revisited," *JR* 49 (1969), 1-17.
18. This is emphasized by Bornkamm, *ibid.*, p. 25. For a recent, thorough analysis of this story and its function in Mark, see Rudolf Pesch, "Berufung und Sendung, Nachfolge und Mission. Eine Studie zu Mk 1, 16-20," *Zeitschrift für katholische Theologie* 91 (1969), 1-31.
19. See Robinson, *A New Quest* . . . , pp. 47, 66 ff., and esp. 95 ff.
20. Norman Perrin has provided a useful statement of how one undertakes systematically to recover Jesus' teachings. *Rediscovering the Teaching of Jesus* (New York: Harper, 1967), Chap. 1. Later in this discussion we will indicate our criticisms of Perrin's unreserved adherence to the negative criteria.
21. For a recent survey of these finds, see James M. Robinson, "The Coptic Gnostic Library Today," *NTS* 14 (1966), 356-401. For a suggestive, recent discussion of canonical and Gnostic gospels, see Ernst Haenchen, "Neutestamentliche und gnostische Evangelien," in *Christentum und Gnosis*, Walther Eltester, ed., Beiheft 37 of *ZNW* (Berlin: Töpelmann, 1969), pp. 19-45.
22. The rubric begs the question because it is derived from the title "Apocrypha"; it is by no means evident that these gospels ever had "canonical" status (though it is exceedingly difficult to know precisely what that term meant in the second century). For a discussion of these and related matters, see W. Schneemelcher's discussions in Hennecke-Schneemelcher, *New Testament Apocrypha*, trans. R. McL. Wilson (Philadelphia: Westminster Press, 1963; 1st German ed., 1959), I, 19 ff.
23. These traditions were collected by Walter Bauer's classic *Das Leben Jesu im Zeitalter der neutestamentlichen Apokryphen* (Tübingen: J. C. B. Mohr [Paul Siebeck], 1909; in 1967 the Wissenschaftliche Buchgesellschaft in Darmstadt reprinted this work). A sample collection was published and discussed by Joachim Jeremias, *Unknown Sayings of Jesus*, trans. from 2nd ed. by R. H. Fuller (London: S.P.C.K. 1957; 1st German ed., 1948, rev. 1951).
24. The Gospel of Truth was translated and analyzed by Kendrick Grobel, *The Gospel of Truth* (Nashville: Abingdon Press, 1960). One Gospel of Thomas concerns the boyhood of Jesus; it can be read in M. R. James, *The Apocryphal New Testament* (New York: Oxford University Press, 1924). A text and English translation of the newly found Gospel of Thomas were published by Harper in 1959. It contains only sayings of Jesus.
25. The recent study of E. P. Sanders corrects and carries forward the analysis of the fate of the Jesus traditions. *The Tendencies of the Synoptic Tradition* (S.N.T.S. Monograph 9) (London: Cambridge University Press, 1969).
26. What is in view here is the sort of work done by Dieter Georgi's *Gegner des Paulus im 2. Korintherbrief. WMANT* 11 (Neukirchen-Vluyn: Neukirchner Verlag, 1964); a brief statement of the topic can be found in Hans Dieter Betz, "Jesus as Divine Man" in

Jesus and the Historian (Colwell Festschrift), ed. F. T. Trotter (Philadelphia: Westminster Press, 1968), pp. 114-33.

27. Of course, many scholars have long preferred to rely on the Johannine chronology for the passion story.

28. See, for example, the extensive discussion of this problem in Raymond E. Brown's commentary, *The Gospel According to St. John* (*Anchor Bible*) (Garden City, N.Y.: Doubleday, 1966), Vol. I. Brown—unnecessarily, I think—still connects the earliest stratum with the Apostle.

29. The most thorough recent investigation in this vein is that of C. H. Dodd, *Historical Tradition in the Fourth Gospel* (London: Cambridge University Press, 1963).

30. *The Synoptic Problem* (New York: Macmillan, 1966). Whatever be the outcome of this debate (one must not rely only on consensus; this may, after all, simply reflect scholarly inertia), Farmer has not only provided an excellent survey of the course of the discussion but shown how the priority of Mark nourished the life-of-Jesus research as carried on in the late nineteenth and early twentieth centuries. This does not, however, invalidate the solution.

31. Manson saw the issue clearly: "It is a case of Mark's order or none at all." *The Teaching of Jesus* (London: Cambridge University Press, 1931), p. 26. In 1943, almost as if recognizing the vulnerability of his view, he wrote, "While many concessions may have to be made to the disruptive criticism of Mark, it is nevertheless the case that a good deal of structure remains. When the lath and plaster is removed, it appears that there is some solid masonry underneath. The *main* [his italics] outline is an outline of what really happened." "The Life of Jesus: A Study of the Available Materials," in *Studies in the Gospels and Epistles*, ed. Matthew Black (Philadelphia Westminster Press, 1962), p. 26. But on what did the foundation itself rest? A year later, Manson argued that the author was John Mark (Acts 12:25), who was also an eyewitness of some events (he was the youth mentioned in 14:51-52) and in contact with Peter. "The Foundation of the Synoptic Tradition: The Gospel of Mark," *Studies in the Gospels and Epistles*, pp. 28-45. Petrine tradition rests on the statements of Papias, and their repetition in the early church. Little in Mark itself points to Peter's own narratives, least of all the central section—the Caesarea-Philippi story. The course of the discussion really reveals how criticism has come to rely more on its own reading of the text (internal evidence) and less, if at all, on early Christian traditions about Mark (external evidence). The same shift has occurred in connection with the rest of the New Testament.

C. H. Dodd defended the historical tradition of Mark's outline on another basis: when Mark's summaries are read in sequence, they produce a somewhat coherent narrative; from this Dodd inferred that the framework is an old outline into which Mark placed individual pericopes! "The Framework of the Gospel Narrative," reprinted in Dodd's essays, *New Testament Studies* (Manchester: Manchester University Press, 1953). D. E. Nineham effectively refuted this in "The Order of Events in St. Mark's Gospel—an Examination of Dr. Dodd's Hypothesis," in *Studies in the Gospels* (R. H. Lightfoot Festschrift), ed. D. E. Nineham (Oxford: Blackwell, 1955), pp. 223 ff. Harry Sawyerr's criticisms of Nineham, on the other hand, have not been effective. "The Marcan Framework," *SJTh* 4 (1961), 279-94.

32. The following random examples illustrate the vehemence with which Q has been rejected: Joachim Jeremias: "The written 'sayings source' is in our opinion pure fantasy." *Unknown Sayings of Jesus*, p. 3, n. 1. Austin Farrer: "Try as I may, I cannot believe the Q hypothesis." *St. Matthew and St. Mark* (London: Dacre Press, 1954), p. viii. C. Stewart Petrie: " 'Q', which might well stand for 'quirk,' should be wholly forgotten and promptly dispatched (hand in hand with 'John the Elder') to the limbo of forlorn hypotheses." "The Authorship of the 'Gospel According to St. Matthew': A Reconsideration of the External Evidence," *NTS* 14 (1967), 32. See also his " 'Q' is Only What You Make It," *NovTest* 3 (1959).

33. For recent discussions of Q and sayings traditions, see, e.g., Helmut Koester, "One Jesus and four Primitive Gospels," *HTR* 61 (1968), 203-48.

34. Bultmann has explicitly affirmed the priority of the words of Jesus over everything else. See *Jesus and the Word*, trans. Louise Pettibone Smith and Erminie Huntress Lantero (New York: Scribner's 1934; paperback ed., 1958) pp. 10-11.

35. "The Quest of the Historical Jesus" (1956), in *Studies of the Historical Jesus*, trans. Andrew Scobie; *SBT* 42 (1964), p. 21.

36. *The Mission and Achievement of Jesus*, *SBT* 12 (1954).

37. This is aptly observed by Paul J. Achtemeier, *An Introduction to the New Hermeneutic* (Philadelphia: Westminster, 1969), pp. 151 ff.

38. Two elements in Jesus' words have received special attention: the parables and the Son of Man sayings; the former effort has produced the more solid results, largely through the careful work of Joachim Jeremias, *The Parables of Jesus*, trans. S. H. Hooke (New York Scribner's, 1963; 1st German ed., 1947, repeatedly revised). Son of Man research, on the other hand, has not been able to move beyond an impasse, despite prodigious labor.

39. This is the clear burden of his *Church and the Reality of Christ* (New York: Harper, 1962).

40. Ernst Haenchen's suggestive article shows how the church trans-mitted Jesus-traditions that were in tension with its own views. See "Die frühe Christologie," *ZThK* 63 (1966), 147-48.

41. Perhaps the best-known formulation of these criteria is that by Ernst Käsemann in "The Problem of the Historical Jesus," *Essays on New Testament Themes*, trans. W. J. Montague, *SBT* 41 (1964), p. 37. Norman Perrin's book (see note 20) is an extensive and rigid application of these criteria. Thus he asserts that what is "most characteristic of Jesus . . . will be found not in the things

which he shares with his contemporaries but in the things wherein he differs from them" (p. 39)!

42. For example, Philipp Vielhauer's important essay on the Son of Man builds its case largely on the assumption that because proclamation of the kingdom of God has no place for a coming Son of Man, and vice versa, the future Son of Man sayings are not genuine. See "Gottesreich und Menschensohn in der Verkündigung Jesu" (1959), and "Jesus und der Menschensohn" (1963), in his essays *Aufsätze zum Neuen Testament* (Munich: Kaiser Verlag, 1965).

43. Bultmann's epoch-making book, after relating Jesus to his milieu, divides the material into three groups: the coming of the kingdom, the will of God, and "God the Remote and the Near"—the whole being restricted to his words. Bornkamm's *Jesus of Nazareth* follows this, though with significant modifications. Between the discussion of Jesus' times and of the eschatological message he inserts what Robinson called a personality sketch, and after the chapter on the will of God, he deals with discipleship, the Passion, the Messianic question, and the resurrection faith.

44. This reversal of fronts has been clearly described by Ernst Käsemann, "The Problem of the Historical Jesus," p. 17.

45. Robinson speaks of kerygma as "a whole unified theological position which has just as nearly swept the field in twentieth-century theology as did the theology of the historical Jesus in the nineteenth century." *A New Quest* . . . , p. 43. For a critique of the "enthusiastic" insistence that Christ is present in the kerygma, see Wolfhart Pannenberg, *Jesus—God and Man*, trans. W. Wilkens and D. Priebe (Philadelphia: Westminster Press, 1968), pp. 21 ff. On the other hand, Peter C. Hodgson has accused Pannenberg of overreacting to existentialism. "Pannenberg on Jesus," *Journal of the American Academy of Religion* 36 (1968), 374.

46. Pannenberg, *Jesus—God and Man*, pp. 33-34.

47. It was Martin Kähler who was shocked by the possibility that believers might be made dependent on professors. *The So-called Historical Jesus*, pp. 61-62.

2

THE HISTORICAL JESUS AND THE CHARACTER OF FAITH

"The belief that something exists is an experience of a wholly different order from the experience of reliance on it."

H. RICHARD NIEBUHR

"To believe in someone . . . , to place confidence in him, is to say 'I am sure that you will not betray my hope, that you will respond to it, that you will fulfill it." . . . But it is abundantly clear that the assurance which we have proposed is by no means a conviction; . . . . it is a jump, a bet—and, like all bets, it can be lost."

GABRIEL MARCEL

In the previous chapter, we saw why the historian's reconstructed Jesus is delineated in lines that run quite differently from those drawn by the Gospels. The latter portray Jesus according to early Christian understandings of Jesus which, with considerable diversity, view Jesus as the decisive act of God for the sake of men and the world. The historian, in contrast, cannot make this conviction and perspective the starting point of his work without derailing his enterprise and mutilating it into an apologetic treatment of Jesus. Martin Kähler doubtless oversimplified the matter when he said that the Gospels are concerned to present the sinless Christ rather than a Jesus to whom apply the ordinary aspects of human development and probability.[1] Nevertheless, he rightly sensed that a Jesus drawn according to the canons of secular histori-

47

ography is not completely congruent with the portrait of the Gospels. But whereas Kähler used this insight to repudiate the theological and religious significance of the historically reconstructed Jesus, this essay contends that such a reaction is as unnecessary as it was unfortunate; that is, we are contending that the historical Jesus (the historian's Jesus) does have a role in Christian faith, though it is not the liberal one that Kähler rejected.

This possibility requires us to see clearly what faith means; more precisely, it compels us to see that faith itself may be understood differently and not merely our image of Jesus. This correlative reconstituting of faith makes our topic significant and controversial.

Because we are shaped by the controversy's recent history, we can be freed from it only if we are clear about its contours and consequences. Hence, we shall review briefly certain important contemporary views of the role of the historical Jesus in Christian faith. Our own view will emerge in conversation with these; however, since the whole discussion has them in mind, this chapter inaugurates our critical reflections more than it states them fully.

I. The Contour of a Debate

Rudolf Bultmann is the most important figure in this discussion. While he did not discover the issues, he did formulate them as we presently know them. The Enlightenment figure, G. E. Lessing, and the father of existentialism, Søren Kierkegaard, formulated them first and gave influential answers.

A. Since Lessing was concerned to undermine orthodoxy,[2] he sought to deprive it of its right to rely on miracle and fulfillment of prophecy as a demonstration of the truth of Christian dogma. For Lessing, whose views on this point are representative of the Enlightenment and of Deism,[3] historical events are accessible only through reports whose authority diminishes with time. Hence he wrote, "The problem is that this proof of the spirit and of power no longer has any spirit

48

or power, but has sunk to the level of human testimonies of spirit and power" (p. 52). Because "historical truths cannot be demonstrated," he articulates the dictum, often repeated: "accidental truths of history can never become the proof of necessary truths of reason" (p. 53). If one were to aver that the Gospels were written by inspired historians who could not err, Lessing rejoins, "Unfortunately, that also is only historical certainty, that these historians were inspired and could not err." This gap between the historical fact and certitude is what Lessing called "the ugly, broad ditch which I cannot get across, however often and however earnestly I have tried to make the leap. If anyone can help me over it, let him do it, I beg him, I adjure him" (p. 55). Like Ariadne's thread, this insight concerning the inadequacy of historical fact as the basis of absolute certitude of faith or of reason runs through the entire subsequent story of Protestant theology.

It was Kierkegaard who deliberately accepted Lessing's challenge to help him over the ditch by inviting him to take the leap of faith. We cannot review Kierkegaard's whole argument, especially its dependence on Hegel, but can only note its relation to Lessing's problem. Kierkegaard forces a choice between Socrates and Christ in the sense that "Socrates" represents the view that man already knows and needs only be reminded, in which case the teacher has no inherent, indispensable relation to what is known, but is merely a catalyst in the process.[4] Knowledge of Christ, on the other hand, is given only by God in the Absolute Paradox that God became man and that God himself makes it possible to know this, in which case what is taught is inseparable from the Teacher. On this basis, contra Lessing,[5] there is absolutely no difference between the historical contemporary of Jesus and the modern believer. For both, the Teacher is utterly indispensable to what is known, and chronological proximity or distance from Jesus is of no importance.[6] Rejecting Lessing's eyewitness knowledge, Kierkegaard insisted that the sort of knowledge faith needs is of a radically different kind. In effect, Kierkegaard tells Lessing[7] that only God can transport him across the ditch.[8] In this argument, based on the view that the incarnation is not self-evident to man's reason

49

but an Absolute Paradox that appears as offense,[9] lies the modern source of the relentless relativizing of historical knowledge of Jesus for faith.[10] What dominates the discussion is the role of history as the insufficient cause for absolute faith.

B. Even though Bultmann's view is well known, it is necessary to rethink his position since he remains the key figure in the debate. While his response to the "new quest" [11] is of major importance for our theme, his work is an organic whole marked by very little change in direction;[12] hence we can draw on the total Bultmann corpus to delineate his argument. We will reserve comments until his major theses are before us.

Axiomatic for Bultmann is the conviction that neither God nor anything immediately pertaining to God (e.g., his Word, kingdom, salvation) is an object, a phenomenon of this world.[13] As for Kierkegaard, so for Bultmann, man has no inherent knowledge of God but depends radically on God's Word, which excludes historical criteria.[14] In other words, because faith is in *God*, the object of faith cannot be susceptible to any examination, historical or rational, whatever;[15] similarly, the integrity of *faith* precludes moving from historical data to faith by way of inference. "Faith does not at all arise from the acceptance of historical facts." [16]

In this light, Bultmann's disinterest in the historical Jesus for faith is intelligible. To be sure, he insists that the gospel presupposes the historical Jesus, for "without him there would be no kerygma." [17] It genuinely matters for Bultmann *that* Jesus lived and was crucified, for this single fact (the famous *Dass*) prevents the gospel from being only a myth.[18] Bultmann is not making a virtue of necessity, as if his critical analyses of the Gospels left him no substantial Jesus anyway. Actually, it does not matter one whit for him whether the pile of facts about Jesus is large or small, because he is opposed in principle to assigning any role to the historical Jesus for faith. Jesus is a mathematical point to which one must refer, but he may not be a line to be analyzed as the basis for faith or as its object, because "it is the Christ of the kerygma and not the person of the historical Jesus who is the object of faith." [19] He asserts that "the Christ of the kerygma has, as it were, displaced the historical Jesus." [20]

Clearly, Bultmann denies that the historical Jesus can be the Word of God, for that would give the Word historical content —a narrative[21]—and make it a phenomenon: Jesus. But for Bultmann, there is "no 'content' . . . that can be conclusively exhibited." [22] When he declares it to be theologically illegitimate to ask questions about the kerygma, he is not saying it is impossible to know anything about Jesus historically or that it is illegitimate to inquire. He is saying that the Word is a self-attesting event that can only be rejected or obeyed, never interrogated. He views his position as a deliberate application of the Reformation principle of faith and works to the problem of faith and knowledge: "There is no difference between security based on good works and security built on objectifying scholarship." [23]

While Bultmann would not restrict the Word to one mode of occurrence, he does correlate closely the Word of God and Christian preaching. What he says about the New Testament is his own view as well: 'The preaching is itself revelation and does not merely speak about it, so that it mediates a content that one can understand or to which one can relate himself through knowledge and thereby 'have' the revelation." [24] Because the kerygmatic Christ is present as Word in preaching,[25] Bultmann can agree with Erich Frank's statement: " 'For although the advent of Christ is an historical event which happened "once" in the past, it is, at the same time, an eternal event which occurs again and again in the soul of any Christian in whose soul Christ is born, suffers and dies and is raised up to eternal life.' " [26] This is why Bultmann is not interested in merely repeating the words of the historical Jesus,[27] or in emphasizing Jesus' deeds as acts of love with "word character." [28] That too would be an attempt to base faith on the "once-upon-a-time" Jesus instead of on the once-for-all-time Christ of the kerygma who is repeatedly present as Word.[29]

The presence of the kerygmatic Christ in the Word is parallel to his presence in the sacraments. Bultmann avers that "baptism and the Lord's Supper are only a special means of re-presenting the salvation-occurrence, which in general is represented in the word of preaching." [30] Whereas the Reformers insisted that the sacraments must be seen as Word, Bultmann sees the Word as sacrament, extending the theme of "real presence" to the sermon.[31]

Though he says little about it, Bultmann implies a particular view of the church as well. He admits that "there is no faith in Christ which would not also be faith in the church as the bearer of the kerygma; that is . . . faith in the Holy Ghost." [32] On another occasion he wrote, "The church's preaching, founded on the Scriptures, passes on the Word of Scripture. It says: God speaks to you *here!* In his majesty he has chosen *this* place! We cannot question whether this place is the right one; we must listen to the call that summons us." [33] To be sure, he also insists that by "church" he means not simply the institution but "an eschatological event. It is not the guarantor of faith, but is itself the object of faith. It is just as much a scandal as the cross." [34] This is why he can write that the "Church is genuine Church only as an event which happens each time here and now . . . it is only in a paradoxical way identical with the ecclesiastical institutions which we observe." [35]

At every point Bultmann's argument is propelled by a concern to protect God and His Word from any kind of objectification which he sees coming from historically ascertained data. Correlatively, authentic faith in God can in no way rest on such data or be a movement over a bridge across Lessing's ditch between the history of Jesus and the certitude of the gospel. Only a God-given leap is permitted.

Our response to Bultmann centers in the relation of faith to fact, and in the relation of the Word to the church.

(1) This conception of faith is not a fixed point but a historically conditioned one with a clear lineage in which Luther, Kierkegaard, and Wilhelm Herrmann are prominent forebears.[36] In all of them, faith is understood as the crisis of the individual and of his capacity to believe, not as fidelity and trust, as in the Old Testament understanding of faith.

Bultmann was deeply influenced by his teacher, Wilhelm Herrmann, who contended that the object of faith and the ground of faith are identical,[37] that is, only God makes possible faith in God. On this basis, Bultmann is free to pursue his critical analysis of Scripture without anxiety over its results, for its role as Word of God in the act of faith does not depend on critical conclusions.[38] He observed that it was his critics who seemed most nervous about rescuing this or that item from the critical fire, while he could calmly "let it burn" because what he saw being consumed was nothing but "phantasy pictures of the Life of Jesus theology." [39] Throughout, of course, Bultmann is concerned to theologize on the basis of the New Testament.[40]

Moreover, Bultmann also allied himself with the early Barth[41] and with his use of Kierkegaard to overcome the collapse of liberalism after World War II;[42] at the same time, Bultmann continued liberalism's historical method.[43] Like Barth, Bultmann excoriated liberal theology for regarding human experience as the subject matter of theology. To make God the subject matter is to negate man in this role.[44] He saw liberal theology's interest in the historical Jesus as destroying faith as being truly in God.[45] So he adopted Kierkegaard's understanding of faith as the antithesis to Christendom's assurances,[46] embodied at the turn of the century in the work of Harnack[47] and Troeltsch. The dialectic of participating simultaneously in the world and in its end did not concern them,[48] but is central for Kierkegaard and Bultmann.[49] In other words, when World War I made the collapse of Christendom inescapably evident, Kierkegaard's conception of faith was coupled with Herrmann's view of its role in order to overcome the dissolution of those things which previously had been seen as faith-supporting and faith-inducing, especially the historical study of Jesus and the Jesus it produced. But Barth and Bultmann had roots on the other side of the disaster. While Bultmann has denied that his theology was affected by World War I and its aftermath,[50] this only suggests that he may not be aware of the impact of the times on his thought. In any case, Bultmann was heard and appropriated by those who, after Verdun and Versailles, saw Christendom in shambles. In this setting, it was easy to turn inward to find the absolute center in the self's relation to the Word, a Word that in no way whatever is dependent on man's work, study, or disposition.[51]

Yet our own situation is more drastic, for we live not amid the dissolving of Christendom so much as on this side of the dissolution that has already occurred. This makes it more than questionable whether Bultmann's view of faith is germane.[52] When fewer persons have any vital memory of Christendom or residual relationship to the church, be it in Prague or Pittsburgh, Manila or Munich, it is less and less convincing to be told that if one so much as asks for the credentials of the gospel or for the content of the word "Jesus" the game is lost at the outset. This is not Bultmann's intent, but it is his effect.

Another unsatisfactory dimension of Bultmannian faith is its hiatus between research and faith. In his favorable response to Barth's early work, he wrote, "Historical science cannot at all lead to any sort of result which could serve as a foundation for faith, for all its results have only relative validity." [53] In this way, Bultmann made an end run around the liberal/orthodox argument over historical facts necessary for Christian faith; that is, Bultmann showed that such a controversy was fruitless because both sides were being defined by the wrong issue, since no fact or amount of facts could do what either combatant assumed it could do. But, helpful as this exposure may have been in moving Protestant theology beyond its impasse, it can lead only to a rigid compartmentalization of faith and historical knowledge. One cannot learn what we have learned about the Bible as a historical work without having his entire understanding of revelation, and of God himself, undergo a basic change. And it is not merely concepts that have changed, but the character of faith itself—often painfully, as every conservative Christian who has wrestled with biblical criticism can testify. A pastor, for example, who has appropriated a critical theological education often finds himself at odds with his congregation because his mode of believing as well as his beliefs have been transformed through biblical criticism. If in this case historical study modified faith already present, can we insist that historical work plays no role at all in *coming* to faith? One need not argue that faith is the inevitable step in historical reasoning[54] in order to seek a more adequate understanding of how faith and research are related.

A third reason for uneasiness concerns the way Bultmann grounded his view of faith in the Reformation doctrine of justification. Claiming that historical study is a form of "works righteousness" is a premature judgment. Surely the historian knows that "history proves nothing," that no invulnerable bastion against religious doubt can be built upon historiography alone. We must ask whether Bultmann's appeal to the Reformation is not misplaced, and whether it would not be more proper to speak of law and gospel. To put it differently, the historical Jesus functions not as a secure basis for faith but as a crisis-creating figure who makes hearing the gospel and coming to faith possible, though not inevitable. This is an alternative to be explored in the next chapters.

There is a fourth side to the disquiet with Bultmann's concept of faith—his insistence that faith is absolute and certain while historiography is at best uncertain and probable. Bultmann himself has repeatedly spoken of faith as venture.[55] But if faith is absolutely certain, where is its venturesomeness? If faith is unhesitating, unequivocal response to the self-validating Word that attests itself as God's word as it occurs, where is its risk? Surely it is not only the observer who notes that the believer is risking his existence on the Word. To be sure, Bultmann wrote that "faith is certain of itself only in looking to its object, which is also its source [God's word], in looking at itself it is always uncertain." [56] But this does not really help, because if faith is utterly certain with respect to its object and source, it does not remain venture for the believer. To the contrary, it is precisely by taking seriously the venturesomeness of faith that we can also take seriously the historical, probable Jesus. Rather than destroying faith, keeping one's eyes on the historical Jesus is precisely what preserves faith's risk, and does so in a way that the believer always knows that he is risking his life on that of Jesus. Moreover, one ought to ponder whether the absolutism of Bultmann's view of faith does not deny the Reformation's *simul justus et peccator* to the act of believing, whether Bultmann unwittingly describes faith in perfectionist terms.

(2) The relation of Word to church is also problematic, for Bultmann insists that "the man whom the kerygma addresses may not inquire behind the kerygma for a legitimation," [57] for this would be asking God's Word for its divine credentials. Now it may be granted that in the moment of encounter no one asks to see God's passport—*if* he is convinced that it is really God whom he meets and hears. But can one so easily equate hearing the kerygma and hearing the Word? If not, then what is said about the moment of hearing the Word cannot be transferred so easily to hearing the kerygma. Kerygma, of course, is heard first of all as human words and traditions,[58] as those who labor over sermons (and those who hear them) know quite well. This has important consequences. In the first place, if God's Word occurs through the agency of human words, then it occurs through ambiguous, fragile, inadequate, historical, problematic, and unstable words (or acts of compassion). But if God's Word is not nullified because it is borne on such words of men, why must one deny that his Word cannot occur through ambiguous, changing, probable delineations of the historical Jesus? To insist that "the historical Jesus is not the kerygma" (as Word) misses the point, for neither is the sermon or the New Testament as such. They can become instruments of the kerygmatic Word. There is no persuasive reason why the reconstructed Jesus is less serviceable to the Word than is a constructed sermon (unless, of course, one argues that because the sermon intends to proclaim the Word it does so[59]). Besides, it is gratuitous to speak of *the* kerygma, even in the New Testament. It is precisely this plurality of "gospels" which requires us to "inquire behind the kerygma" in order to make some judgment about what we hear. On Bultmann's terms, one cannot distinguish between the Word of the Lord and the Word of the angel Moroni. Where there is a consensus (or pre-understanding) that what is preached in

56

church is indeed the Word, one may perhaps assume that there is but one kerygma to be encountered. But in a pluralistic, post-Christendom situation marked by competing traditions and multiple churches with diverse kerygmata traced to the same New Testament, Bultmann's *modus operandi* is inadequate. The pluralism of the American scene is more important for the way we believe and theologize than what Bultmann asserts about the Word and the Church.[60]

Unfortunately Bultmann's own experience in Germany did not contribute what it might have precisely at this point. His participation in the Confessing Church and his treatment by the post-Hitler ecclesiastical establishment are well known.[61] Still, were there but one self-validating kerygma, the phenomenon of the Confessing Church pitted against the "German Christians" would be difficult to explain. Did not both claim to preach the kerygma? Was it not imperative to show by historical evidence that Jesus was not an Aryan but a Jew (thus going beyond the mere *Dass*)? Did not Bultmann himself undertake to show that one cannot force a choice between Jesus and Paul? [62]

In this light, we see again that the theological question that evoked Bultmann's answer was more the intellectual heritage from Lessing[63] and Kierkegaard, who concerned themselves with the problem of the basis of absolute faith, and less with the theological issues embedded in today's concrete situation of actual belief and disbelief.[64] Moreover, it is not accidental that Bultmann's impact has been greatest on those whose "Christian world" has been shaken by historical and scientific knowledge but who nevertheless seek a way of maintaining their traditional faith—the Protestant seminary students who come from traditional, often pietistic, backgrounds. But as soon as one theologizes in a different setting, as soon as one begins to interpret the Christian gospel to those without such roots, as soon as those without such roots struggle to believe and begin to theologize and to interpret for others, Bultmann's refusal to talk about the historical Jesus shows itself to be inadequate. Within Christendom's church, withdrawing the Word from criteria derived from Christian culture and Christian scholarship is a prophetic protest (as was Kierkegaard, with whom it began[65]) against that domestication of the divine which the Establishment represents. In Christendom's church, precisely in order to press for a personal decision of faith, one must assert that faith is not to be confused with habitual reliance on institutions, customs, Christian scholarship, etc. But in our pluralistic setting, relying on a series of self-validating moments of encounter which are always beyond question leads the church to sophisticated *Schwärmerei*. Beyond the church itself, Bultmann's weapon also misfires because on this side of Christendom it has the effect of shifting the offense from the message to the messenger whenever he forbids ascertaining how his kerygma is related to the historical Jesus.[66]

So, Bultmann's view is too close to tacitly requiring prior faith in the church. How else will one admit that when the church says, "God speaks to you here, in the Scriptures," questions are out of order? [67] How much Bultmann is willing to assume about the concrete church is disclosed by his reply to Hans Bolewski.[68] Bultmann admits that for him the *sine qua non* of church is its self-understanding as eschatological phenomenon created by the Word, and adds that there is no relation between this self-understanding and any particular order and polity; more important, he avers that the day-to-day life of the church is the responsibility of church administrators, but not of theologians. Here it appears that the two-realms doctrine has been extended to the church itself. Yet there is little reason to think that if the church's life is left solely in the hands of its bureaucrats it will be able to hear or proclaim the Word, for life and thought, institution and gospel, inform each other. In a word, Bultmann's attitude toward the church is problematic because he does not find it so.

C. A radically different approach has been signaled by Joachim Jeremias, who has not expressed himself as fully or as repeatedly as Bultmann. Instead of viewing Jesus as a fact behind the kerygma but not its substance, Jeremias appears to regard only the historical Jesus as able to empower Christian preaching.

Jeremias admits[69] that the Gospels do not allow us to write a biography of Jesus, yet he still contends that they insist that Christianity did not arise with the kerygma or with Easter faith but with Jesus himself, especially in his preaching. Besides, the kerygma itself compels us to go behind the message to the man. Wherever we pick up the kerygma, we are led back to Jesus himself, he argues. This inescapable Jesus-centeredness is the result of the incarnation: it not only permits but demands historical study. Against Bultmann's contention that such efforts deliver God's act into the hands of men for scrutiny, Jeremias flatly says that this is what the incarnation means: that God has surrendered himself to man. Apparently he means that by incarnation God made himself subject to historical study! Against this, Ernst Käsemann registered a vehement protest.[70]

What kind of Jesus does Jeremias find? He is a Jesus who makes the same claim for faith as the kerygma. This historical Jesus, reached by sophisticated methods, he finds to be completely without parallel with respect to his demeanor, his message, his audacity in calling God Father. But the decisive thing is what Jeremias infers from this: in the historical Jesus, the recovered and reconstructed Jesus, we are set before God himself! But then Jeremias backs away: whoever deals with the historical Jesus must deal with his claim to authority, and this puts to us the question of faith. Jesus' own proclamation and the preaching of the church about him are related as call is to answer. Despite this uncertainty about the direction in which he wants to move, Jeremias locates the issue in the concept of revelation. He contends that according to the New Testament, revelation does not occur on Sunday morning during the worship of the church, but solely in Jesus and his resurrection. Preaching is not revelation but witness to it. The idea of a continual revelation (his paraphrase of Bultmann's point about the eternal event which recurs in preaching) he labels a Gnostic heresy.

How shall we assess this outspoken alternative to Bultmann? Apart from the rather too optimistic expectation of success in the quest for the real Jesus, the most important flaw is the confusion in the statement that when the historian reaches the real Jesus he reaches God because Jesus acts with unparallelled authority. By what criterion does Jeremias know that Jesus' claim to authority is legitimate? Here Christian confession is confused with methodology. In fact, Jeremias' statements are mutually incompatible, for on the one hand, there exists no historiography for studying God himself but only for the study of men, while on the other, confession that in Jesus we deal with the act of God cannot be made the *sine qua non* for the historical study of Jesus. Closely related is the assumption that the historical Jesus is somehow self-validating. Only in Christendom can one assume that historical study will demonstrate that Christian theology is true. Jeremias appears even less viable than Bultmann, though he is correct in his contention that the historical Jesus belongs to the content of the gospel, as in his view that Jesus' audacity provokes a response.

D. A quite different alternative to Bultmann has been advanced by Gerhard Ebeling.[71] As for Bultmann, so for Ebeling faith is the central and constitutive factor in Christianity,[72] though in a somewhat different way.[73] Whereas Bultmann insists on contrasting the historical Jesus with the proper object of faith, the Jesus who is present only in the preached word, Ebeling argues that Christian faith is faith in Jesus himself.[74] Against Bultmann, Ebeling is not afraid to go behind the kerygma to ask whether it is legitimate. Moreover, he insists that one must do so in order to determine whether believing in Jesus accords with Jesus' own intention, or whether he is, in effect, the unwitting victim of Christian preaching. If faith has no basis in Jesus himself, then it is not Christian faith, he writes.[75] Constantly, Ebeling insists that "Jesus" and "faith" belong together in closest association, so "that the question of who Jesus is and the question of what faith means cannot be answered apart from each other, but only in conjunction with each other." [76] Or, to put the matter differently, he asks, How is it that the New Testament regards Jesus not as an obstacle to faith but as its source and occasion? With what right does Heb. 12:2 call Jesus the author and pioneer of our faith?

To answer such questions, Ebeling does not ask merely for data about Jesus, but asks what Jesus was all about. What was his inmost intent? What made him what he was? These questions require him to do more than ascertain hard-core facts about Jesus' deeds and words; they obligate him to penetrate this data to that core of the self which holds the diverse data in a living relationship. Hence he rejects Bultmann's contention that when we get behind the kerygma we get to pure facts that emasculate faith. Rather, when we get to Jesus we see that we are dealing with an event that was "pure Word," since Jesus sought but one thing— faith.[77] Jesus is not a fact needing interpretation but an event with Word of God character because he makes possible the right response to God and so makes God effective. When the church's kerygma expressly calls for faith in Jesus, it simply brings into verbal expression what was already latent in Jesus.[78]

How does Ebeling know that Jesus was committed to evoking faith?[79] Only partly on the basis of Gospel texts. To a large extent it is a logical argument, as it must be because there are almost no data in which Jesus talks about faith. If Jesus is concerned to awaken faith, one cannot make him a bystander to faith; to the contrary, if one tries to evoke faith, he must engage his own faith without speaking of it.[80] Therefore, Jesus' own faith is everywhere involved whether or not this is reported in the texts.[81] We see Jesus' own faith in his use of "Amen," an originally cultic word spoken in the presence of God.[82] This fact leads him to conclude that Jesus regards his own words as spoken to men and before God in such a way that God will stand behind them (as in a cultic pronouncement). In this way Jesus intends to awaken faith, that is, to make it possible for his hearers to share his faith. This is how Jesus is the source and object of faith at the same time.[83] Faith arises when one encounters this Jesus who is bent on evoking faith. He is a confidence-creating Word[84] because he himself had confidence. Jesus' certainty is not an aspect of him but the constitutive quality in the man himself.[85] What was it that made Jesus what he was, that came to expression in him? With tenacity, Ebeling insists it was faith.[86]

Because faith is what Jesus himself was all about,[87] it is not only legitimate but necessary for the kerygma to repeat and reformulate this, since this is the only way Jesus himself can be made effective (*zur Sprache kommen*[88]). Because Ebeling sees the task of defining the phrase "the historical Jesus" as "the task of giving expression to what came to expression in Jesus,"[89] there is no fundamental hiatus between the historical Jesus and the kerygmatic Christ. Instead of asking, like Bultmann, How did the subject of a message become the object of one (the proclaimer become the proclaimed)? Ebeling asks, "How did Jesus, the witness of faith, become the basis of faith?"[90] In accord with the New Testament, Ebeling answers by pointing to the resurrection, for in the appearances "he appeared as what he really was, namely, the witness of faith"[91]—because appearance and coming to faith coincided. But the heart of the matter is that it is faith which establishes a relation of Jesus to the self. Faith in Jesus means "to let him, as the witness of faith, be the basis of faith, and thus to have to do with him and to enter upon his way."[92] Moreover, once this has occurred, it must not be inferred, as Bultmann did, that the explicit kerygma no longer needs what is implicit; that is, the gospel and faith in Jesus cannot dispense with the historical Jesus whence they arose.[93] To the contrary, Jesus is the criterion of the kerygma.[94]

Before assessing Ebeling's alternative to Bultmann, it is appropriate to take note of the similar position taken by Ernst Fuchs. For convenience' sake, we will concentrate on his still untranslated essay in which he comments on his concerns in the historical study of Jesus.[95]

Like Ebeling, Fuchs insists that throughout the New Testament faith is concerned to interpret (*auslegen*) the historical Jesus (p. 1). This leads him to defend his position that Jesus' call to decision and faith echoes his own action (see note 81) by reminding us of his his view that Jesus, having responded to the Baptist's message of the nearness of the end, through the death of John grasped the *time* of the kingdom in a new way, not a conception of it. Then he asks, What was present for Jesus existentially? Answer: the kingdom of God. Consequently, a temporal coefficient was included in Jesus' word. Jesus claimed *his* presence as *God's* presence (p. 11). Therefore, Jesus' summons was itself his decisive deed, for it expressed his understanding of time as the presence of God in his own hour. What Jesus sought was to impart God's presence to his hearers (p. 13). Jesus' word is his deed; therefore one can infer backward to his understanding of existence as conditioned by the presentness of God. The problem in the New Testament, as today, is the extent to which God's presence in Jesus' time can be his presence for us as well (p. 15); since already the New Testament interpreted Jesus' person, we are not permitted to refuse to do so (p. 14). In this way, he turns Bultmann's prohibition against asking behind the kerygma, into an obligation to do so.

Fuchs further insists that "faith does not believe in facts, but in a person; specifically, in his word with which he 'pledges' himself" (p. 15; referring to Gogarten). Fuchs insists that what Jesus *said* is the kernel of his *action* (p. 19). In his preaching he made God effectively present to a generation existentially devoid of God.[96] Therefore, whoever accepted his words understood himself as participating in the kingdom. Thereby God himself "came to speech" (was made actual) in Jesus' word. This speaking is "the medium which united Jesus with the early church and with the church afterwards. . . . *This* speech was experienced by the disciples and by others. In it they received Jesus' secret. Thereby Jesus' secret became also the secret of their own existence." (P. 23) It is not surprising that Fuchs can say that in faith we know ourselves to be at one with Jesus. Moreover, "just as our faith rests on the authority of Jesus, so our authority rests on the faith of Jesus" (p. 26).

How does faith arise? That remains hidden, says Fuchs. Nor is it adequate to say that it occurs through public preaching, for that merely moves the question back a step. But what one must say is *when* faith is present—namely, when the person of Jesus *comes* to speech (or is made effective—see note 88), for then it is manifest that God *came* to speech in Jesus (p. 29). In a later essay, he carries this point farther and says that "whoever speaks of Jesus is to think of God. The converse is also true: whoever wants to speak of God is to think of Jesus. Jesus and God belong together. In this the old creed and the New Testament are at one." [97] Here it is an either-or: Was God at work in the mission of Jesus, or not? If Jesus was justified in what he undertook, then his person is part of faith in God.

There is no doubt that Fuchs and Ebeling have moved the discussion beyond the Bultmannian impasse. While it will become evident to what extent the present argument is parallel to theirs,[98] as well as where it diverges, it is useful here to take note of important gains before calling attention to certain reservations.

To begin, it is but natural that we should applaud their conviction that the New Testament is concerned to interpret what Jesus is all about (*die Sache Jesu*, as they sometimes put it), and that this requires us to avoid taking Lessing's and Kierkegaard's assumption about the impotence of the past (i.e., the historical Jesus) for granted. They correctly see that it is insufficient to say that Jesus is the presupposition of the kerygma, and that he must be regarded as its center and criterion. Ebeling can make this shift because he does not see knowledge as a threat to faith, but understands them to be intimately interrelated.[99]

In the second place, Ebeling is on target when he insists that the historian's Jesus is not a set of data looking for an interpretation—brute facts—but evidence of a life grounded in a clear perception of God and his kingdom. Ebeling is also moving in the right direction when he observes that "object of faith" is not really the appropriate way to speak of Jesus. In the same way, Fuchs rightly says that faith does not believe in facts but, as I prefer to say, trusts a person. It is because a person is a network of words, deeds, motives, aims, etc. that one is required to ascertain critically what he was all about;

to do this critically means to continually compare his reading of the man with the evidence. This is why it is necessary to go behind the kerygma.

Third, Fuchs and Ebeling see that rehabilitating the centrality of the historical Jesus for Christian faith means rethinking the nature of faith. Bultmann's work is marked by his allergy for anything that might even suggest "legitimation"; their problem, however, is how faith is possible, specifically, how faith in Jesus is possible. Whether their proposed answer to to this question is appropriate is another thing.

Finally, Fuchs (like Jeremias) is correct in saying that given Jesus' audacity it is a matter of either-or; either he speaks for God validly or he does not. Unfortunately, neither Fuchs nor Ebeling makes as much of this as he should. In fact, it is at this point that our reservations begin.

Four reservations are important to note here.

(a) The position taken by Fuchs and Ebeling is reminiscent of Wilhelm Herrmann and Wilhelm Bousset, who emphasized the power of Jesus' own inner life.[100] Its ultimate roots go back to Schleiermacher. Whereas these liberals used the category of Jesus' religion, Fuchs and Ebeling speak of his faith, his certainty and confidence. But the structure of the argument is similar. Whether one speaks of the generative power of Jesus' religion or of his faith, it is far from self-evident that either in Jesus' own day or in ours meeting his confidence elicits the same from those whom he encounters. It is an assumption to say or to imply that Jesus' own faith (or self-understanding) is the sufficient cause of the rise of faith in another, though it may very well be a necessary factor.[101] It is because the whole effort was set in motion to correct Bultmann that they, and the new questers generally, emphasize the capacity of the historical Jesus to create the same faith that the kerygma calls for. What is minimized, therefore, is the offense of Jesus—despite the emphasis on Jesus' audacity. Not surprisingly, Fuchs repeatedly insists that the disciples' faith did not break down between Good Friday and Easter, so that Easter faith is the renewal, confirmation, and release of pre-Easter faith.[102]

(b) It is by no means clear what it means for Ebeling to say Jesus was "pure word." If this means merely that his entire career was controlled by his passion to communicate the kingdom, by word and deed, the statement may be apt enough. Yet, it appears that this terminology is used chiefly to facilitate the movement from Jesus as word to kerygma as word, and less for historical considerations. Moreover, was Jesus more pure word than John the Baptist or the Teacher of Righteousness? [103] And what are the criteria for making such distinctions? Surely not historical ones. Ebeling's question, What made Jesus what he was? is appropriate, but his answer appears too much shaped by the needs of a certain mode of theology after Bultmann to be convincing historically. The farther one reads, the more one suspects that Jesus is portrayed as the first post-Bultmannian Lutheran. Again, the strangeness—historically, the Jewishness of Jesus—is neglected. Where is his passion for Israel, for the righteousness of God—which is what the kingdom means, not simply God-relatedness in faith?

(c) Important aspects of faith in Jesus appear not to get their due. Among them are the communal character of faith (What is the role of the believing community in the rise of faith?); Jesus' own expectation that the future will vindicate him (Is Jesus more adequately grasped in terms of faith than of hope?); Jesus' expectation that the kingdom will bring the manifest righteousness of God for creation and the definitive defeat of the demonic (Can Jesus really be disabused of apocalyptic?). Since these elements of the historical Jesus lead directly to important dimensions of our believing in him, their neglect inevitably means that the analysis of our believing has been shortchanged as well.

(d) Since we will deal later with this theme, we can be content here simply to record a fundamental objection to the insistence that Jesus made God "present," that the kingdom came when Jesus "came to speech." This contention is nothing less than a thorough Johannizing of the historical Jesus, for whom, as we shall see, this kingdom came anticipatorily.

Before we indicate something of the direction that discussion will take it is useful to formulate several theses which have emerged from this survey and which will guide the subsequent chapters.

1. Against Bultmann, to concentrate on the historical Jesus is not to attempt to legitimate faith. (a) To the contrary, faith in Jesus requires us to know the content of the word "Jesus," if he is named in Christian preaching in our time at all. (b) Moreover, the historical Jesus forces an either-or decision about his validity. (c) Faith must remain venture and risk. Only when the ambiguous historical Jesus (ambiguous in the sense that he is not self-validating, not simply in the sense that "historical Jesus" contains probabilities) is central does faith retain its venture. Above all, the church cannot guarantee the validity of its message. (d) There is no reason why the reconstructed Jesus is less serviceable as a vehicle of the divine Word than an exegetical sermon. (e) Going behind the kerygma of the church is necessary to keep the church's proclamation honest. Only in Christendom can one assume that the church's message has validity *a priori*.

2. Against Jeremias, the historical Jesus is not self-validating or self-evidently "God at work." With Jeremias, it is the audacity of Jesus which forces the either-or.

3. With Fuchs and Ebeling, "Jesus" is not a set of brute facts at the bottom of the Gospels but a life with a discernible commitment. Moreover, he is the core and criterion of Christian faith and life.

4. Against Fuchs and Ebeling, it is not evident that Jesus was pure Word or can be grasped fully under the rubric faith. Nor is it clear that his faith is the sufficient cause for Christian faith in him.

II. The Proposed Mode: Trust

A. In the theme "the historical Jesus and faith" the difficulty lies not only in ascertaining "the historical Jesus" but in delineating "faith" appropriately, especially in view of the way faith has been developed since the time of the Enlightenment and its battle with Orthodoxy. Today, there are two difficulties of a rather elemental sort which need to be seen. In the first place, it is common to point out that faith is a noun for which we have no verb in English. Inevitably, when we use "believe" we distinguish "believing that" from "believing in," affirmation from commitment. Or we reach to the Latin distinction between *fides qua* and *fides quae*; helpful as this may be, the fact is that I do not "live in Latin" and therefore no distinctions that depend on this language really help the act of faith. Closer to home, the very phrase "act of faith" reveals the English difficulty because "faith" is an abstract noun that loses part of the reality in the process of abstraction. It reifies a living reality. This reification is manifest in such common expressions as "I have lost my faith," or "I have come to faith" or "I want to have more faith." Inescapably, therefore, discussions of Christian believing regularly disavow such distortions in order to insist that faith is a stance, a commitment, a process of deciding, a way of life, trusting. This simply shows how incapable the word "faith" is of saying directly what must be said.

In the second place, more serious is the fact that faith-believe polarizes into faith-doubt, belief-disbelief. Imperceptibly, the problem of faith becomes the problem of believing something, and of doing so by overcoming doubt. In the case of the gospel concerning Jesus, a credibility gap between fact and faith emerges, a problem we have traced from Lessing onward. Faith, in this heritage, repeatedly mainfests itself as certitude that overcomes doubt [104] or lack of adequate evidence. It does this either by efforts to demonstrate historically that Jesus is congruent with the kerygma or by requiring a leap over Lessing's ditch. Faith as persistence, as loyalty, as trust in the face of ambiguity, scarcely receives adequate attention. Finally, far too many discussions of faith are controlled by the need to avoid heretical pitfalls more than by the effort to give conceptual clarity to the phenomenon of believing and relying actually done by Christians.

B. Reasons such as these make it necessary to ask whether it is not time to seek a somewhat different terminology, less freighted with difficulties. We are not declaring "faith" to be legal tender no longer. Rather, we are suggesting that if most analyses of faith come around to speaking of it as trust, it is worthwhile to see whether we cannot say what needs to be said by using this term directly.

There are several reasons why trust is a more adequate way to say what needs to be said.

(1) Trust is so basic to human existence that it is universally accepted as a central dimension of life. One who is no longer capable of trust is often diagnosed as paranoid and in need of psychiatric help. Trust is a fundamental ingredient of life, virtually from the moment of birth. While one might say, "I have no faith" because definitions of it leave him out, he would scarcely say he has no trust. Trust is not an option. Therefore we have a "pre-understanding" of what trust is in a way and to an extent we no longer have for faith. One can therefore speak of trust and be understood much more readily than when one begins to speak of faith, for in the latter case one must immediately exclude misconceptions.

(2) More important, trust is an act of the self as a self in response to a self. We saw that Fuchs and Ebeling insisted that faith is not in facts but in a person, a response to a person in trust. The opposite of trust is not disbelief, incredulity or doubt, but suspicion, distrust, infidelity, hostility, or despair. In trust, one places himself at the disposal of another,[105] relies on him, and commits himself to him. Trust, being both noun and verb, allows one to see more clearly the central point—that one's relation to Jesus and to God is a movement of the self toward reliance and fidelity to another. One may believe statements or claims, but one trusts persons.

(3) Moreover, while trust is an intensely personal act it is by no means private or solitary but profoundly social. From childhood onward, trust arises in a texture of relationships, often over an extended period. Precisely because "I" am a network of relationships to others and to the structure of society, trust arises in the act of living, not as an

instantaneous "Yes" to a word. Furthermore, the trust-relation has a social quality because it is directed not toward a verifiable object but toward a life. This brings into play the entire network of relationships that constitute the self. Therefore there can be no split between "faith" and "ethics." Trusting is an ethical act, and acting manifests what one trusts. As H. Richard Niebuhr once put it, the supreme ethical question is, In what does a man trust? [106]

C. The decisive question concerns how the historical Jesus is related to the act of trust. What does it mean to trust Jesus? Because the rest of the book returns to this theme again and again, only a preliminary sketch is called for here in order to set the horizon.

First of all, just as Bultmann is correct in saying that faith does not arise from the acceptance of historical facts about Jesus, so it is true that trust is not the result of ackowledging the factuality of certain Jesus-data or of assenting to historical probabilities. In addition, more is involved than Jesus' own trust. At least three factors are at work: an elemental confidence in the historian's work, trust in the witness of those who commend Jesus as trustworthy, and one's own "reading" of Jesus' trustworthiness (which includes the character of Jesus' own trusting and the character of the One he trusted). In the post-Christendom situation, it is difficult to see how trust in Jesus can arise apart from the functioning of all three elements. One not predisposed to hearken to the church will simply not trust the Jesus it proclaims because it is the church which does so; he will insist on going behind the kerygma to inquire about the person for whom so much is claimed.[107] At the same time, the Jesus he finds will not be self-attesting, self-validating, self-legitimating. Therefore, the witness of those who say, "We have found him trustworthy" is essential. And, one's willingness to trust Jesus with his life emerges in conjunction with the other two elements. We must respect Fuchs' wisdom in saying that *how* this arises remains a mystery. Saying that trust is a response to the Word of God is an interpretive theological statement

70

made by the man who trusts, not a phenomenological one; nor can a theological statement be used as a censor against phenomenological analysis here any more than divine election can be used legitimately to explain historically the fact that in a given family one brother believes and the other does not.

In the second place, since trust is the bond of reliance and fidelity of one life to another, trust is an entirely appropriate way to speak of one's relation to Jesus. We recall Ebeling's point that "Jesus" is not a pile of data but a life. It is inadequate to say that faith is commitment to the kerygma, because this points beyond itself to Jesus, as Jeremias saw. If believing the gospel does not mean trusting the Jesus to whom it refers, it can only mean affirming a theological statement or a myth. One does not trust a proclamation or entrust himself to it; trust is directed toward a person, and the function of the kerygma is to make it possible for trust in Jesus to commence.

In the third place, it is appropriate to ask if Jesus is trustworthy, as trustworthy as the church claims. How does one conclude that the kerygma rightly and truly interprets Jesus? Two ways are important. One has already been noted—historical inquiry. To what has been said we would add only this: Given man's infinite capacity to rationalize as well as the fact that Jesus has been made the warrant for every sort of theological or social program, it is utterly essential to press the historical question critically against the church and its kerygma. This is a necessary move against the ideological use of Jesus. (This will be pursued in the next chapter.) The other way of testing the kerygma is the sheer act of living in the world. The daily encounter with the manifold mystery of life's inequities as well as its sudden glories, one's dealing with the misery of bondage to tyrannies of every kind as well as with the gift of freedom now and again—these put to test daily the claim that Jesus is the adequate disclosure of man's life before God. The deepest obstacles to trusting Jesus and the gospel are not lack of adequate data or an outmoded Weltanschauung but the moral enigma of life, personal and cultural. If the pressure of life, constantly threatened by evil

71

and disintegration, does not perpetually call into question the Christian claims about Jesus and God in such a way as to require these affirmations to be clarified and perhaps corroborated anew, then Christianity has indeed removed itself from life in order to pursue more convenient matters. The decisive question is not whether the historian can produce a sufficient quantity of data to justify making Jesus the object of absolute faith or whether the philosopher can provide a mode of thought and a hermeneutic capable of translating kerygmatic concepts into a viable idiom that does not embarrass the sophisticated Christian. Rather, it is whether he who trusts Jesus and the gospel finds power to live in the world without cutting himself off from it, whether by trusting Jesus he can take up the task of reconciling man to man and man to God.

If we grant, then, that it is not only permissible but essential to make a place for the testing of the kerygma by critical study and critical reflection, and if we grant that the man to whom the kerygma refers is a historical person who, by definition, does not validate himself, how shall the gospel be preached so that genuine trust in him can arise? That is the theme of the next chapter. But first it is useful to explore further the phenomenology of trust and to relate it to the wider horizons of Christian theology. Our aim is to suggest the potential of working with the category of trust.

III. The Potential of Trust

We will explore the potential of trust for Christian theology by setting up a rather ordinary, though grossly simplified, situation involving two men—Jones, who is a trustworthy man of integrity, and Smith, who is not only untrustworthy himself but cannot trust Jones. We are constructing not an allegory, but a suggestive analogy. After all, not every facet of intrahuman relations is directly transferable to theological reflection.

The character of trust may be approached through the crescendo of its opposite, specifically by noting elements of the dynamics of the movement away from trust: non-trust, disappointment, suspicion, distrust, hostility.

Non-trust is simply the want or absence of trust. This is often expressed with reference to a new neighbor. "I don't know yet whether I can trust him." This is a relatively open situation because one expects to ascertain, by various means, whether the man will prove to be trustworthy. As yet, absence of trust implies no moral judgment on the newcomer, or on the established resident. Moreover, this level suggests that non-trust is temporary, and that the normal situation is a network of trusts or "distrusts." Life is as much a process of learning whom and what one may count on as it is a matter of ascertaining (or acquiring) concepts to hold.

Disappointment expresses a sense of misplaced trust which has not yet solidified. One still trusts the person even though a particular expectation was not fulfilled. The capacity and willingness to trust is not yet overridden by experience. On the other hand, in *suspicion* one trusts his own surmise about another more than he trusts him. Suspicion frequently emerges from a series of disappointments. It lives by the disparity between the apparent and the probably real in the other. Jones, for example, is suspicious of Smith because disappointing experiences have made it likely that Smith will promise more than he will deliver. Consequently, Smith's assurance, "This time I'll really be there with the boat," is met with suspicion precisely because the past disparity between promise and act is extended into the future. Jones does not trust the real Smith, whom he now thinks is unreliable. Jones relies more on his experience with Smith than on Smith's assurances.

A factor now appears which will become increasingly important in the descending steps away from trust: bondage. At this level, bondage is not yet severe because Jones's suspicion can be allayed by Smith's arriving with the boat as promised. Should this be the case, Jones's bondage to his own experience of Smith would be reduced because Smith has not been as unreliable as expected. Moreover, Smith's arriving with the boat also reduces his own bondage to his past. For both men, Smith's fidelity to his word, his adherence to his pledge, is a liberating event. Furthermore, Smith's keeping his word this time also begins to make possible Jones's trust in him: "Perhaps I misjudged the man; he may be more reliable than I thought." In other words, the removal of suspicion is marked by a critical stance toward one's own perception as well as by a new readiness to trust the other. Put more abstractly, in a situation of suspicion, faithfulness to one's word creates a measure of freedom. On the other hand, if Smith does not bring the boat, Jones's suspicion is confirmed: "I knew he wouldn't do it! Why did I depend on him? Why didn't I make other arrangements? Next time . . ." In other words, repeated disappointment tightens the bondage under which both men live: Jones has moved from disappointment to suspicion to *distrust,* and Smith himself may begin to see that it is ever more difficult to establish his integrity with Jones. Bondage to history has settled over both men: Jones distrusts Smith, and Smith—in his candid moments—may distrust himself because he sees his words over-commit him repeatedly.

With the hardening of suspicion into distrust, the credibility gap that occasioned the suspicion has become a gulf. On this level, words readily come to be seen as strategies instead of commitments. Even though Jones remains a man of his word, he is not prepared to believe Smith or to act on what he tells him. It is, of course, also possible that Jones himself is affected so that he begins to deal guardedly with Smith. Words now no longer reveal and commit the men to each other but veil them from each other. Soon each begins to ask, "I wonder what's really behind that. What is being said? What is being withheld?" Each then must act not on the basis of words but on the basis of his own reading of the intent imputed to the other.

People who distrust each other commonly prefer not to have any relation to each other at all, and frequently restructure their lives in order to avoid each other altogether if possible. If these lives cannot be separated readily, one is doomed to live, or work, or worship (!) with persons between whom distrust reigns. Now the bondage of this situation is difficult to conceal, and we may speak of it as *alienation.* Not only do such persons find little they can speak honestly about with each other (because doing so would entrust their views to the other and so commit a part of themselves to the other), but they have no basis for discussing anything significant with each other. In the presence of the other, each pulls into himself because he is persuaded that movement toward the other will be met not with integrity but by feigned response, manipulation, or even exploitation ("If I tell him how I feel or what I think, he will take advantage of me sometime; when I'm in a bind he'll use it against me"). Because external relations must be maintained (the couple is still married, the man remains on the staff and cannot be fired, neither neighbor will sell his house and move), the breakdown of trust produces a hellish situation, for there appears to be no escape from the self-destroying network. It is not merely that the persons have become strangers and aliens to each other but that they must confront each other and deal with each other as the estranged and the alienated, often in situations in which this must be concealed from the public. Even if Jones does not respond in kind to Smith, alienation is the fate of both; if Smith's distrust evokes the same from Jones, each exacerbates the situation.

It is almost inevitable that now one begins to justify himself by accusing the other of "starting it all" or of being "too stubborn to admit he's wrong," etc. Another way of asserting one's fundamental innocence is to steel oneself for such a life by shifting the blame onto a third person or external factor. In estranged situations, it is virtually impossible for a neutral observer to factor causes and to assess blame accurately, for the more each party offers his assessment to the judge, the clearer it becomes that neither is telling the whole truth and that both are justifying themselves at the expense of the other. With this we reach actual or covert *hostility*, for each rebels at the move of the other or takes a defensive posture against him. As in the cold war, balance of terror becomes a way of life, and each counts on it for his security. Now, trusting the other is shrugged off as fantasy and wishful thinking.

The urge to defend oneself ought not to be equated with the urge to justify oneself, though they often overlap. One justifies himself before a third party (or before himself) from whom he expects a vindicating word, one which affirms his rectitude. But one defends himself against the threat directly. This is why one moves easily from alienation to hostility. Behind this move lies a sensed need to reconstitute oneself because he has been defiled by being held untrustworthy, especially if one believes he is distrusted without sufficient warrant. To be distrusted is to have one's integrity impugned, to have one's being called into question. Seen from the other side, unwarranted distrust is an attack on another's being, a pollution of his integrity. This is why defensive moves are really acts designed to reconstitute the self by getting rid of what is defiling and debilitating.

The foregoing remarks have had in view primarily a reciprocal alienation in which there was mutual, even if not equal, responsibility. In order to allow our phenomenological reflection to become more serviceable, more translucent for explicit theological thinking, we need to ponder the dynamics of a situation in which a person of moral integrity and fidelity to his word is distrusted nevertheless.

Christian theology, like its parent Judaism, has consistently understood this to be the true analogue. The faithfulness of God is by no means to be taken for granted, either in the history of the biblical tradition, or in the general history of religion or in contemporary theology (the "death of God" can be viewed as the assertion that God has not been able to keep faith with himself or with men in modern times as the living God but has simply "died out").

In the history of Hebrew-Christian theology, the faithfulness of Yahweh to himself became a dominant motif, though in the process the earlier tradition of the capriciousness of Yahweh was not obliterated entirely, as the story of his trying to kill Moses en route to Egypt clearly shows (Exod. 4:24-26). Later in the face of repeated national disaster, the prophets insisted that God was indeed faithful; in fact, his fidelity was manifested precisely in the disaster because his moral integrity could be counted on—that is, he took himself and them seriously enough to punish a faithless people. Furthermore, the same faithfulness was the basis for affirming that disaster was penultimate and not final, for God could be counted on to keep his covenant-word with his people: he would redeem the exiles in order to keep faith, even if this was but a remnant of the people. The same faithfulness-of-God motif generated the apocalyptic theology and the theodicy problem, for now the problem was intensified: where is the fidelity of God when those who are faithful to him are slain?

This development can be appreciated better in light of ancient alternatives (they have modern equivalents, of course). Neither a henotheistic theology nor a polytheistic religion must grapple profoundly with such matters. In the former case, historical disaster could mean that the victor's god has shown himself the stronger; and in the latter case, the whole human situation is subject to the capricious outcome of intramural struggles of the gods and the natural forces they embody. Only a monotheist religion must grapple with the moral integrity of God in the face of human experience, and struggle to affirm that the One is trustworthy and worship-worthy. If it is unable to make this affirmation, it must settle for a capricious God who cannot be counted on (or who can be counted on to be capricious!), or for one who is indifferent.

This development of the understanding of God's faithfulness to his goodness and to his word took place in the course of the Old Testament; it is foundational for the New. In fact, this is what the righteousness of God is all about—the vindication of the integrity of God. For Christians, this occurred pro-leptically and paradigmatically in Jesus. We shall return to this theme in the last chapter.

How does it happen that someone trustworthy is not trusted? It is difficult to claim that the trustworthiness of Jones is so well concealed from Smith that he never learns of it, for by definition moral integrity cannot be self-concealed. If Jones is utterly trustworthy, the only way for Smith not to know it is to remain unrelated to him; if, on the other hand, they are neighbors, colleagues, or partners, Jones's trustworthiness will manifest itself steadily at each encounter and level of relation. Even though Jones is affected by Smith's distrust, he will resist retaliation in kind, for he will be consistent with his own character.

If Jones's "word is as good as his bond," and if his word is consistent with his character—that is, we are dealing with the integrity of goodness—why does Smith not trust him? Since normally we instinctively trust what we know to be trustworthy, we can scarcely avoid seeing Smith as a tragic figure. His distrust of Jones violates the nature of things, for like calls to like. Something must have gone wrong in Smith, for distrust (like trust) is a historical relationship, not one traceable to genes. As we shall see in Chapter III, the theological analogue to this tragedy is the myth of the Fall.

For our analogy it is not necessary to draw up a master list of reasons; it will suffice to note several major possibilities. Smith may simply doubt that Jones is really trustworthy. "Every man has his price," he may reason, and infer that Jones has been trustworthy simply because thus far no one (or no situation) has yet offered him sufficient inducement to compromise. In Genesis 3, it will be recalled, the serpent begins the enticement by raising precisely this question: "Did God really say . . . ?" That is, Is his word reliable? The movement away from trust (distrust and disloyalty) is the root sin, not lack of certainty as Ebeling says.[108] Or he may doubt Jones' integrity because he claims he does not know enough about Jones. Were he to know the real Jones he would find clay feet there too. (Here we touch the theme of knowledge and trust which runs through this entire essay. Trust is not possible without some kind of knowledge or perception. But it is equally clear that trust is not the inevitable outcome of accurate information.) But it should not be overlooked that Smith does not know enough about Jones to warrant not trusting him because on each occasion Jones shows himself to be trustworthy. For Smith to be distrustful, then, can only mean that Smith projects knowledge of himself and of other men onto Jones. The habituated life-style of Smith manifests itself in his refusing to trust the trustworthy Jones. In this situation, Smith's not trusting tells us a good deal about Smith, but nothing about Jones himself. By analogy, this is why the phrase "death of God" is so ambiguous; it says a good deal about our culture but nothing about God.

It does, however, tell us how Smith will "read" Jones. He responds not to the real Jones but to the imaged (and imagined) Jones, the Jones he thinks is but another instance of untrustworthy persons he has met again and again. The longer this confusion and misinterpretation exist, the more Smith's life is built on false premises about Jones—premises that, of course, are taken to be realistic and true. Genuine trust of the trustworthy will not emerge until knowledge of the truth about Jones penetrates Smith, for valid trust is impossible without truth. (It has often been observed that atheism, as we know it in the West, is really the rejection of the God of the church, the ideological God as I would prefer to say it.)

How does the truth penetrate Smith, and what sort of truth will this be? It is not merely evidential truth (truth for which evidence and accurate facts can be adduced) that is requisite because trust is not simply the result of rational decision or the outcome of being confronted by facts. Trust is a response of the total self, not simply of the mind or the will. Hence, the distrusting self must be healed at the center. This occurs when the capacity to trust, debilitated by a series of experiences which shaped a distrusting life-style, is restored. It is not necessary here to outline clinically the several ways this may be achieved. But it clear that no incapacitated person comes to trust by being accosted with the demand, "Trust!" just as he is not enabled to trust by hearing reasons why he must or can. (The pertinence of this observation for the Bultmannian perspective should be clear.) Nothing short of being trusted, and of being in a context in which persons trust one another (thereby including him), perhaps on a rather elemental level at first, will heal his ability to trust. By trusting one another, this community witnesses to the trustworthiness of persons. In short, it is experiential truth, not merely evidential truth, which is needed. This observation is a hint of the role of the church as the community that witnesses to trust not merely by commending it but by facilitating it.

It is necessary to reflect not only on what is requisite for Smith, but on what can be expected of Jones if Smith is to be helped. It is difficult for Smith to conceal from Jones that he

79

does not trust him. (In Genesis 3, it will be recalled, Adam and Eve hid themselves from God because they could no longer face him.) Since distrust offends one's being, Jones can be expected to deal with the situation, for his own sake as well as for Smith's, since it would be a strange moral integrity that "didn't give a damn" for Smith. But how will Jones maintain his integrity in order to help Smith? Surely not by conditional trust: "If you don't trust me, I won't trust you," for then Jones's integrity would have been mortgaged to Smith. The only way for trust to emerge from Smith is for Jones to persist in not allowing Smith's distrust to govern the future totally. Theologically, the Pauline understanding of justification by faith expresses the freedom of God to deal with man on his own terms and not to be tethered to a *quid pro quo*. This is especially clear in Rom. 9–11, which is but the obverse of the argument in Rom. 1–8.

Jones need not permit Smith to escape the consequences of distrust. (Theologically, this is what is meant by the "wrath of God," or the "judgment of God.") but Jones does need to maintain his integrity and freedom. Smith can begin to trust Jones only if the latter is steadfast enough for Smith to encounter his fidelity.

Because Smith's distrust does Jones an injustice, coming to trust Jones not only brings with it a new self-understanding but an emergent new life-style. (As we shall see in Chapter 4, this is what is meant by repentance.) Smith may actually confess to Jones that he had wronged him. Though the consequences of the past cannot be repealed, the new relationship will nevertheless manifest a certain freedom from the tyranny of the past. Smith will discover that Jones does not hold a grudge against him and never has; that is, Smith will know that he is forgiven. Moreover, Smith's pilgrimage is a response to what Jones's fidelity to himself and to Smith made possible. Theologically, one would speak of the prevenient grace of God, of the *extra nos* dimension of the gospel, and so on.

We must now reflect further on the role of a third party in this new relationship. Since Smith distrusts the trustworthy Jones, what is required is an event or deed by Jones which intersects this situation in such a way as to evoke a fundamental realignment of perception and trust; otherwise each incident is but an extension of the past. Ideally, this will occur in Smith's own encounter with Jones. If not, Smith must come to learn about that intersection from those who can attest to it. (Here we allude to the difference between the event of Jesus himself and the accessibility of that event to contemporary men through the Gospels and historiography. We also allude to the role of preaching as witness by the church.) In telling about Jones, the reporters invariably confront Smith with a perception of Jones which challenges his. Moreover, because the reporters themselves trust Jones, perhaps even because by a certain event they came to do so, they report their own convictions as well as Jones's integrity: "He really came through for us."

Now let us take a further step. Suppose the event they report concerns a man who found Jones utterly reliable when he trusted Jones in a crisis. (Again, we anticipate the argument of Chapters 4 and 5 in which the death of Jesus will be given special attention.) Should Smith begin to trust Jones on this basis, he will begin to trust him the way the reported man did (and the reporters do). In Smith's growth toward mature trust, he will assimilate the reported test case because it is this which made the trust possible and did so in a particular way.

Thinking analogically of trust in persons and trust in God soon reaches its limits because the reality termed "God" is *sui generis*. God, after all, is not present to us the way Jones can be present to Smith. More important, Smith is not contingent on Jones the way man is contingent on God. To pursue our analogy requires us to restructure the *given* relation between Jones and Smith so that they are no longer equals who may or may not have a relationship. It is inherent in the concept "God" that we understand him not as man's peer but as his Ground. God has a right, then, to be trusted; this consideration escalates the analogy to the breaking point.

The Bible uses metaphors such as king, shepherd, husband, or father to give articulation to this crucial dimension. Each of them includes the natural right of the sovereign: the trust-worthy king has a right to expect allegiance from his subjects; the reliable shepherd can expect his flock to follow; the faith-ful husband can expect fidelity from his wife—who in that society was not his equal; the responsible father can expect trustful obedience from his son. These metaphors no longer convey directly their inner logic because our total situation has changed. Monarchs are subject to constitutions imposed on them, often against their will, or they are in danger of being deposed; shepherds are replaced by sheepherders and fences; husbands are partners (frequently exchangeable junior part-ners); and sometimes fathers are but sires and bill-paying sponsors. Still, something of the old symbols often remains.

In any case, we are not altogether without analogies. Even though our democratic society has so eroded the hierarchical relation of sovereign-subject, we do not live without hierar-chically structured relationships altogether. No institution exists without them. Today's turmoil reflects this because it is the symptom of the breakdown of trust in scaled responsibility and accountability. Conversely, the power of certain figures—whether a Martin Luther King, a Kennedy, or a Ronald Reagan—is directly proportionate to the amount of trust they generate among their constituents, who constitute the base of the pyramid of power. Persons trust invisible hierarchies because they confer meaning and direction on those who trust them, whether it be the academic, political, or financial game, for each has ways of conferring status and advancement—ways regarded as sufficiently trustworthy to be appropriated as the rules of the game. These implicitly trusted structures have value-valence.

Where trust in these structures begins to fail, there is aliena-tion from the system and from the values it embodies, as well as from the person who epitomizes the system. Because one is a participant in the system and not only its beneficiary, loss of trust produces alienation not only from the system, but from the self, because the self cannot extricate itself fully from it. Conversely, alienation from the system, which may have been provoked by a variety of factors, leads to loss of trust in its values, warrants, and symbols (including person-symbols). Put theologically, loss of trust in the Ground of being means not only loss of trust in religion and theology but gross guilt and various symptoms of rebellion. This usually occurs in the name of something alleged to be more trustworthy. This is the meaning of idolatry. (The dynamics of Exod. 32 ought not be overlooked: when trust in Yahweh and Moses declined sufficiently [he had not returned from Mt. Sinai] Aaron was encouraged to "make a god," a bull [the symbol of power] who would not desert them.) In short, we trust what confers value and being on us and our fellows; this constitutes the self and society as well.

A final word about our friends, Jones and Smith. When Smith begins to trust Jones, Smith himself begins the process of becoming trustworthy. Theologically, this can be termed "salvation." Furthermore, when Smith begins to trust Jones, he begins to trust what Jones does. Theologically, the man who trusts God begins to accept life and to trust it.

NOTES TO CHAPTER TWO

1. *The So-called Historical Jesus*, pp. 53-54.
2. Henry Chadwick shows that Lessing's plan was to state the case for orthodoxy with sufficient clarity to expose its untenability, and thereby to hasten its downfall. *Lessing's Theological Writings*, ed. Henry Chadwick (London: A. & C. Black, 1956; Stanford: Stanford University Press, reprint, 1967), p. 13. Page references are to this edition.
3. *Ibid*, pp. 32-33. For an analysis of the theological milieu of Lessing, see Karl Aner, *Die Theologie der Lessingzeit* (Tübingen: Max Niemeyer, 1929; reprinted by Georg Olms in Hildesheim in 1964).
4. *Philosophical Fragments*. Howard V. Hong's revision of David Swenson's translation (Princeton: Princeton University Press, 1962), p. 76. Unless otherwise stated, all references to the *Fragments* are to this edition.
5. At the outset of "On the Proof of the Spirit and of Power" Lessing wrote, "Fulfilled prophecies, which I myself experience, are one thing; fulfilled prophecies, of which I know only from history that others say they have experienced them, are another." After repeating the point with regard to miracles, he concludes,

"If I had lived at the time of Christ, then of course the prophecies fulfilled in his person would have made me pay great attention to him. If I had actually seen him do miracles; if I had no cause to doubt that these were true miracles; then in a worker of miracles who had been marked out so long before, I would have gained so much confidence that I would willingly have submitted my intellect to his, and I would have believed him in all things in which equally indisputable experiences did not tell against him." *Lessing's Theological Writings*, pp. 51-52. In contrast with Lessing's view that the power of the past diminishes in time, almost like radiation, T. A. Roberts expresses a modern opposite—that by critical historical study, we understand the past better than participants in it. "It is not misleading to draw attention to the fact that we may 'know Christ' better than his disciples ever knew him. And this positive result is the complete, as it is the sufficient, justification of historical criticism of the gospels." *History and Christian Apologetic* (London: S.P.C.K. 1960), p. 80 (see also p. 90).

6. *Philosophical Fragments*, p. 125: "If the fact in question is an absolute fact [incarnation] . . . it would be a contradiction to suppose that time had any power to differentiate the fortunes of men with respect to it, that is to say, in any decisive sense. Whatever can be essentially differentiated by time is *eo ipso* not the Absolute . . . [The Absolute] remains itself ever the same; and though it enters continually into relations with other things, it constantly remains *status absolutus*. But the absolute fact is an historical fact. Unless we are careful to insist on this point our entire hypothesis is nullified; for then we speak only of an eternal fact. The absolute fact is an historical fact, and as such it is the object of Faith." Kierkegaard also denied that the credibility of the contemporary witness of Jesus is decisive (p. 129). Nevertheless, the historical contemporary is important, though not decisive: "The successor believes by *means of* (this expresses the occasion) the testimony of the contemporary, and *in virtue of* the condition he himself receives from the God." (P. 131. His italics.) See also pp. 109, 106-7.

7. Kierkegaard not only knew Lessing's work (through Strauss's quotation of it in *Die Christliche Glaubenslehre* [1840-41], which had been translated into Danish) but expressly commented, "Lessing uses the word *leap* as if its being an expression or a thought were a matter of indifference; I understand it as a thought." (Quoted from Niels Thulstrup's Commentary in *Philosophical Fragments*, p. 149.) It is not accidental that the *Philosophical Fragments'* title page sets the problem in terms that take up Lessing's question: "Is an historical point of departure possible for an eternal consciousness; how can such a point of departure have any other than a merely historical interest; is it possible to base an eternal happiness upon historical knowledge?" Still, Lessing and Kierkegaard understood the leap somewhat differently. See James Brown, *Kierkegaard, Heidegger, Buber*

and Barth (originally published as *Subject and Object in Modern Theology*, 1955) (New York: Macmillan, 1962), pp. 58-59.

8. In the same paragraph from which the penultimate quotation in the foregoing note was taken, Kierkegaard wrote, "Only one who receives the condition from God is a believer. (This corresponds exactly to the requirement that man must renounce his reason, and on the other hand discloses the only form of authority that corresponds to Faith.)" (p. 129). For an exposition of Kierkegaard's view, see the important book by Hermann Diem, *Kierkegaard's Dialectic of Existence*, trans. Harold Knight (London: Oliver & Boyd, 1959; German ed., 1950), esp. chaps. 11, 13.

9. When Kierkegaard grants, not without irony, that the contemporary of Jesus has the advantage of seeing the Teacher, he immediately asks, "May he then believe his eyes? Why not? But may he also believe that this makes him a disciple? By no means. If he believes his eyes he is deceived, for the God is not immediately knowable. But then perhaps he may shut his eyes. Just so; but if he does, what profit does he have from his contemporaneity?" *Philosophical Fragments*, p. 78. Kierkegaard is explicit on the relation of understanding to Paradox: "We do not ask that he [the learner] understand the Paradox, but only understand that this is the Paradox." (P. 72).

10. "The historical fact that the God has been in human form is the essence of the matter; the rest of the historical detail is not even as important as if we had to do with a human being instead of with the God. Jurists say that a capital crime submerges all lesser crimes and so it is with Faith. Its absurdity makes all petty difficulties vanish. Inconsistencies which would otherwise be disconcerting do not count for anything here; they make no difference whatsoever. . . . If the contemporary generation had left nothing behind them but these words: 'We have believed that in such and such a year the God appeared among us in the humble figure of a servant, that he lived and taught in our community, and finally died,' it would have done all that was necessary; for this little advertisement, this *nota bene* on a page of universal history, would be sufficient to afford an occasion for a successor, and the most voluminous account can in all eternity do nothing more." *Philosophical Fragments*, pp. 130-31. Hermann Diem insists that one must not forget that "Kierkegaard's arguments are determined by his adversary's position [Hegel], in which he had to make a breach." Consequently this is "no independent exposition of dogmatic ideas but only observations *ad hoc.*" *Kierkegaard's Dialectic of Existence*, p. 191. In twentieth-century appropriation of Kierkegaard, however, the anti-Hegel front was generally ignored, and his works were used as quarries for cornerstones in a construction of "existential systems" —as Diem sees (p. 205). Richard Campbell has also seen that the polemical quality of the "experiment in thought" leans on Hegel for its character, and has suggested that Kierkegaard there-

fore proposed "a thesis to end all theological theses"—the alternative to the Hegelian synthesis. "Lessing's Problem and Kierkegaard's Answer," *SJT* 19 (1966).

11. Originally a paper presented to the Heidelberg Academy of Sciences and published by Carl Winter in Heidelberg in 1961, it is now available in English as "The Primitive Christian Kerygma and the Historical Jesus" in *The Historical Jesus and the Kerygmatic Christ*, ed. Carl E. Braaten and Roy A. Harrisville, pp. 15-42. All references are to this translation.

12. Walter Schmithals points out that Bultmann not only received his theological training in pre–World War I liberalism and then became, with Barth and Gogarten, one of the leading proponents of dialectical theology but that he expressly sought to combine the decisive insights of the latter with the heritage of the former, assuming a critical stance toward both. (Expressed in "In eigener Sache," a response to Rene Marle's interpretation of Bultmann; now in *Glauben und Verstehen* III [Tübingen: J. C. B. Mohr (Paul Siebeck), 1960], p. 178.) Moreover, Schmithals rightly points out that Bultmann's discovery of Heidegger, his colleague in Marburg from 1923-28, did not cause him to abandon or modify his dialectical theology. *An Introduction to the Theology of Rudolf Bultmann*, trans. John Bowden (Minneapolis: Augsburg, 1968; German ed., 1966), pp. 14 ff. On the other hand, Dan Otto Via has suggested that with respect to the question of the place of the historical Jesus for faith and theology, Bultmann has become somewhat more negative. *The Parables* (Philadelphia: Fortress Press, 1967), p. 195. Nevertheless, Schubert Ogden and Van A. Harvey have argued persuasively that Bultmann's views have not changed (against Robinson). See "How New Is the 'New Quest of the Historical Jesus'?" in *The Historical Jesus and the Kerygmatic Christ*, pp. 197 ff.

13. In 1924, Bultmann showed his affinity with the dialectical theology newly launched by Barth. "Liberal Theology and the Latest Theological Movement" in *Faith and Understanding*, I, trans. Louise Pettibone Smith (New York: Harper, 1969), pp. 28-52. Even before, Bultmann spoke of God as hidden and mysterious, "full of contradictions and riddles," so that "if we want to see God, then the first thing we should say to ourselves is that we may not see him as we have conceived him." See his Pentecost sermon of 1917, "The Hidden and Revealed God," in *Existence and Faith*, trans. and ed. Schubert Ogden (New York: Meridian, 1960), pp. 23-24; cf. esp. pp. 26 ff.

14. "To believe in the Word of God means to abandon all merely human security. . . . Faith is the abandonment of man's own security and the readiness to find security only in the unseen beyond, in God. This means that faith is security where no security can be seen. . . . This faith can become real only in its 'nevertheless' against the world. For in the world nothing of of God and of His action is visible or can be visible to man who seeks security in the world." *Jesus Christ and Mythology* (Lon-

don: SCM Press, 1960), p. 40. Compare these sentences with those of Kierkegaard in note 11.
15. See his statments in "Die Krisis des Glaubens" (1931) in *Glauben und Verstehen* II (Tübingen: J. C. B. Mohr [Paul Siebeck], 1952), pp. 16-17.
16. "The Primitive Christian Kerygma," p. 25.
17. *Ibid.*, p. 18.
18. When Bultmann compares the Gnostic theology of redemption with that of early Christianity, he finds a great deal of similarity in pivotal matters. Yet two things distinguish Christianity: the historical Jesus and the conception of the Word and the faith it elicits. Regarding the former he writes, "It is the appearance of Jesus of Nazareth and his crucifixion, events whose historicity is vouched for by eye witnesses and by the tradition of which they are the source. All the same it would be wrong to lay too much stress on this. For to begin with the historical person of Jesus was very soon turned into a myth in primitive Christianity. Furthermore, the Gnostics also believed that the advent of the redeemer was a real event, and the source of the tradition enshrined in their worship and doctrine." As far as the Word of preaching is concerned, it diverges from Gnosticism precisely because it calls for repentance of the integral self from itself as a self, not for the freedom of the essential, divine spark from the rest of man, as in Gnosticism. This means in effect, that virtually the sole distinctive of Christianity is the self-understanding of man's historical existence. *Primitive Christianity*, trans. R. H. Fuller (New York: Meridian, 1956), pp. 200-201. The similarity between Bultmann's own theology and that of Gnosticism has been alleged from time to time. For a reasonably judicious discussion see W. Rordorf, "The Theology of Rudolf Bultmann and Second Century Gnosis," NTS 13 (1967), 351-62.

David Cairns sees Bultmann's appeal to the historical Jesus as the hallmark of Christianity in contrast with Hellenistic mythology to be a contradiction of his insistence that the historical Jesus is of no real significance for us today. *Gospel Without Myth?* (London: SCM Press, 1960), p. 155. Implicitly, then, Bultmann concedes that should historical study prove that Jesus never lived, the historical basis of the kerygma would have been dissolved. But for him this is only a hypothetical, not a real, possibility. On the other hand, a pure "that-ness" of Jesus is impossible to conceive, as Ernst Haenchen also sees. "Probleme des Johanneischen 'Prologs' " in *Gott und Mensch* (Tübingen: J. C. B. Mohr [Paul Siebeck], 1965), pp. 121-22, n. 37.
19. "The Primitive Christian Kerygma," p. 17.
20. *Ibid.*, p. 30.
21. "In the Christian proclamation, man is not at all offered an historical report about a piece of the past which he could check or establish critically or reject; rather he is told that in what then occurred, whatever it may have been like, God acted and that through this act of God the Word of divine judgment and of

forgiveness which now encounters him is legitimated, that the meaning of that act of God is nothing other than the effectualizing of this Word, the proclamation of the Word itself." "Die Krisis des Galubens," p. 16. Bultmann's understanding of kerygma and narrative has been challenged on the basis of the New Testament itself. For example, Siegfried Schulz formulates: "Proclamation as Narration, that is the program of the Markan Evangelist." *Die Stunde der Botschaft* (Hamburg: Furche-Verlag, 1967), esp. p. 45. A still different consideration is offered by Ernst Käsemann, who insists not only that a kerygma without narrative becomes an idea, but that the narrative form is grounded in apocalyptic. "The Beginnings of Christian Theology" (1960) now in *New Testament Questions of Today*, trans. W. J. Montague (Philadelphia: Fortress Press, 1969), pp. 96-97.

22. "The Concept of Revelation in the New Testament," in *Existence and Faith*, p. 91; see also "The Primitive Christian Kerygma," pp. 20 ff.

23. *Jesus Christ and Mythology*, p. 84. This statement is preceded by the claim that demythologization is nothing less than a radical application of justification by faith to the sphere of knowledge since it deprives the interpreter of all security. More than three decades earlier, Bultmann had also contended that the Reformation principle of the sanctity of all work must not be interpreted to mean that any labor serves God directly. Only indirectly does one serve God. *Ergo*, the exegete has only mediate access to God and his Word. "Liberal Theology and the Latest Theological Movement," pp. 41 ff.

24. "The Concept of Revelation in the New Testament," p. 78. Kierkegaard argued the same point. As Hermann Diem put it, "Faith must always contain an echo of the scandal that has been traversed. The believer cannot once for all have decided for faith and against scandalisation, but at every moment in which he believes he must still overcome the possibility of scandal. "This distinguishes the experience of scandalisation from mere *sacrificium intellectus* which is made once for all, and as a result of which the difficulties are decisively overcome." *Kierkegaard's Dialectic of Existence*, p. 69.

25. *History and Eschatology* (Gifford Lectures 1955) (Edinburgh: University Press, 1957), p. 151. The American edition bears the title *The Presence of Eternity* (New York: Harper 1957).

26. *Ibid.*, p. 153. In addition, Bultmann speaks of the Christ-event as "the once-and-for-all eschatological event, which is continually re-enacted in the word of proclamation. . . . The Word of God is what it is only in event." "Bultmann replies to his Critics" in *Kerygma and Myth*, ed. H. W. Bartsch, trans. and ed. R. H. Fuller (Harper Torchbook; New York: Harper, 1961), p. 209.

27. "The Primitive Christian Kerygma," p. 40.

28. "All possible demonstrations that the historical Jesus loved this man or that, many men or all men, do not say what has to be be said, i.e., what is said by the proclamation of Christ—that God has loved us in Christ and reconciled us to himself (II

Cor. 5:18; John 3:18). For the love directed to *me*—and this alone can make me a new creature—cannot be demonstrated by historical observation. It can only be promised to me directly; and this is what is done by the proclamation." "The Concept of Revelation in the New Testament," p. 87.

29. "As an eschatological event this 'once for all' is always present in the proclaimed word, not as a timeless truth, but as happening here and now. Certainly the Word says to me that God's grace is prevenient grace which has already acted for me; but not in such a way that I can look back on it as an historical event of past." *Jesus Christ and Mythology*, p. 82. Bultmann insists that this "nowness" of the Word by no means dissolves the once-upon-a-time-ness of the event. "Zum Problem der Entmythologisierung," *Kerygma und Mythos II*, H. W. Bartsch, ed. (Hamburg: Herbert Reich, Evangelischer Verlag, 1952), p. 204.

30. "Jesus and Paul" in *Existence and Faith*, p. 200.

31. In "A Reply to the Theses of J. Schniewind" (who had responded to Bultmann's essay on demythologizing) Bultmann referred to the kerygma as a "sacramental event" because "it re-presents the events of the past in such a way that it renews them, and thus becomes a personal encounter for me." *Kerygma and Myth*, p. 115. John L. McKenzie sees this too: "In Bultmann's hypothesis there is only one real sacrament, the proclaimed word, and only one real sacramental effect, faith." McKenzie's inference that this is close to the Old Testament symbolic acts is wide of the mark, however, for he himself admits that they do not reenact the saving event—precisely what Bultmann says about the Word (*see New Testament Theology*, I, 135). "The Sacraments in Bultmann's Theology" in *Rudolf Bultmann in Catholic Thought*, T. F. O'Meara, O.P., and D. M. Weisser, O. P., eds. (New York: Herder and Herder, 1968), pp. 160-61. Karl Barth has criticized Bultmann, and certain Catholic theologians as well, for such a view. *Church Dogmatics*, IV, 1, p. 767.

32. "The Primitive Christian Kerygma," p. 41. Whether this view is more Protestant than Catholic or vice versa is debated. Hasenhüttl reports that in lectures (Summer, 1961), Ernst Käsemann saw it as clearly Protestant, citing Schleiermacher's point that for Protestants the individual belongs to the church because he belongs to Christ, whereas the Catholic belongs to Christ because he belongs to the church. But is Schleiermacher's dictum a valid guide here? *Der Glaubensvollzug: Eine Begegnung mit Rudolf Bultmann aus Katholischem Glaubensverständnis* (Essen: Lugderus Verlag Hubert Wingen, 1963), pp. 88, n. 12. In any case, Hasenhüttl gocs much too far when he says there is no individualism in salvation for Bultmann because the church is always prior to the act of faith (p. 105-6).

33. "How Does God Speak to Us Through the Bible?" in *Existence and Faith*, p. 168.

34. "The Primitive Christian Kerygma," p. 41, n. 80.

35. *Jesus Christ and Mythology*, pp. 82-83.

36. Finding the roots of Bultmann's views has apparently become

a new indoor sport. Barth links him with Catholic mysticism of the passion (*Kerygma and Myth*, *II*, 99), and Hasenhüttl has compiled a wide range of proposed influences: Marle saw chiefly Luther in the background, but Karl Adam thought it was Calvin more than Luther; Ethelbert Stauffer linked him with Origen, Ian Henderson with Thomas Aquinas; many, of course, see mostly Heidegger. *Der Glaubensvollzug*, pp. 18 ff. Lutheran theology has been reluctant to accept its child in Bultmann. On the other hand, Carl Braaten has reminded Schubert Ogden that he overlooked Bultmann's Lutheranism and cited important emphases in support. "A Critical Introduction" for *Kerygma and History*, Carl Braaten and Roy Harrisville, eds. (Nashville: Abingdon Press, 1962), p. 13.

But Bultmann's theology has other roots as well. Günther Bornkamm refers to an unpublished Heidelberg dissertation by Y. Kumazawa in which it is shown that Bultmann's critical freedom is rooted not only in the Reformation freedom of the Christian man but in the tradition of liberal theology and of humanistic freedom of man in general. "Die Theologie Rudolf Bultmanns in der neueren Discussion," *TR* 29 (1963), 127. This magisterial essay is now included in *Geschichte und Glaube*. 1. Teil *BhTh* 48 (Munich: Kaiser Verlag, 1968). This wider intellectual heritage, including Kant and German idealism, partly explains why Roman Catholic response to Bultmann has been largely indirect, according to Gotthold Hasenhüttl, "Rudolf Bultmann und die Entwicklung der Katholischer Theologie," *ZThK* 65 (1968), 54.

37. "True faith is not demonstrable in relation to its object. But, as Herrmann taught us long ago, it is just here that its strength lies. For if it were susceptible to proof it would mean that we could know and establish God apart from faith, and that would be placing him on a level with the world of tangible, objective reality. In that realm we are certainly justified in demanding proof." On the next page he writes, "As Herrmann used to say, the ground of faith and object of faith do not fall apart, but are identical, for the very reason that we cannot say what God is like in himself, but only what he does to us." "Bultmann Replies to His Critics," in *Kerygma and Myth*, pp. 201-2.

38. "Historical science can not at all lead to any sort of result which could serve as a foundation for faith, for all *its results have only relative validity*." He illustrates this with the variety of pictures of Jesus produced by liberal scholarship. "Liberal Theology and the Latest Theological Movement," pp. 30-31. (His italics.)

39. "On the Question of Christology," in *Faith and Understanding*, I, p. 132.

40. Schmithals rightly points out that it is this concern to be a theologian on the basis of the New Testament, coupled with his undoubted use of the Reformation's *sola sciptura*, that has led him to forge the hermeneutical question. *An Introduction to the Theology of Rudolf Bultmann*, p. 221. (See also Bultmann's

response to Ogden's charge of inconsistency in *JR* 42 [1962], 225 ff.)
41. See also Schubert Ogden, *Existence and Faith*, pp. 14-15.
42. Schmithals quotes a letter to this effect, written in 1926. An *Introduction to the Theology of Rudolf Bultmann*, p. 9.
43. See Bultmann's "Reply" in *The Theology of Rudolf Bultmann*. C. W. Kegley, ed. (New York: Harper, 1966), p. 257.
44. "Liberal Theology and the Latest Theological Movement," p. 29. Bultmann explicitly rejects idealism's tendency to speak of God as that which actualizes itself in man's rationality on the basis that this would in effect divinize man. "God represents the total annulment (*Aufhebung*) of man, his negation, calling him in question, indeed judging him." "Liberal Theology . . . ," p. 46.
   It is evident that Cairns does not see the problem that Bultmann sees, and therefore he misunderstands the issue when he writes: "Bultmann cannot have it both ways. Either our talk is about God, in which case it must certainly be inadequate to the reality and in that sense 'mythical.' Or else it is talk about ourselves, and ourselves alone." *A Gospel Without Myth?*, pp. 99-100. What Bultmann sees is the need to talk about God in such a way as not to make him an object (see notes 13, 37). This becomes evident also in his reply to the charge that he ought not really speak of "act of God" any longer: "If such language is to have any meaning at all it must denote an act in a real, objective sense, and not just a symbolical or pictorial expression. On the other hand, if the action of God is not to be conceived as a worldly phenomenon capable of being apprehended apart from its existential reference, it can only be spoken of by speaking simultaneously of myself as the person who is existentially concerned. To speak of the act of God means to speak at the same time of my existence. . . . This event, our being addressed by God here and now, our being questioned, judged, and blessed by him, is what we mean when we speak of an act of God." "Bultmann Replies to His Critics," in *Kerygma and Myth*, pp. 196-97.
45. Because the content of theology is God, shifting the content to man's experience means robbing theology of the *skandalon*. Hence Bultmann criticized liberalism thus: 'In all these [foregoing] formulations the 'stumbling block' . . . has been removed from Christianity. All of them totally lack the insight that God is other than the world, he is beyond the world, and that this means the complete abrogation of the whole man, of his whole history. Their common aim is to give faith the kind of basis which destroys the very essence of faith, because what they seek is a basis here in this world." "Liberal Theology and the Latest Theological Movement," p. 40.
   It is important not to overlook the fact that Bultmann was poised polemically not only against the intellectual theological tradition but against its effects in the church as well. This is seen in his treatment of the statements found in the "daily

91

devotions" materials published by the church press and in his repudiation of current slogans: "kingdom-work," Christian-socialism, Christendom, etc. He rejects on theological grounds all efforts to "actualize a situation of the world which is somehow more pleasing to God." For him, "there is no deed which could be directly related to God and to his Kingdom." "Liberal Theology and the Latest Theological Movement," p. 44.

46. This is evident also in his critique of Martin Dibelius' *Geschichte u. übergeschichtliche Religion im Christentum?* (Göttingen: Vandenhoeck & Ruprecht, 1925; reprinted in 1929 as *Evangelium u. Welt*) in *Faith and Understanding*, pp. 95-115, esp. p. 109.

47. In his Preface to the re-issue of Harnack's *What Is Christianity?* he criticized Harnack not only because he never caught "a glimpse of the utter strangeness of the image of primitive Christianity" discovered by the history of religions approach but because he diluted the core of Christianity which Kierkegaard saw: "How is a Christian existence possible in this world, when one in both his work and pleasure, shares in its culture, its tasks and its worldly goods?" (Torchbook: New York: Harper, 1957), pp. x-xi.

48. Troeltsch was prepared to accept the possibility that with the dissolution of Western civilization, Christianity would disappear as well. The strength of Christianity lies precisely in its inner congruence with the Christian epoch. For a recent analysis of Troeltsch's thought, in contrast with Barth's, see Thomas W. Ogletree, *Christian Faith and History* (Nashville: Abingdon Press, 1965), Part I, esp. pp. 37, 42, 55-58.

49. One ought to be more careful in making sweeping generalizations about the liberal theologians; far too often they have been described strictly from the point of view of their critics, as Bultmann has done, and especially James Robinson (in *A New Quest* . . . , Chap. 2). Harnack, for example, is much more aware of what history "demonstrates" and does not demonstrate. He began his famous lecture course on the essence of Christianity by disavowing as cheap apologetics all efforts to demonstrate the claims of the Christian religion. *What Is Christianity?*, pp. 7, 14. The entire lecture series ends on precisely the same word of caution. Yet here, Harnack's rootage in Christendom is also evident: knowledge "does, indeed, instruct us in facts; it detects inconsistencies; it links phenomena. . . . But where and how the curve of the world and the curve of our own life begin . . . and whither this curve leads, knowledge does not tell us. But if with a steady will we affirm the forces and the standards which on the summits of our inner life shine out as our highest good, nay, as our real self; if we are earnest and courageous enough to accept them as the great Reality and direct our lives by them; and if we then look at the course of mankind's history, follow its upward development, and search . . . for the communion of minds in it, we shall not faint in weariness and despair, but

become certain of God." (p. 322) It is precisely this under-standing of the "summits of our inner life" as congruent with God and the willingness to trust inferences from this which separates Barth and Bultmann from their liberal teachers.

50. See note 42 and the statement to which it refers.
51. I am pleased to find that Peter Berger has made a similar analysis of the relation of theology to history. See *The Sacred Canopy* (Garden City, N.Y.: Doubleday, 1967), Chap. 7, esp. p. 151. On the other hand, the independence of existentialism from the milieu in which it emerged has been asserted repeatedly. See, e.g., H. J. Blackham in *Six Existentialist Thinkers* (London: Routledge and Kegan Paul, 1952), p. 163, and John MacQuarrie, *Existentialist Theology* (Torchbook; New York: Harper, 1965; 1st ed., 1955), p. 95, who disassociates Heidegger's withdrawal to the Black Forest from the existential "system."
52. The difference between our situation and Bultmann's is even clearer when we are reminded that for him the transcendence of God is presupposed. See Johannes Körner, *Eschatologie und Geschichte.* "Theologische Forschung 13" (Hamburg-Bergstedt: Herbert Reich, 1957), p. 84.
53. "Liberal Theology and the Latest Theological Movement," p. 30.
54. Or, as Julius Schniewind aptly put it, "*Notitia, assensus,* and *fiducia* do not follow one another in strict chronological sequence. To take 'notice' of Jesus at all is in itself *fiducia.*" "A Reply to Bultmann" in *Kerygma and Myth,* pp. 77-78. Bornkamm also observed that Anselm's *fides quaerens intellectum* has no place in Bultmann's thought. "Die Theologie Rudolf Bultmanns," p. 140, n. 1.
   One can agree with Wolfhart Pannenberg that "Christian faith must not be equated with a merely subjective conviction that would allegedly compensate for the uncertainty of our historical knowledge of Jesus. Such a conviction would only be self-delusion." But he overcompensates when he says knowledge of Jesus' history "has the peculiarity that it leads to faith," for this sounds as if the process were natural and inevitable. "The Revelation of God in Jesus Christ," in *Theology as History.* "New Frontiers in Theology III," James M. Robinson and John B. Cobb, eds. (New York: Harper, 1967), pp. 129 ff.
55. E.g., "Faith as Venture" in *Existence and Faith,* pp. 55 ff.
56. *Ibid.,* p. 57.
57. "The Primitive Christian Kerygma," p. 17.
58. Schniewind was near this point when he chided Bultmann for playing off Jesus present in human memory against Jesus pres-ent in kerygma. Schniewind contended that memory not only plays a vital role in historical existence and in the presentness of the Christ-event, but that "the tradition is identical with the Gospel and the Word (see I Cor. 15. 1-3, etc.)." "A Reply to Bultmann," in *Kerygma and Myth,* p. 80.
59. Bultmann sees, of course, that there is no guarantee, a course in homiletics included, that proclamation will actually occur. See, e.g., his reply in Kegley, *The Theology of Rudolf Bultmann,*

p. 277. See also his "Das Befremdliche des Christlichen Glaubens" (1958) in *Glauben und Verstehen*, III (Tübingen: J. C. B. Mohr [Paul Siebeck], 1960), 206.

60. Peter Berger has seen the "market situation" in this country. *The Sacred Canopy*, Chap. 6. When Norman Perrin asks whether Bultmann might not turn out to be the last great German Protestant theologian, he sees something of the same thing—that Bultmann's work gathers up an intellectual legacy from which we are ever more estranged—especially in America. (In fact, on the American scene the theological motifs that actually shaped our religious life have never been those which shaped Bultmann's theology, despite the assiduous importing of Continental Protestant theology in theological schools.) *The Promise of Bultmann* (Philadelphia: Lippincott, 1969), p. 12.

61. Unhappily, W. F. Albright appears to have denied this in his review of the Gifford Lectures. *JBL* 77 (1958), 248. A clearer picture is given by H. W. Bartsch in *Kerygma and Myth*, II, trans. R. H. Fuller (London: S.P.C.K., 1962), pp. 4 ff. For a résumé of anti-Bultmann reaction in the German church, see Günther Bornkamm, "Die Theologie Rudolf Bultmanns," pp. 33-141, esp. p. 77.

62. See "The Significance of the Historical Jesus for the Theology of Paul" (1929) in *Faith and Understanding*, pp. 220-46, and esp. his "Jesus and Paul" (1936) in *Existence and Faith*, pp. 183-205. The latter is set in motion by Alfred Rosenberg's view that Jewish notions, especially Paul's, ruined the pristine religion of Jesus.

63. Note how Bultmann continues Lessing's point with regard to the cross: "As far as the first preachers of the gospel are concerned . . . the cross was the cross of him with whom they had lived in personal intercourse. The cross was an experience of their own lives. It presented them with a question and it disclosed to them its meaning. But for us this personal connection cannot be reproduced. For us the cross cannot disclose its own meaning: it is an event of the past. We can never recover it as an event in our own lives. All we know of it is derived from historical report." "New Testament and Mythology" in *Kerygma and Myth*, p. 38.

64. On this point, see also Gerhard Ebeling, "Gewissheit und Zweifel," *ZThK* 64 (1967), 323.

65. See his *Attack upon "Christendom*," trans. Walter Lowrie (Princeton: Princeton University Press, 1944; Boston: Beacon Press, paperback, 1956).

66. Bultmann forbids even questioning the reliability of the kerygmatic tradition. "Reply to Schniewind" in *Kerygma and Myth*, p. 116.

67. Dietrich Ritschl contends that because the only function that "church" has for Bultmann is that of an organization in which some preach kerygma and serve sacraments to others, we really have here a contemporary form of Cyprian's and Augustine's

institution for salvation. *Memory and Hope* (New York: Macmillan, 1967), p. 41.

68. See Kegley, *The Theology of Rudolf Bultmann,* pp. 276 ff.

69. Originally an address given at the 500th anniversary of the University of Greifswald in the DDR, this lecture was revised and published in various forms. A German version, "Der gegenwärtige Stand der Debatte um das Problem des historischen Jesus" is found in Helmut Ristow and Karl Matthiae's anthology, *Der historische Jesus und der kerygmatische Christus* (Berlin: Evangelischer Verlagsanstalt, 1964), pp. 12-25. An English version first appeared in *The Expository Times* 69:11 (August, 1958), pp. 333-39. An American version is available as *The Problem of the Historical Jesus* (Facet Books; Philadelphia: Fortress Press, 1964).

70. Käsemann's critique is contained in "Blind Alleys in the 'Jesus of History' Controversy," *New Testament Questions of Today,* trans. W. J. Montague (Philadelphia: Fortress Press, 1969). It is difficult to see what could have led James Robinson to say that Jeremias' view is somewhat analogous to that of Käsemann. *A New Quest of the Historical Jesus,* p. 24, n. 1.

71. In speaking of Ebeling, I do not in the least minimize the importance of Ernst Käsemann in giving new impetus to the historical study of Jesus and its place in Christian theology.

72. Just as Harnack, the historian of Christian thought, attempted to set forth the essence of Christianity in a lecture course for all students in Berlin (the English title obscures this with its *What Is Christianity?*), so Ebeling, the historian of Christian thought, undertook the same task in the same format, but with the title "The Nature of Christian Faith." *Das Wesen des christlichen Glaubens* (Tübingen: J. C. B. Mohr [Paul Siebeck], 1959). Ebeling's title was likewise modified in translation as if the word "Christian" did not matter: *The Nature of Faith,* trans. Ronald Gregor Smith (Philadelphia: Fortress Press, 1961). The centrality of faith is evident by the fact that each of the 15 chapters deals with an aspect of Christian faith; but the absence of the word "Christian" from all titles save the first does not mean that Ebeling is discussing faith generically.

73. Ebeling is concerned to overcome certain problems stemming from the subject-object split. Therefore he sees the question of faith as the "question of man's participation. . . . If however faith is understood as participation [in God], then it cannot possibly be regarded in isolation as a human act, but the thing in which faith participates belongs inseparably to faith itself." "Jesus and Faith" in *Word and Faith,* trans. J. W. Leitch (Philadelphia: Fortress Press, 1963), p. 142. This is also why, in *The Nature of Faith,* Ebeling discusses "God" not as something external to faith but under the title "The Reality of Faith."

74. See *The Nature of Faith,* pp. 45 ff., 70-71.

75. "Jesus and Faith," p. 204.

76. *Ibid.,* p. 202. See also p. 204, where he says "that the *sola fide* corresponds to the *solus Christus* because Jesus is the essence

of faith and faith is the essence of the work of Jesus and consequently no 'organ,' no 'means to an end,' but the gift of Jesus himself." In *The Nature of Faith* he puts it as follows: "Jesus and faith are joined together as closely as possible: first, in that faith is dependent on Jesus, it is faith *in* him; and second, clearly, in that this Jesus is to a certain extent dependent on faith: only faith can recognise him as he wishes to be recognised." (Pp. 45-46.)

77. *Theology and Proclamation*, trans. John Riches (Philadelphia: Fortress Press, 1966; German ed., 1962), p. 58. This book consists essentially of a critical dialogue with Bultmann.

78. *Ibid.*, pp. 77-78.

79. In "Jesus and Faith," pp. 223 ff. he deals extensively with this question.

80. *Ibid.*, p. 234. Ernst Fuchs argues in the same way (appealing to Ebeling!): "Since Jesus does not use the word 'faith' technically, the Old Testament understanding of faith—that is, the firmness of the relation between God and man—is to be accepted as self-evident in his case. In the New Testament, too, faith is to be taken as a firm unwavering faith." "Jesus' Understanding of Time," *Studies of the Historical Jesus*, SBT 42 (1964), 130-31. A clear shift of criteria has occurred between this statement and that on p. 122 where he argues from the same kind of evidence—lack of terminology on Jesus' lips—that he did not require repentance or conversion. Surely if in one case the absence of terminology points to assumptions shared with the Old Testament (and Judaism, I would add), it cannot be used to argue in the opposite direction as well.

81. Also Ernst Fuchs insists that Jesus' call to decision or to faith echoes his own decision and faith. See "The Quest of the Historical Jesus" (1956) in *Studies of the Historical Jesus*, p. 23. On the other hand, Bultmann has consistently rejected this view, insisting that he does not want to know Jesus' inner life because this would be a Christ "according to the flesh." So already in "On the Question of Christology" (1927) in *Faith and Understanding*, p. 152. In his critique of the new quest, Bultmann specifically asks what is to be gained from Fuchs' point, "which can only originate in a biographical interest." Moreover, he sees this as a "relapse into the historical-psychological interpretation." "The Primitive Christian Kerygma and the Historical Jesus," in Braaten and Harrisville, eds., *The Historical Jesus and the Kerygmatic Christ*, pp. 32-33.

82. "Jesus and Faith," p. 236. Ebeling leans on the article "Amen" in Kittel's *Theological Dictionary*, and on Joachim Jeremias' contribution to the Wikenhauser Festschrift (1954), "Kennzeichen der ipsissima vox Jesu," now in *Abba* (Göttingen: Vandenhoeck & Ruprecht, 1966), pp. 145 ff.

83. *The Nature of Faith*, p. 56; "Jesus and Faith," p. 238.

84. *Theology and Proclamation*, pp. 78 ff.

85. *Ibid.*, p. 89.

86. "The Question of the Historical Jesus," in *Word and Faith,* p. 296.
87. See *The Nature of Faith,* p. 59. In "Faith and Unbelief in Conflict about Reality" further light is thrown on Ebeling's persistent assertion that "faith" is the constitutive thing about Jesus. Here he says that "faith has its proper place where it is a case of understanding reality . . . as a whole. This wholeness is not a sum of individual parts, but the experience that at one particular point everything stands or falls together. . . . This one point . . . is the conscience of man . . . conscience in the radical sense as the place where it is decided what man truly is. . . . Whatever binds him in conscience, decides how reality as a whole concerns him." *Word and Faith,* p. 384. In this light, Ebeling can see Jesus' faith as the center that determines the whole man.
88. Ebeling (and Fuchs) are fond of using the phrase "what came to expression" (*was zur Sprache gekommen ist*). They find it useful because it achieves two things: one, it allows them to probe the center of the Jesus-data to locate what is constitutive and to do so in a common German phrase; two, it is a natural bridge to the hermeneutical question concerning the language of the kerygma and theology, and the role of language generally. "What comes to expression" is thus escalated literally into, "What came to language (or speech)." This then allows them to speak of the "linguisticality of existence" (Heidegger), and to explore how reality is expressed in language itself. For a convenient exposition of this point of view, see Robert W. Funk, *Language, Hermeneutic and Word of God* (New York: Harper, 1966), chaps. 2, 3.
89. "The Question of the Historical Jesus," p. 294.
90. *The Nature of Faith,* p. 58. In "Jesus and Faith" he wrote, "Jesus is rightly understood only when he is not an object of faith but its source and ground." (Pp. 201-2.) In "The Question of the Historical Jesus" he put it this way: "The fact that Jesus and faith belong together forms the ground of the continuity between the historical Jesus and the so-called Christ of faith. Jesus is therefore not an object of faith in the sense in which we are accustomed to speak of objects of faith. Rather, he is the ground of faith." (P. 303)
91. *The Nature of Faith,* p. 69. In "The Question of the Historical Jesus," he also insists: "To be sure Jesus did not now meet with faith for the very first time. But now for the first time it is a case of the faith awakened by Jesus and founded on him being proclaimable." (P. 301)
92. *The Nature of Faith,* p. 71.
93. *Theology and Proclamation,* p. 78.
94. *Ibid.,* p. 65.
95. "Zur Frage nach dem historischen Jesus. Ein Nachwort" in *Glaube und Erfahrung.* "Gesammelte Aufsätze III" (Tübingen: J. C. B. Mohr [Paul Siebeck], 1965), pp. 1-31. Page numbers

in parentheses refer to this piece. Paul Achtemeier's *Introduction to the New Hermeneutic* (Philadelphia: Westminster Press, 1969) provides a useful summary of Fuch's general views. See esp. chaps. 6 ff.

96. Here he takes the same line regarding Judaism as Günther Bornkamm, *Jesus of Nazareth*, trans. Irene and Fraser McCluskey (New York: Harper, 1960; 1st German ed., 1956). For a critique of this prejudiced view of Judaism, see my "Bornkamm's *Jesus of Nazareth* Revisited," *JR* 49 (1969), 9 ff.

97. "Der historische Jesus als Gegenstand der Verkündigung," in *Glauben und Erfahrung*, p. 439.

98. For the most part, the parallels were discovered after my own thinking had taken shape, for I have never considered myself a disciple. At the same time my original distrust of important emphases of theirs has not diminished, especially the passion to reduce all currency to the common coin of "word" (and linguisticality) and "faith."

99. See his "Faith and Unbelief in Conflict about Reality" in *Word and Faith*, p. 383, where he writes: "Faith is so little threatened by knowledge that on the contrary, if it is true faith, it sets us free to conscientious examination of what is knowable and takes up the cudgels against unbelief's behaving as if it were knowledge. For that reason faith is never by any means indifferent towards scientific examination of reality. . . . This is what distinguishes it from superstition." Also Fuchs refuses to deny that faith is dependent partly on historical criticism. "Glaube und Geschichte im Blick auf die Frage nach den historischen Jesus" (review article on Bornkamm's *Jesus of Nazareth* [1957] in *Zur Frage nach den historischen Jesus. Gesammelte Aufsätze II* (Tübingen: J. C. B. Mohr [Paul Siebeck], 1960), p. 168. Unfortunately, this essay was omitted from *Studies of the Historical Jesus*.

100. Concentration on Jesus' inner life marks the whole argument of Herrmann's *Communion of the Christian with God*, trans. J. S. Stanyon; 2nd English ed., revised by R. W. Stewart in accord with the 4th German ed. of 1903 (London: Williams and Norgate, 1906). Because of the inner connection between Fuchs, Ebeling, and Herrmann, this work will be republished in the "Lives of Jesus" series, and will be introduced and edited by Robert T. Voelkel. See also Wilhelm Bousset, *Jesus*, trans. J. P. Trevelyan and W. D. Morrison (London: Williams and Norgate, 1911), pp. 103-4.

101. Pannenberg has seen this too. Moreover, he points to the surprising fact that long before the new questers emphasized the authoritative claim or audacity of Jesus, dogmatic theologians such as Werner Elert and Emil Brunner did so. *Jesus—God and Man*, trans. L. L. Wilkins and D. Priebe (Philadelphia: Westminster Press, 1968; German ed., 1964), pp. 53-66.

102. The view is repeated in "Zur Frage nach dem historischen Jesus," p. 18.

103. What Ebeling says to this point is not satisfactory: "If this concentration of a man upon a single point . . . appears from

the historical point of view to be strange and incomprehensible, then we certainly cannot well adduce analogous cases to make it completely clear. For it is only where faith is concerned that this concentration of a man on one single point can take place. But as for the fact that it is true only of Jesus that all that can be said of him may be summed up by saying that faith came to expression in him—that belongs under the head of historical contingency." The Question of the Historical Jesus," p. 297.

104. E.g., Bultmann wrote that "faith always exists only in the overcoming of unbelief." "The Problem of Natural Theology," *Faith and Understanding*, p. 329. Fuchs has observed, "The main error in the debate of our times seems to me to be that *doubt* is the starting-point for the interpretation of faith. Instead of this we must set out from the fact that faith is *fruitful*. Not the frustrations but the achievements of faith give rise to the theology of faith." He also observed that the believers see "that the deeper danger of faith also lies not in its failure but precisely in its successes. . . . Here lies the root of both fanaticism and of legalism." "Language in the New Testament" (1959) in *Studies of the Historical Jesus* SBT 42 (1964), p. 80.

105. What is in view here is suggested by Gabriel Marcel; one has but to substitute "some one" for "something" in the following sentences: "If I believe in something, it means that I place myself at the disposal of something, or again that I pledge myself fundamentally and this pledge affects not only *what I have* but also *what I am*. In a modern philosophical vocabulary, this be expressed by saying that to belief is attached an existential index which, in principle, is completely lacking to conviction." Conviction he defined as a defensive position in contrast with faith. *The Mystery of Being. II: Faith and Reality* (Gifford Lectures 1949-50), trans. Rene Hagie (London: Harvill Press, 1951). p. 77.

106. "Evangelical and Protestant Ethics" in *The Heritage of the Reformation*, ed. E. J. F. Arndt (New York: Richard Smith, 1950), p. 223.

107. Walter Kaufmann once observed that "most of the so-called existentialists, as well as most, if not all, of the theologians who like to call themselves existentialists, have occupied themselves with commitment without ever seeing or saying clearly what distinguishes a responsible commitment from an irresponsible one." *The Faith of a Heretic* (Garden City, N.Y.: Doubleday, 1961), p. 85.

108. *Theology and Proclamation*, p. 79.

3

THE HISTORICAL JESUS AND THE GOSPEL

"In the word which is to be proclaimed there is . . . contained a question which is addressed to the hearer. The hearer is, however, not simply asked if he will accept and hand on a list of doctrinal points. . . . Instead, the proclamation poses the question which the hearer has to answer by his faith. . . . The hearer should not be constrained to limp into place behind a previously established unity of preaching and confession."

ERNST FUCHS

"The Easter faith was the foundation of the Christian kerygma but was not the first or only source of its content. Rather, it . . . took cognizance of the fact that God acted before we became believers, and . . . testified to this fact by encapsulating the earthly history of Jesus in its proclamation. How far are we obliged, or even able, to appropriate to ourselves the decision which was then taken?"

ERNST KÄSEMANN

What role does the historical Jesus play in the actual preaching of the gospel and in the emergence of trust? How shall the Christian preacher present the historical Jesus so that one may begin trusting Jesus? We shall begin by ascertaining more precisely what constitutes "gospel." Then, after seeing how the early church dealt with the matter, we shall address our question directly.

I. What Is "Gospel"?

We cannot speak clearly of the place of the historical Jesus in the gospel until we know what we mean by gospel. It will help us to make important distinctions as well as to note a definition.

A. It is useful to distinguish the *formal* structure of the gospel from a *material* statement of it. "Formal structure" exposes what is constitutive, irrespective of particular content. For example, we analyze patriotism without dealing with particular patriotisms, say in Czechoslovakia. Similarly, we ask what makes a religious announcement "good news" in the Christian sense. Classically stated, it is the news of God's grace in Jesus—God's free manward movement in Jesus for the sake of man's wholeness. The particular material development of this formal pattern comes to light when we ask how man's situation is perceived. If it is perceived as bondage, God's grace appears as liberation; if one sees man as guilty, God's grace is forgiveness. One task of theology is to insist that the material understanding of the gospel adequately expresses the formal understanding. Accordingly, we see that *any* material way of putting the gospel has these correlative components: (a) an understanding of man's plight; (b) a way of conceptualizing a resolution appropriate to the plight; (c) an appropriate way of talking about Jesus as the one who effects the resolution. Thus if one speaks of man's situation as darkness, it is pointless to talk of reconciliation, for this is the appropriate antidote to alienation; rather, one must speak of enlightenment and of Jesus as the light. While each material understanding of the gospel has its own logic and limitations, in each the formal aspect is operative.

It is not only the material expression of the gospel which has become problematic today but the formal aspect as well. This is not a totally new situation, for Paul Tillich observed that (in the West) in twenty centuries there has been but one fundamental alternative to the Christian gospel—Stoicism.[1] Stoicism offers no savior, no grace, and no salvation because none is needed. The Stoic "gospel" is the news that inauthentic man (to use a modern cliché) can become authentic by actualizing what he already is—a rational being. In a way, the radical (Death of God) theology has returned to just such a view.[2] By contrast, built into the formal definition of gospel is the contention that man cannot save himself by resolving to actualize himself, that at the deepest level man is incapable of doing for himself precisely what must be done. This is why the formal aspect of the gospel is more deeply offensive than any particular material expression of it. Even within the church, the preacher faces many persons who prefer the Stoic outlook. In any case, it is not simply certain biblical terms (the material aspect) which have lost their franchise (e.g., new birth) but the formal framework itself.[3]

B. We must see also the difference between *preaching a theology of grace and communicating a grace-full event with theological clarity*. Much more is at stake here than a word game. What matters is putting the news about Jesus in such a way that it reaches the hearer as a grace-event, as good news. The distinction, then, turns on the difference between communicating grace and advocating a concept called grace.

Characteristically, Christian orthodoxy has preached grace. Yet hearing a theological point elucidated and advocated is not yet hearing good news, gospel. Grace has not yet happened when it is explained. More often than not, such a sermon reaches the unconvinced hearer as a required idea. Actually, one should preach so that a new situation is created for the hearer, one in which he is grasped by grace.

A grace-event occurs when the word about Jesus reaches the hearer as good news for him; or, to put it in different terms, in hearing the word about Jesus something decisive can occur which can liberate and reorient the hearer. "Grace" is the theological understanding of this event. It cannot be generated merely by propounding the theology of grace. Theological clarity is needed so that, among other things, one understands this distinction. A major task of theology, in this light, is to clarify the creativity of God through the word of man's preaching and through the Jesus to whom it points so that we are free to present Jesus in ways that allow a grace-event to occur. It is always easier to present Jesus as "law," as an obligatory pattern or teacher of requisite ideas, than it is to present him in a way that makes possible an occasion in which transforming trust can emerge. Developing the basis for this mode of

102

preaching which centers in the historical Jesus is the aim of this chapter.

C. Our third distinction is a double one and is the most crucial. It concerns the need to distinguish *gospel from propaganda, theology from ideology.* It is not helpful to say that propaganda is "biased communication,"[4] because utterly disinterested communication is a self-contradiction. While there are many forms of propaganda as well as diverse functions for it,[5] it is germane to note that propaganda is news designed to achieve influence or power, not simply, as in the past, to promote an ideology.[6] Further, propanganda does not aim for the well-being of the hearer, but enlists him for the aims of the propagandist. Especially since World War I we have had to deal with propaganda in social and political matters,[7] not only because governments of all sorts have undertaken propaganda (it is part of the technique of propaganda to call ours an "information service") but because the technological development of communication media has placed every person within range of multiple propagandas. Moreover, we should dispel the notion that propaganda is incommensurate with facts;[8] rather, propanganda is the skillful use of facts in order to promote a corporation, political party, government policy, or prevalent social ideology (e.g., the American way of life, or the new left).

What, then, is an ideology? It is the theoretical underpinning for propaganda, the rigid rationale from which propaganda flows and to which it points.[9] The word "rigid" is important here, for ideology rules out critical evaluation and projects a closed system, one with no loose ends or unexplained phenomena. Propaganda and ideology tacitly or openly claim to have answers for virtually everything. Moreover, an ideology is immune to modification because new data are seen simply as diverse, though perhaps unexpected, illustrations of the dogma. For example, those controlled by the cold war propaganda and ideology inevitably interpret every Russian overture for détente as a deceitful ruse to lure the West into a trap. Those governed by virulent anti-Catholic propaganda and ideology not only saw Kennedy's candidacy as a Papal plot to subvert the United States but were able to overcome this idea only when Kennedy himself verbalized Baptist ideology and claimed that a man's religion is his private affair!

These observations, may, at first blush, appear to be not only tangential but offensive in the context of a theological discussion. Nevertheless, the church is far from immune from the risk of subverting its faith at precisely these points.[10] First of all, Christian preaching becomes propaganda when it appropriates *uncritically* a current, perhaps latent, social myth or ideology as the means for advancing the gospel. Jacques Ellul has pointed out that "propaganda must not only attach itself to whatever already exists in the individual, but also express the fundamental currents of the society it seeks to influence. . . . A propaganda pitting itself against this fundamental and accepted structure would have no chance of success." [11] What more clearly manifests technological man's myth that ever-new products are increasingly improved than the constant propaganda on behalf of "new theology"? Propaganda for the managerial view of technological urban culture appears also in the form of Cox's *Secular City*, a religious ideology[12] justifying the technocrat's view of civilization.[13] Conversely, though illustrating precisely the same point, Billy James Hargis' "Christian Anti-Communism Crusade" propagandizes on behalf of the ideology functioning in Bible Belt Protestantism.

We have emphasized the importance of a critical relation to a current ideology. One difference between propaganda and preaching, then, lies in the way the communicator relates the message to what is already assumed to be true by his hearers. Christian preaching becomes propaganda when it adopts the current ideology instead of entering into a struggle with it. It becomes propaganda when current myths and assumptions control what is said or not said, whether it be "religious individualism" as the sacred counterpart to "the free enterprise system" (*Christian Economics*), or religious zealotism as the handmaiden of radical reconstruction.

In the second place, the church becomes a propaganda agency in the name of Jesus Christ when its basic concern is recruit-

104

ment, promotion, and power. In this case, what is said and how it is presented are not controlled by a passion to deal with the plight of men for their sakes, but to use the plight of men as the basis for power, more euphemistically expressed as "status." The human situation can be used without dealing with it when the church's message is controlled by the desire to show the public that it is avant garde or conservative, depending on what its clientele expects, when the sermon does little else but repeat whatever analysis of man is fashionable in its circle and then commend "faith" in order to suggest that this church is really with it. In other words, the gospel is debased into propaganda whenever the church's message uses the plight of man, wittingly or otherwise, to enhance the status of the institution, and looks to Jesus as its warrant.

In the third place, when the church begins to propagandize, its theology hardens into an ideology without a sense of mystery. Instead of accepting the fact that the course of history and the vicissitudes of human life continually interrogate the theology in such a way that constant rethinking and reworking are called for, propagandized ideology implies that it knows the answers in advance and that revision is out of place.[14] Wherever theology has been distorted into ideology, the possibility that the church has been wrong appears as an intolerable threat and the call for revision as insurrection. On the other hand, the true power of a theological tradition manifests itself precisely in its openness to restatement and correction. This, to be sure, requires accepting the risk of engendering new errors—as the history of Christian theology amply demonstrates. Clinging tenaciously to a firm tradition can be a prophetic theological act when done critically against the stream, or it can be an ideological stance when promoted on behalf of the stream. In tying itself uncritically to prevailing ideology within or without the church, the church's own theology is withdrawn from revision since popular ideology cannot be challenged or changed. For example, when the church becomes the spokesman for the American way of life, as defined by mass opinion and propaganda, it can scarcely be open to changing its theological or social stance without incurring the charge of being un-American—probably the most feared epithet among those who can remember the Berlin blockade. When this occurs, revised theology is no longer dealt with by criticism developed out of the theological tradition but is attacked as subversive, Communist-inspired, and so on. This tyranny of propaganda explains why, when theological professors and pastors are dismissed for alleged theological reasons, the action does not climax (or initiate) an extended period of theological wrestling with the issues posed but rather the action is designed to keep the ideology or the institution intact.

These distinctions—the formal definition of gospel and its material expressions, advocating a theology of grace and creating a grace-imparting situation, propaganda and good news as well as ideology and theology—have direct bearing on our question: How shall we speak of Jesus so that the formal character of the gospel can be expressed materially in a way that it reaches the hearer as good news for his sake and not as church propaganda? Specifically, how shall one articulate the good news so that the historical Jesus comes through in a way that the hearer may trust him for his salvation?

II. Gospel in the Early Church

Because the New Testament offers a precedent recognized as normative, at least wherever the import of canonization has not been entirely dissipated, we will do well to inquire how the gospel was made known in the earliest decades of Christianity. This will not only give historical perspective to our task, but call us to follow in the wake of the apostles. They were, by and large, far more venturesome than the church that admires them.

A. *Gospel in a Jewish Setting.* It is regrettable that the New Testament does not contain a sample of earliest Christian preaching by Jews to fellow Palestinian Jews.[15] Because Peter's Pentecost sermon (2:14-36) is part of a network of sermons and speeches reworked and largely composed by the author,

106

we cannot simply equate it with earliest Christian preaching.[16] Nevertheless, the consistent picture drawn by Acts is doubtless correct in two interrelated points: (a) Appeal to Scripture was central. This is confirmed by Paul's own words, for I Cor. 15 says he had received a tradition that "Christ died for our sins in accordance with the scriptures, that he was buried, that he was raised on the third day in accordance with the scriptures" (RSV), etc. Because Paul received this tradition near the time of his conversion, we are led to the first decade of Christian preaching, even though it cannot be proven decisively that this formulation was first made in Aramaic.[17] (b) Doubtless earliest preaching to Palestinian Jews stressed the good news that the Messiah was Jesus,[18] that the new Aeon was therefore under way, and that the consummation of all things was very near. Inevitably, the question arose: Is the news true? Is it trustworthy? After all, as far as politics, economics, and religion were concerned, nothing appeared to have changed. Moreover, while Jesus awakened Messianic fervor in some hearts, he apparently did not act like a Messiah[19] or claim to be one,[20] and he certainly died in an un-Messianic way,[21] though indicted for being a Messianic pretender. How, then, could early Christians formulate "Christ (Messiah) died in accordance with the scriptures?" Evidently, they rebuilt the understanding of the Messiah's career in light of Jesus' life and death on the one hand, and transferred the regal role of Messiah to the hour of his imminent Coming. The initial meaning of the resurrection, apparently, was his installation into the office of Son of Man,[22] an office to be manifest at the impending end.[23] The New Testament, and I Cor. 15:3 in particular, does not report this interpretive process but reflects its already having occurred. Clearly, it was precisely the life of Jesus (for them, of course, not the historian's Jesus) that required the reconstruction of the idea of Messiah.[24] So quickly and so solidly did this occur that within two decades, Paul could refer to Jesus simply as "Christ," almost as if this were his proper name.

It is important to note that the claim that Jesus is the Christ was not left as a bald assertion. Rather, several things began to take place rather swiftly. First, Jewish Christians undertook to show specifically that Jesus truly fulfilled Scripture,[25] in his earthly life as well as in his exalted role. The fact that we, governed by a concern to determine what the authors themselves meant to say, are unimpressed by this mode of argument must not impede our appreciating the fact that the early church found this a natural and necessary approach. Judaism as a whole believed Scripture to be the oracles of God whose meaning is independent of the situation in which they were committed to writing, but, conversely, dependent on the mind of God. In this context, correlating texts with the story of Jesus was a persuasive way of proclaiming the good news that the hoped-for hour was now here.[26] Second, the earliest church began to formulate its message with the help of Old Testament phrases and overtones,[27] and to use Scripture language to narrate events of his career.[28] Third, because the career of Jesus, capped by his execution between criminals, by no means could be presented simply as the fulfillment of what had been expected, it was necessary to re-read the Scriptures in order to find texts that could be seen as pointing to Jesus. Not only were texts already Messianically interpreted in Judaism, such as Ps. 2 or 110, applied to Jesus, but texts not previously associated with the Messiah were now understood as having their real fulfillment in Jesus (e.g., the Suffering Servant passages were now taken to refer not to the nation Israel but to Jesus).[29] That is, early Christians not only interpreted Jesus in light of Scripture, they also interpreted the Synagogue Bible in light of Jesus,[30] thereby beginning a process [31] that eventually made it into a Christian book, designated "Old Testament." [32]

Reminding ourselves, even in this briefest way, of the mode of preaching the gospel by Jews to Jews makes three important contributions to our subject. First, what Bultmann says about preaching hardly describes this phase of Christian proclamation.

(a) Inherent in the text-fulfillment scheme is an invitation to go behind the kerygma to ascertain its truthfulness by comparing the Jesus-tradition with the text of the Bible.[33]

Accepting the gospel was not a matter of accepting the message because it claimed to be a word from God that precluded investigation, but was a matter of persuasion that the message was true enough to believe with one's mind and to trust with one's life. It is not to be concluded, of course, that accepting the gospel was equated with merely assenting to an exegetical *tour de force,* for the life-witness of the apostles, whether by their own wondrous deeds [34] or by a new style of life, was an essential ingredient from the start.

(b) Moreover, implicit in the foregoing considerations is the contention that the earliest Christians did include in their preaching a brief narrative (or narratives) about Jesus —a piece of history. Making this observation is not yet to rehabilitate C. H. Dodd's views about a "historical section" in the kerygma,[35] for Robinson rightly points to the modernizing language used by Dodd (historical facts, data).[36] But it is to undercut the alleged illegitimacy of any narrative at all. Nor ought we to regard this earliest form of preaching as something that the church fortunately outgrew when it advanced through Paul to John, as Bultmann views it.

(c) When one comes to the New Testament evidence for earliest Christian preaching, such as it is, from a reading of Bultmann, one is struck by the overall absence of interest in "encounter." A full critique of encounter theology is very much needed, but it is precluded here. Suffice it to say that certain modern assumptions, such as that the early Christian kerygma made possible an encounter between the hearers and the existential selfhood of Jesus, do not give us entrée to the texts in a historically persuasive way. Even if, given our historical awareness, we should find encounter theology necessary, it is surely unwarranted to make it the hermeneutical prerequisite for interpreting the kerygma of those without this problem. Besides, having to make a decision regarding Jesus and oneself in relation to him (which earliest preaching certainly called for) is not yet having an encounter in the pregnant sense in which Bultmannians commonly use it. Moreover, the reign of encounter theology is a symptom of the Kierkegaardian legacy in which immediate confrontation with

109

the Word is the sole event that appears capable of overcoming the shock of discovering the ambiguity of history, on the one hand, and the debilitating sense of temporal distance from the event (Lessing), on the other. Above all, encounter language impeded movement toward clarity because when properly used it is confessional language, not explanatory language for phenomena. Consequently, it is unwarranted to use the confession as a criterion either for phenomenological analysis of speaking and hearing or for determining what may and may not be said. If this is not borne in mind, the "new" quest may prove to be even more an effort to build one's own security through hermeneutics than was the "old" quest with its "facts." Since the redemptive selfhood and intention of Jesus are to be inferred from the evidence, encountering this inferred reality is no less a transaction with one's own works than was being captured by the maligned nineteenth-century construct, the inner life of Jesus. One also suspects that once this need for encounter is overcome, the fascination with the relation of *Historie* to *Geschichte* will dissipate as well.

Second, it is evident that the earliest Christian mode of gospel preaching is germane only where the classical Hebrew texts are accepted as Scripture and function as God's Word, not merely as background material. To one unacquainted with these texts or standing apart from the community that accepts them as Scripture, hearing that Jesus fulfills the Scriptures of the Jews is a curious item of information, but not yet good news for him. For faith's reflection, as we shall see, Jesus' relation to the Hebrew Bible is of major importance. But the two roles ought not be confused.

Third, in light of what we said previously, it is clear that early Christian preaching cannot be classified as propaganda. Such would have been the case had the apostles simply absorbed the current expectation and promoted Jesus as its embodiment. Precisely because the life of Jesus was so starkly un-Messianic, the Apostles were prevented from such propagandizing; conversely, because they were nonetheless convinced by the resurrection that Jesus was the pivotal act of God at the turning of the Aeons, they were compelled to conclude that titles such as Messsiah, Son of Man, Prophet, *must* apply to him because they could conceive of none other than Jesus to fulfill these roles.[37] Hence, in light of Jesus and their conviction, they had either to surrender these categories for understanding Jesus or to reinterpret them in accord with the Jesus who actually had lived among them (as well as in light of the hour in which they now found themselves). It was, then, just this process of revising fundamentally certain inherited conceptions without surrendering the formal scheme of promise and fulfillment that made theologians and not ideologues out of the apostles, and permitted them to announce a message of good news and not mere propaganda. Put in terms of our first distinction, the scheme of promise-fulfillment was part of the formal setting of the news of God's grace while the reworked understanding of that fulfillment constituted the material substance of the gospel.

B. *Gospel in the Hellenistic Milieu.* The New Testament also reveals how the gospel was preached to those who were aliens to the biblical tradition and for whom the Bible was not Scripture to start with—the gentiles. Here too we regret that the New Testament does not give us a sample sermon to a wholly gentile audience, though Acts intends to do so. Just as Acts 13 is to exemplify Paul's preaching to Hellenistic Jews, so Acts 17 puts him before the sophisticated Greek world in Athens. Scholarly opinion generally regards both as Luke's idea of how Paul preached to these diverse audiences rather than as reliable accounts of what was actually said. Nevertheless, again the basic point is doubtless correct—that Paul adapted the content of his message so as to make contact with the hearers before him. Hence just as the synagogue sermon relates Jesus to the history of Israel and to the Old Testament, so the Mars Hill sermon explicitly quotes a pagan poet (and merely uses Isa. 42 phrases) and relates the gospel to the character of popular religion in the Hellenistic world. Nothing is said about prophecy-fullfillment.[38]

But is it probable that Paul himself shifted the content of the gospel in this way? Some support for Acts comes from

111

Paul's own letters. In I Cor. 9:19-23, he says that to Jews he became a Jew, to pagans a pagan in order to win some to the faith. Probably Paul had in mind more than a free attitude toward customs (e.g., observing dietary laws), for the previous verse explicitly speaks of his gospel-preaching.[39] Doubtless this freedom to be "all things to all men" made him vulnerable to criticism from both sides. Yet only a person free of ideology could think through afresh each time what the gospel meant when the situation of hearing changed. Elsewhere Paul can be *seen* recasting the traditional Christian language. Instead of talking about the forgiveness of sins, as the older Jewish Christian theology had done, Paul spoke of being set in right relation to God. Likewise, although he appears to know the theology of the Son of Man, he never uses this phrase but speaks instead of the Son of God. The likelihood that already the Hellenistic church before Paul had begun to use new categories does not change the point we are making, but only moves the process back and allows for more than one step.[40]

It is clear, of course, that this sort of shift did not mean abandoning the Old Testament. Not even the sermon in Acts 17 does that altogether, for it has points of contact with Old Testament and with Hellenized Jewish thought, as well as with current Stoic ideas; and it includes the resurrection and coming judgment—ideas rooted in Jewish apocalyptic theology.[41] Moreover, I Cor. 15 expressly says that the Scripture-related gospel was transmitted to the Corinthians, a predominantly gentile church. Nevertheless, the decisive thing was *how* the Old Testament was interpreted to gentile audiences. In a word, Paul, and the church on gentile soil, interpreted the gospel and its Old Testament roots by taking up a new mythic pattern.[42]

Central to this myth is the divine savior who descends to earth to save men and subsequently returns to his heavenly point of departure.[43] Now it is perfectly true that we do not have a clearly pre-Christian pagan text that narrates this myth as explicitly as do certain Gnostic (and Christianized Gnostic) texts afterwards.[44] It may well be the case that one impact of Christianity on the Hellenistic world was to precipitate a clear myth of the descending/ascending savior out of the somewhat diffuse mythic ideas and patterns already extant in the culture.[45] But whatever critical judgment in this complex and controversial matter may prove to be the correct one, for our purpose it can be said that in preaching to the Greek world Christians took up mythic patterns and themes not at home in the original Jerusalem church.

Important evidence for this is embedded in Paul's letters, thereby showing that he took for granted that his readers needed no explanation or defense of his allusions and assumptions. Thus I Cor. 2:8 says that the rulers of this age (aeon) did not understand what was happening in the Christ-event, for if they had they would not have crucified the Lord of glory. These "rulers" are not Pilate and Herod but the cosmic principalities and powers who dominate this time-space, this aeon.[46] This is an allusion to the myth of the savior's secret and incognito descent into the cosmos—a theme spelled out much more fully in later texts but already assumed here. Nowhere in the literature associated with Paul is this myth clearer than in Eph. 4, which takes for granted Christ's having descended to earth and then having ascended to God's glory.[47] The same descent/ascent pattern is built into the hymn that Paul quotes in Phil. 2,[48] according to which he who was in the form of God assumed the form of a slave (presumably a slave to the cosmic powers,[49] not a purchased servant) and after death was exalted above the cosmic powers to which he had formerly been subjected. So firmly did this descent/ascent pattern root itself in the Christian tradition that the Fourth Gospel has Jesus himself say that he came down from heaven and will ascend once again to his Father (6:38).[50] In such texts, we have elements of the myth of a pre-existent heavenly being, the Son of God, who descended to the realm of existence and left it after his salvific work was accomplished. Jesus is understood as the low point in a U-shaped Christ-event.[51]

In other words, just as Jerusalem Christianity interpreted Jesus in terms of text and fulfillment, so Hellenistic Christianity interpreted him as the one who descended into the cosmos

113

to save men and then returned, exalted, to his heavenly origin. To oversimplify it visually, Palestinian Jewish Christianity set Jesus in a horizontal framework of past promise and present (and future) fulfillment of Israel's hope, while Hellenistic Christianity set Jesus in a vertical scheme of descent/ascent. True, the early Son of Man theology also operated with a descent scheme (on clouds), but the decisive difference is the fact that the Son of Man was expected to descend in the imminent future, whereas the Hellenistic myth regarded Jesus as the one who had already descended and ascended. The older view of Jesus as one exalted to the role of the Son of Man did not speak of his pre-temporal status in heaven to which he returned after descending/ascending.

In this grossly oversimplified sketch what must not be overlooked is that both modes of interpreting Jesus were used to make plain the gospel meaning of Jesus.[52] In both, the formal character of the gospel as the news of God's manward grace was maintained; the one insisted that God had kept his word of promise in a startling way in making this Jesus the Messiah, the other that he had sent his Son from heaven for the sake of man's liberation from hierarchic invisible powers of tyranny. In this way, the material content of the gospel changed precisely in order to maintain the formal character— good news of God's decisive act for mankind.

One more thing must not escape notice. Because the Hellenistic church took up the Old Testament, it also reread it a fresh in order to relate this mythic pattern to the Scripture. But how could Hellenistic mythic patterns be correlated with the Old Testament? To be more precise, how could the Old Testament be understood to speak about this syncretistic myth, both being understood as referring to Jesus? Two examples [53] show how this interpretation was accomplished.

In Gal. 4 Paul interprets the law as a manifestation of this aeon's tyranny over man. He does not explain the law's power in terms of the tyranny of Moses or of Judaism's concen to order the whole of life according to the law; rather, he sees it as a mark of bondage to this aeon, which is under control of the principalities and powers (the

114

Stoicheia).[54] Then he says, "And when the fullness of time had come, God sent out his Son, born of woman, born under the law, so that those under the law might be brought free, so that we might receive adoption as sons." The "fullness of time" is a concept rooted in Jewish apocalyptic theology (according to which God sets times and seasons and acts when the time is ripe, "full"), whereas the sending of the Son refers not to Jesus' decision to leave the shop in Nazareth [55] but to his coming from God himself (an allusion to the descent [56]) and entering the realm of men (under the law). Here the prophecy-fulfillment theology and the descent/ascent myth are interlocked by the claim that the descent occurred at the set time. In this way, the mythic pattern was historicized and the historical Jesus cosmologized; the former for the sake of precluding a timeless descent, the latter for the sake of relating Jesus to the cosmic dimensions of man's dilemma.

Hebrews 2 affords another example. In Chap. 2, the author appeals to Ps. 8, which in its Hebrew form uses parallel lines of thought to extol the dignity of man:

> What is man that thou art mindful of him,
>   and the son of man that thou dost care for him?
> Yet thou has made him little less than God,
>   and dost crown him with glory and honor.
> Thou has given him dominion over the works of thy hands;
>   thou has put all things under his feet. (RSV)

Our author uses this in a highly instructive way (2.8-9). He writes,

Now in putting everything in subjection to man he left nothing outside his control. As it is, we do not yet see everything in subjection to him. But we see Jesus, who for a little while was made lower than the angels, crowned with glory and honor because of the suffering of death, so that by the grace of God he might taste death for every one. (RSV)

The author uses the Greek translation of the Old Testament which speaks of man's being lower than "angels" instead of "God." Moreover, he evidently takes "son of man" not as

115

mankind (as did the Hebrew) but as the heavenly Son of Man.[57] Next, he understands "a little less than angels" to mean "for a little while lower than angels" because the Greek word can mean either a little space or a little time. Thereby he is able to allude to the brief span of time when the Son of God (Man) was indeed lower than the angels (i.e., while on earth as Jesus). The reference to the dominion over all things then means the Lordship that Christ attained by his resurrection, which exalted (taken spatially as elevated) him to such status. The author points out that at present this status is not yet manifest; it is "visible" only to the eye of faith (faith as the conviction of things not seen, 11:1). What we do see now is Jesus' subservience to the angels. But the present phenomenon is no accurate index to the impending reality. This is why the whole discussion begins, "for it was not to angels that God subjected the world to come" (2:5). It is not over the phenomenal world that Jesus is Lord, but over the coming world.

That Hebrews is to us a strange and forbidding book must not prevent our seeing what is going on as this text comes into existence. First, because the pattern of descent/ascent is taken for granted, it can be used to apply Ps. 8 to Jesus. Second, in accord with common Christian practice of using parts of this Psalm [58] the author divides elements of it among the moments of Jesus' career. Third, the apocalyptic eschatology is Hellenized by the ensuing discussion, which emphasizes the solidarity of the Savior and the saved—a theme common to the Gnostic redeemer theology. In contrast with Gnosticism, it must be stated, this solidarity is not inherent (ontic or metaphysical), so that it could be said to "pre-exist," but is established only by the Son of God's identifying himself with the lot of man, including suffering. This is the aim of the descent. This act of solidarity (which John terms "incarnation) makes it possible for Jesus to be the "author of faith" (not in Ebeling's sense!) and the "pioneer" of salvation, which consists of deliverance from death and the Devil and in bringing men to God (as a triad of Old Testament quotations in vv. 12-13 aims to make clear). The whole discussion is

116

a fascinating example of how Hellenistic categories (including descent/ascent), Old Testament exegesis, and the historical Jesus [59] mutually affected one another.

In light of the previous section, the decisive question is whether this reinterpretation of the gospel, which took up the Hellenistic myth, was an ideological-propagandistic step or a genuinely theological-evangelical one. That is, did Christians simply appropriate a "going" myth in order to promote Jesus and the church's salvation, or did they at the same time criticize and modify the myth in the light of Jesus? There is no doubt that extensive propagandistic assimilation of Jesus to current Hellenistic myths did take place; after all, Christianity was not uniform or "pure." The more widespread and diversified it became, the more multiform it came to be. Inevitably, forms of Christian propaganda developed. What matters for our discussion is whether the church was able to criticize and restrict them.

To see what full assimilation of Jesus to Hellenistic myth was like, we must go beyond the New Testament to certain Christianized Gnostic systems current in the second century. True, one cannot tar all second-century Gnostic Christians with the same brush, for the recent finds in upper Egypt [60] confirm our surmise that this mode of Christianity encompassed not only bizarre beliefs and rites but a highly sophisticated and but slightly mythologized Christianity as well [61] (as did the "orthodox" counterpart!). Our purpose, nonetheless, is served by noting one of the two diverse reports concerning Basilides. Because it is the character of these theologies which interests us, it does not matter here whether Basilides himself is accurately portrayed in either report.[62]

According to Hippolytus' complex report, (*ref.* vii 7-15), Basilides taught a quite sophisticated system. Since no known category is applicable to the true God,[63] especially "being" which is appropriate to time-space, God is the "non-existent" One.[64] He spoke a word through which a cosmic seed containing three sonships came into being: the refined (spirit); that needing refining (soul); and the gross (body), which contained the souls of Gnostic men. The salvation of the

117

latter occurs by an elaborate process, according to which transcendent knowledge moves downward, manward, eventuating in the Light (power) that descended on Jesus. His resurrection separates the mixed nature of man (body and spirit) and thereby enables all who are of the same substance [65] as Jesus to follow him upward out of the cosmos toward the Father. This "resurrection" is really his being factored into component parts—a step necessary for undoing the mixed nature of every man.[66]

In what ways is this interpretation propagandistic and ideological? First of all, it is apparent that the myth dominates the historical Jesus completely; further, Hippolytus reports that Basilides wedded widespread anti-Semitism to resentment against the Creator and his creation—this evil world of matter was the work of the Jewish God. Second, the Basilideans in no way challenged the idea that man's situation stemmed from his soul's being entombed in the body or mixed with matter, and that his salvation consisted of release from it. Accordingly, by definition the specifications for a savior were known in advance; Jesus was merely the name for the figure. In no way did his life or death or resurrection question or modify the system; he simply was absorbed into it. Third, within the churches the Basilideans appropriated the Gospels and wrote commentaries on them, thereby claiming to have the true meaning of what Christians at large held without understanding.[67]

Though the church opposed Gnosticism, it continued to use the descent/ascent myth without succumbing to it completely. First, it refused to describe the relation of the pre-existent Son or Logos to the aeons, just as it refused to narrate his descent into the cosmos[68] or ascent to the Father. It simply stated the movement, generally eschewing curiosity about its details.[69] Second, pre-existence was limited to the Savior. Man's soul was not held to be pre-existent, for only the divine is eternal.[70] At precisely this point the myth was broken, for its whole power rested on the consubstantiality of Savior and saved—a consubstantiality marked by the pre-existence of both. In saying that created man could become immortal, the church denied "natural" immortality to the soul. Third, in refusing to accept *en toto* a myth of a pre-existent savior who descended to save pre-existent souls and lead them upward to reintegrate the divine totality, the church implicitly rejected the contention of the Gnostics that the non-Gnostic Christian was incapable of "doing theology" properly because this required consistent adherence to the myth and the adjustment of the history of Jesus to it. Where the historical Jesus was permitted to retain his integrity over against the mythic patterns, the gospel (and its theological [formal] substructure) was preserved from becoming transformed completely into propaganda for an ideology.[71] Fourth, some Gnostics also composed their own gospels and their own traditions of Jesus in which Jesus said and did what Gnostic theology required him to have done. Because the main channel of the church was also reformulating, expanding, and contracting the Jesus-tradition, the struggle with Gnosticism was in effect a struggle over the limits of interpretation with regard to the historical Jesus.[72]

But it was not only in the second and third centuries that there was struggle. The New Testament itself reveals how steps were taken to restrict the absorption of Jesus into an ideological structure. The Gospel of Mark contains a number of miracle stories with hallmarks of a Hellenistic milieu and perspective (4:35-5:43; 6:31-56). They contain no conflict with Judaism, no debate about Jesus' authority—motifs found in stories rooted in Palestine. Nor do they relate his work to the kingdom or the forgiveness of sins. Rather, they present Jesus as operating through supranatural power within him the way a Hellenistic wonder-worker did. In short, they glorify Jesus as a divine-man (*theios anēr*). Certain stories, then, circulated in which Jesus was portrayed as a common Hellenistic miracle man.[73]

But the decisive thing to see is how Mark counterweights their effect by the way he builds them into his narrative. Whereas they were told originally to *manifest* Jesus' divine power, Mark used them to accent their *inability* to disclose Jesus' true identity and the character of the gospel. He not only operates with the "Messianic secret" but repeatedly emphasizes the disciples' inability to comprehend, climaxed by Jesus' rebuke after the second feeding of the crowd (8:21). Moreover, Mark emphasizes the point that what is decisive about Jesus was his suffering and the call to follow in that way. This, not stories of Jesus' divine power, constitutes the good news for Mark.[74] In this way, he checked the propagandizing use of Jesus' miracle stores.[75]

C. *Conclusions.* What has this complex precedent from early Christian times taught us? First, neither the earliest Jewish nor the subsequent Hellenistic mode, taken as it stands, is a live option today. Even though the church has claimed the Hebrew Bible as its own Old Testament, the fact is that contemporary men outside the church, and many within it as well, are as alien to this "Old Bible" [76] as were Paul's hearers in Athens. There is little gain in centering the good news about Jesus in his fulfillment of the Old Testament if the hearer does not acknowledge that it is decisive to begin with. That the Old Testament and Hebrew/Jewish theology are important historical backgrounds for Jesus and the gospel no one will dispute; but to speak of background is by no means the same as announcing that Jesus is God's good news because in him Israel's hope is made actual. It is no better if one proclaims that Jesus is good news because he came down from heaven and returned, for in a day when heaven is no longer "up" this is either incomprehensible or misleading. A creature from outer space is not at all what the early Christians meant when they spoke of God's Son coming to earth. Merely repeating New Testament formulations and arguing for their truth might conceivably convince the Christian preacher that he is faithful to the Bible, but his message would scarcely be heard as good news by the man who is not. In fact, to perpetuate biblical language doggedly and defensively would have the effect of turning the gospel into propaganda for an ideology.

Second, the New Testament shows that it was (is) possible to restate the gospel in different ways without surrendering its "gospel-hood." At this point, the authority of the New Testament, if one wants to speak in such terms, manifests itself in authorizing us to do in our time what our forefathers did in theirs.[77] Undertaking this is not easy, nor are the results without risks, as the battle with Gnosticism shows. In reformulating the gospel so that it remains gospel, we sail on but partly charted seas, encouraged by the precedent of earlier mariners who, convinced that in Jesus they had a trustworthy answer for life's question, sought new routes for letting others share that conviction.

Third, just as our observations about earliest Jewish Christian preaching advanced our criticism of Bultmannian views, so we can now comment further on the Fuchs-Ebeling line. It is the divine-man Christology that crystallizes our uneasiness, already noted, about the lack of offense in the Jesus they portray. The watermark of the divine-man is that he manifests his power in such a way that beholders perceive enough of his identity and power that they can acknowledge him rightly. One must therefore ask whether in the historical Jesus portrayed by Fuchs and Ebeling—the confident Jesus who makes us confident, the one who so brings God to speech that in his words God is effectuated also in us—we have not been brought, unwittingly to be sure, dangerously close to a modern form of the divine-man. Do not the Gospels show that Jesus made disbelief and unfaith as possible as faith and trust?

Our task, then, can be restated: How shall one present Jesus so that the hearer today receives the word as good news and can entrust himself to him? More precisely, how does the historical Jesus—the Jesus accessible through historiography—function in Christian proclamation that is not mere propaganda? If he is not to be regarded as a divine-man, how shall he be presented?

III. The Historical Jesus as a Question

The thesis is simple: in the proclamation of good news to post-Constantinian hearers, the historical Jesus should be presented in such a way that he evokes a question; this allows trust in him to emerge. The remainder of this chapter explores this thesis from several angles, but first we must identify what is *not* intended by it.

121

A. *Five Caveats.* Obviously, in the first place, we are not saying that the preacher announces his historical questions concerning Jesus or that he undertakes to disabuse the hearer of his historical misinformation, though in certain cases it may be necessary to illumine the character of the Jesus-tradition in order to crack solidified positions.

Nor does it mean, second, that one presents the historical Jesus so as to produce hero-worship. In such presentations, Jesus increases "in stature and wisdom and in favor with God and man" in direct proportion to the extent to which his contemporaries decrease—that is, they are invariably portrayed as narrow-mided legalists (Pharisees), fanatical nationalists (Zealots), sophisticated skeptics (Sadducees), esoteric sectarians (Essenes), and persons devoid of religious sensitivities altogether ('Am ha-arez). When Jesus is played off against such a milieu, his appeal is purchased too cheaply. The error of the old liberal lives of Jesus lay precisely here—they lionized Jesus by playing him off against both Christian theology and the Judaism of which he was a part in order to present an appealing hero of liberal religion and ethics. As we saw in the previous chapter, the same error is made by Fuchs and Bornkamm; Jesus "brings God to speech" in a culture existentially devoid of God.

Third, our suggestion must be dissociated from one element in the new quest—namely, the effort so to delineate the existential continuity between Jesus' understanding of existence and that of the gospel that Jesus becomes the embodiment of the existentialist message. This swallows up the particularity and concreteness of the historical into categories that are as self-evident to the existentialist as the liberal categories were to the liberals. Not accidentally does the issue shift from whether "what Jesus was about" is valid, to whether what is valid about man is linked inseparably to Jesus himself. We hope to retain the functional centrality of Jesus in the gospel in such a way as to guard against merely appealing to him as the historical point of reference to what is true in any case.

Fourth, the proposal to present Jesus in such a way that he evokes a question does not mean foreswearing the Christian conviction that Christ is the answer or silencing this claim. What it does mean is taking today's hearer and his situation with sufficient seriousness that one holds back the answer until the hearer's own question is uncovered and crystallized. Making "the Christian answer" central in the sermon easily bypasses the hearer or misdirects his attention to the concepts of the classical Christian tradition. As we saw, that turns the answer into a law—an obligatory set of ideas. The underlying reason for presenting the historical Jesus as a question-evoking figure is to make it possible to offer the hearer a gift.[78] When the hearer finds himself drawn into a situation that evokes a re-examination of the mystery of his own life because Jesus has been introduced into his orbit, he is in a new situation, one not generated by himself. The theological interpretation of this development is grace. The immediate aim of preaching is to create such a situation; to this end the historical Jesus functions as a catalyst.

Fifth, therefore, in speaking of the historical Jesus' function as we do, we are not denying in any way the theological interpretation of what occurs in preaching—e.g., that God calls the hearer to faith and enables him to respond. Rather, what we are trying to understand is what occurs phenomenologically when one begins to trust Jesus. This no more denies or excludes the activity of God "in, with and under" this process than analyzing the process by which our Gospel of John came into existence takes it out of the Word of God. Phenomenological analysis and theological interpretation are neither competitive nor complementary (as if one required the other); rather they are discreet language systems and modes of discourse developed to deal with the same process. The mode used at any given moment is appropriate to the task at hand—i.e., it expresses the relation of the speaker to the subject matter. In analyzing a process, such as the one before us here, he is an observer or a knower (even of himself); in giving a theological account of it, he articulates his understanding of how this process as a whole is related to the One who is not analyzable. That is, he confesses and celebrates his participation in the process in a particular way, as one known by God. This is why theological interpretation rapidly atrophies if it is not nurtured by praise.

B. *Jesus as Catalytic Question.* Having tried to put distance between our intent and possible malformations of it, we are now in a better position to lay out its rationale and potential.

First, it is instructive to see an analogy; presenting the historical Jesus as a question-inducing figure is to treat him as one treats a canonical text today. In times past, preacher and hearers alike stood within a Christianized context in which "what the Bible says" was assumed to have a claim to obedience, moral or conceptual—as in the Jewish situation of earliest preaching. Since the dissolution of Christendom, such an unspoken context of preaching and hearing is no longer present. Consequently, the clearer and sharper the exposition of the text becomes, the more pressing grows the question, Is this really valid? Even within the church the day is long past when one could win a theological point by showing that it says just what the Bible says. Rather than being jettisoned or reduced to a historical source book, the canon is to be retained partly for the sake of continuity with the Christian community through the years (the New Testament, after all, is the only *thing* Christians have in common), and partly for the sake of locating central questions. By using the text as a window into reality, one does not provide the congregation with the self-evident answer but exposes a question that invites a response.

In regarding the historical Jesus as a canonical text, we are consistent with this view of biblical preaching.

(a) As with the text, so the historical Jesus does not inevitably evoke an acknowledgment that he is valid and trustworthy.[79] Rather, in both cases, the exposition generates a situation in which one may decide for or against him, and the immediate purpose of the message is to create the occasion for an authentic decision with regard to an authentic issue.

(b) Moreover, the text's canonicity manifests itself less as an authority to legitimate the preacher's words and more as that material through which the preacher focuses the hearer's attention on what is decisive. The preacher neither states nor argues his theological understanding of Scripture as the prerequisite but allows that understanding to undergird the way the Scripture functions in his preaching. In the same way, Christology is not the burden of the sermon, but the basis for presenting Jesus as the one who focuses the issue of man and God. What is so desperately needed in some quarters is freedom to use Jesus as the surprising uncoverer of our deepest questions, and to stop arguing about him or his beliefs.

(c) The preacher's understanding of the content of the text depends on the critical conclusions and probabilities advanced by biblical scholarship and critical theology. To the extent his faith is shaped by his perception of what the text says and what is going on in it, his faith is contingent on scholarly probabilities. Yet one scarcely confuses this with trust in God himself. In the same way, while one's perception of Jesus relies on reconstructions, this is not confused with religious trust in him. Just as scholarly work assists—at least intends to—in understanding the text, so it helps us—at least in principle—see what the name "Jesus" refers to. Historical work helps to identify the subject matter that calls for attention.

The scond consideration grows out of what has been sketched. Centralizing precisely the *historical* Jesus is more conducive to producing a grace-laden occasion than is presenting the Christ of Christian dogma, since the Christology of the church is not the door to faith.

Several reasons can be advanced to support the claim that the historical Jesus serves adequately the aim of offering (and accepting) a gift. (a) Because the name "Jesus" refers to a historical figure accessible to public knowledge, he serves as the common point of departure which does not first need to be verified as a legitimate subject of reflection. (b) Because he is not self-validating, he himself requires a decision. This is inescapably an act of faith, whether the decision is for or against the man. The more sharply Jesus is perceived, the clearer becomes the need to take some position with regard to what he was. Establishing beyond reasonable doubt that he was an exorcist who regarded victories over demons as signs of the kingdom's power settles the matter, if at all, only for him who already believes that whatever Jesus did and thought is valid; for him who has not yet made this decision, the exorcistic side of Jesus poses the question: Are such deeds a reliable index of Jesus' standing with God or of the character of the kingdom? The Synoptics know this well, for they report that his exorcistic power was traced also to collusion with Satan. Similarly, the more evident it becomes that Jesus presumed to speak and act on God's behalf, the more pressing is the question, Is this really valid? Even if one could prove unequivocally that Jesus believed himself to be the Messiah, the Son of God, or the Son of Man (in whatever sense), this would only press the question whether this self-interpretation is justified. Precisely the same point applies to Jesus' understanding of existence, though the new quest does not make the ambiguity of this point as prominent as it should.[80] By grasping the ambiguity of the historical Jesus (the historian's Jesus) one avoids the danger so important to Bultmann's argument—that concern with the historical Jesus is inimical to faith because it legitimates it. Actually, the ambiguity inherent in the historical Jesus precludes such an inference, since the more accurately (historically) he is seen the less legitimation can be "read off." Seeing the historical Jesus does not make faith easier or more self-evidently justified but makes it clearer that trust is not the inevitable last step in a series of historical inferences. It is important to note that the ambiguity of the historical Jesus and the probability factor in research are not surds to be overcome by faith or logic, because these factors keep faith from being confused with sound historical reasoning and grace from being identified as the good fortune of finding a reliable historical portrait of Jesus. And in presenting such a Jesus, the sermon must resist the temptation to argue the Christian case and so distract from the centrality of Jesus, since it is with regard to him that decision is invited.

One disclaimer must be noted at this point. The foregoing argument does not mean that the closer one gets to the facts the more untenable becomes the Christian understanding of

Jesus. That would be a return to Reimarus. Here it is absolutely essential to distinguish between assuming that the historical data validate faith, invalidate it, or permit it without requiring it. It is the latter that is implied here. As the burden of Van Harvey's recent book makes clear, it is immoral to believe something for which *no* warrants can be adduced.

A third aspect, therefore, of our suggestion concerns the Christian stake in sound historiography. It is at this juncture that our foregoing reflections on the nature of ideology and propaganda are specially germane. In a word, historical study of Jesus serves the gospel by requiring the church to be honest, thereby controlling the tendency to incorporate Jesus into an ideology that can appeal to facts for support.

The historical Jesus helps to keep the church honest through the constant pressure of having to do with a real human, historic figure. The controversy over the historical Jesus in theology is simply the modern form of the old question of Docetism, that ancient (and perennial) theological tendency so to absorb Jesus into the current theological understanding that he becomes its construct.[81] The concrete historical reality of the whole fabric called "Jesus" cannot be inferred from the Christian conviction that the ever-living Lord is known in faith and is present in the heart of the believer, just as the character of that Jesus is not to be inferred from the believer's heart or theology. These rest, rather, on the fact that he is as available to historiography as is Socrates. It is precisely the public character of historical knowledge which prevents the church from appealing to its private Jesus as the content of faith and proclamation, a Jesus whose lineaments are subject to no verification or correction—an ideological Jesus.

Further, the good news does not concern a Jesus who can be collapsed into the various forms of gospel-preaching as they develop from era to era but concerns a Jesus who stands over against them all. The gospel has salvific power because it invites the hearer to see Jesus through the proclamation, not merely to accept Christian (self-) understanding. Insisting on the historian's Jesus, in Bultmann's terms narrating a piece of history, is one essential means for making clear that it is Jesus

127

to whom trust is directed, and that the church is the community that acknowledges this freely and gladly. In other words, its foundational reliance on Jesus must be perfectly clear; otherwise, the church becomes presumptive.

Fourth, what is implicit in what we have been saying is that this centrality of the ambiguous historical Jesus is nothing less than the extension of the "skandalon of the cross" through the entire career of Jesus. Bultmann, on the other hand, has appealed to Paul, who gave us the phrase, to argue that the historical Jesus was unimportant to Paul and hence a matter of indifference to us as well. A full and adequate discussion of the matter is yet to be written;[82] nevertheless, at the risk of being arbitrary in interpretation and apodictic in presentation, three considerations are consistent with Paul, though they cannot, and need not, be designated as what Paul said.

(a) There is no justification for thinking that the offense of the cross is derived solely from the means of execution, regarded as offensive already in the Old Testament (cited in Gal. 3:13). Nor is there any evidence whatever that Paul proclaimed that somebody crucified was resurrected, as if the man on the cross were irrelevant to the meaning of resurrection. To the contrary, what makes the cross truly offensive theologically is the man on it, as I Cor. 2:8 and Phil. 2:5-11 imply. This does not mean that today one must first believe that Jesus is the Son of God in the flesh before the cross appears as offense. Rather, the contours of his human life make the cross offensive to us more than predicated divinity, because the cross is what it all came to, an absurd cross among crosses. In a word, the historical Jesus as a whole is an offense because the cross climaxed his career; hence it stands for his life. The cross, in this sense, offends our deepest understanding of life. If in New Testament times it was the pattern of descent/ascent which served to expose the offense of Jesus' life, today the same sort of offense-quality can be made evident by strict attention to the history of Jesus, because just as the former challenged the prevailing idea of divinity, so the latter challenges the prevailing idea of man. In the former, the idea of man was more latent; in the latter, it is the understanding of God which

128

is latent. That is why the historical Jesus is not an item in an ideology but the challenge to it.

(b) Paul's marked, and to us distressing, silence concerning the words and deeds of Jesus should not be used to justify our disinterest, for possibly the Synoptics provide us a more extensive body of Jesus-tradition than was available to him. In any case, it is indeed an odd procedure to insist, as Bultmann does, that we should ignore the full potential of what we have for an accurate repristination of an earlier situation! Moreover, it is at least possible that Paul declined to emphasize even what he did know because the descent/ascent framework in which he thought of Jesus focused on the weakness of the historical Jesus (the low point in the U-shaped Christ-event), not on his power (whether by word or deed) as certain traditions about him may have been doing. If so, then our mode of emphasizing the historical Jesus (as not self-validating) is continuous with the direction of Paul's thought, though it uses quite different means. It also raises the question whether the new hermeneutic's concern to show that the kingdom came when Jesus preached or ate with sinners reverses the flow of Paul's thought.

(c) It is far from evident that Paul's epistles, written to believers who had already heard the gospel, can be used the way Bultmann uses them. Not only do they discuss only what is at issue, but they can allude in shorthand phrases to whole complexes of thought which Paul can take for granted. Can one draw firm conclusions from such material concerning the way Paul presented the good news for the first time? I find it impossible to imagine Paul preaching in Ephesus or Corinth without telling a rudimentary story of Jesus,[83] just as I do not see how he could write II Cor. 10-13 if his self-interpretation were grounded only in a myth of a descended god who had been executed before he returned to glory.

If up to now we have concentrated on questions associated with the *historicality* of Jesus, our fifth consideration concerns the centrality of the historical Jesus: Why *Jesus* and not someone else? If the function of a historical figure is to evoke a question, why could not one use another person, such as Francis

129

of Assisi or Bonhoeffer of Berlin? In principle, of course, such persons can function in the same way, since their lives do interrogate our own and since the historical Jesus was not *sui generis* but continuous with men of history. Yet, using such men would not displace Jesus from the center, because they understood themselves, rightly, as being contingent on Jesus.

If, on the other hand, one prefers to think of figures outside the Christian tradition—say Gandhi or Socrates (whose death was more impressive than was Jesus')—an even more profound aspect of our suggestion is exposed, namely, that the centrality of Jesus is constitutive of historical Christianity. Continuity with this tradition is evidenced in concentrating on Jesus as the decisive event, and one must do this without denigrating figures outside this tradition. This looking to some figure as the paradigm or clue to reality is not peculiar to Christians, for everyone stands in some tradition, some stream of understanding,[84] and no one begins from the brow of Jove. So it is not surprising that no Christian community exists which is not earmarked by what appears to others as preoccupation with Jesus. The preacher expresses the church's foundational conviction when he speaks of Jesus in a way in which he does not speak of others, and there is no reason to be on the defensive about it. Part of the confusion in today's pulpits is anchored in the widespread flight from identification with the Christian community, as if one could speak for God-as-such to man-as-such as an interpreter of faith-as-such in order to be legitimated by modern man. But post-Christendom culture will never license the church to talk about Jesus in terms consistent with Christian insight. The church must be clear about its own reasons for trusting Jesus and for commending him, and bear witness to that.

But the pivotal factor in the decision to make Jesus the center of preaching to another so that he too may entrust his life to Jesus is the trust of the witness himself. Not that the preacher says, "Look at my trust!" thereby making himself into a "divine man" by appealing to the success stories of his faith. (In fact, this was precisely what the Corinthians demanded of Paul, who finally acceded to their demands by

130

reciting with irony his case history of "weakness" in II Cor. 10–13.) Rather, in view here is the fact that the preacher can bear effective witness only to what he himself trusts, regardless of what he proclaims. One can scarcely come to entrust himself to Jesus if the preacher does not bear witness to what trusting Jesus means and does not mean. This testimony is not identical with verbalization, though it includes it, but is also the contour of life itself. One does not need to reinstate Donatism in order to see that the life-style of a trusting witness gives moral warrant for commending Jesus as trustworthy. Clearly, for example, Bonhoeffer's death as the climax of a career gave his writings moral authority that they would never have achieved had he retired to the Black Forest to think about "the cost of discipleship." Nor would Martin Luther King's commendation of nonviolence have been persuasive had he carried a knife. Congruence of life and word does not create proof capable of overcoming doubt in Lessing's sense, but it does give power to the word of witness without which preaching becomes propaganda.

C. *From History to Gospel.* This role of the historical Jesus (the historian's Jesus) in preaching seems to run counter to his role in historiography. Even if the historian learns to discriminate between what he can know with reasonable confidence, what can probably be inferred, what must remain a possibility, and what cannot be known at all, nevertheless in the nature of the case historical reconstruction implies a critical "answer" to historical questions. (Nor should it be forgotten that sheer curiosity is an elemental form of a question.) Even a provisional reconstruction, a working hypothesis, is a provisional answer to inquiry. How, then, does the historian's answer become the preacher's question? Our problem is not simply, What makes a fact questionable? for that is an issue of critical historiography. Rather, How does a reported "fact" become a question to the hearer? Specifically, How does the reconstructed Jesus question the hearer as a self? Up till now we have argued that Jesus can play this role; now we must ask how this transfer of roles occurs. Another way of putting this is to recall

131

that the historian interrogates the texts and the Jesus of whom they speak; but how does the recovered Jesus come to interrogate the hearer?

An example may help. For purposes of discussion we may assume that Jesus said, "Blessed are you poor, for yours is the kingdom of heaven (or God)," that in saying this he did not make the kingdom into an ideological warrant for the aspirations of the underprivileged but cited a concrete instance of the impending inversion of the present state of things, that this inversion was grounded in the conviction that God's kingdom was not the fulfillment of the present but an alternative to it in accord with the integrity of God, and so on. Even if one might readily reconstruct a coherent understanding of God and man implicit in this single saying and be reasonably sure that he has recovered the theology of the historical Jesus, he would only describe the outlook and convictions of Jesus (including his understanding of existence!). In presenting him, the preacher will place this reconstruction before the hearer, thereby inviting him to ponder it. But since the historical Jesus is not self-validating, and because the preacher (whatever his own stance) cannot assume that Jesus is valid for the hearer just because it is *Jesus* (only when one speaks to another Christian can one assume that the word of Jesus has authority), how does the preacher allow the historian's conclusion to become a question to the hearer about himself so that trust may arise?

To begin, this movement can be put in grammatical terms: the change from assertion to question. Sometimes the change in relation to the subject matter is manifest in the syntax of the sentence. In a statement ("Jesus said [or did say] x") the speaker asserts something to the hearer about Jesus; the hearer is the more or less passive recipient of information. If the words are rearranged ("Did Jesus say x?"), the speaker invites the hearer to determine whether or not he did so say. Unless the question is ignored, the hearer now becomes a participant in the search for an answer. But the change of roles can also occur without a syntactical change: "Jesus said x?" Here the punctuation (?) indicates that a different relation is asked from the hearer. The point is that any movement from assertion to question realigns the relationship between speaker, hearer, and subject matter. It is the task of preaching to set this process in motion.

The possibility of personal trust in the described Jesus comes when the question of the validity of the subject matter, not the accuracy of the statement, comes into view. (Not, Did Jesus say this? but, Was he right in saying so?) This question may arise in more than one way, but it is the task of the preacher to press it. What is distinctive about the preacher is that he himself escalates the reflection to another level by adopting another role. That is, he moves from the role of notary public (historian) who attests that the statement is accurate to that of witness who testifies that it is also true, that he ("he" includes the whole Christian community, of course) has found Jesus trustworthy, that life has not exposed his trust as untenable, and so forth. This is why preaching the historical Jesus engages the whole self in a way that neither descriptive historiography nor announcing kerygmatic theology does. Dealing with the validity of the subject matter requires the preacher and the hearer, furthermore, to have entree to it and to stand on common ground in apprehending it. That is, the preacher must identify with the hearer sufficiently to deal with the issue where the hearer must deal with it. There the witness invites the hearer to look with him, to stand with him in trusting Jesus and in perceiving reality from this standpoint which can be also the hearer's own. The witness is more like a painter or poet than a traffic cop commanding. "Obey!" This mode of speech is more than an assertion and less than an imperative; it is, as it were, a blend of both—an invitation to share in the affirmation that the subject matter is valid and trustworthy.

In making this witness the preacher shows that the hearer's question about Jesus' validity leads to a question about himself. That is, the preacher leads the hearer in a double movement of thought. For example, by presenting what Jesus said in the first Beatitude, he focuses the hearer's attention on Jesus in such a way as to facilitate a second level of reflection—the validity of what Jesus said and perceived. But when one begins to question the validity of Jesus he must engage his own grasp of what is valid. Furthermore, because the self is constituted by what it trusts, raising the question of what one holds to be valid exposes the question of what one ultimately trusts, or the question of God. Conversely, questions about Jesus and the God he trusts lead to questions about the self and what it deems trustworthy to the uttermost. In presenting the historical Jesus, then, the preacher juxtaposes Jesus and the hearer so as to make possible a genuine response to him. A trusting response occurs when this reflection about one's own trusts leads to their restructuring in accord with Jesus. (The traditional word for this is repentance.)

In this light, Robinson's assertion that the kerygma and historiography are alternate routes to the same decision situation[85] falls wide of the mark, for kerygma and historical report are not alternates to be chosen but complementary dimensions of preaching. Kerygma without narrative is sheer church assertion; narrative without witness is ambiguity and offense.

Finally, this role of a narrative about Jesus comports with what we said earlier about the function of Jesus being comparable to that of a text. But not any kind of text. Specifically, the narrative of his life is the text of a parable that calls for a response. Just as the parable does not prove an argument or illustrate a point but tells a story in such a way as to invite the hearer to self-examination and to restructured commitment, so the story of Jesus calls for a decision when it is not forced to become a self-evident truth or a proof for an assertion. This is not to obliterate the difference between a constructed story and a reconstructed history; but it is to call attention to the analogous functions of these two kinds of narrative. Furthermore, just as the parable reorders perception as well as commitment, so the story of Jesus, when it functions as the lens into reality, restructures our understanding of God. This is why the last chapter will return to the role of Jesus as the parable of God.

In trying to achieve some clarification of the shift from narrative to invitation to share trust, we have perceived again, implicitly, that a clear grasp of any significant life leads easily to a re-examination of one's own. What is decisive about Christian preaching, therefore, is not this catalytic function as question but the claim that Jesus is at the same time the definitive answer. The subject of the next chapter, therefore, is the difference that trusting Jesus makes.

NOTES TO CHAPTER THREE

1. *The Courage to Be* (New Haven: Yale University Press, 1952), pp. 9 ff.
2. William Hamilton, "The Death of God Theologies Today," in *Radical Theology and the Death of God* (Indianapolis: Bobbs-Merrill, 1966), pp. 40-45.
3. The criticism some have aimed at Bultmann for not demythologizing radically enough because he clings to the mythic view of the Word and because he insists that the kerygma is necessary if man is to attain "authentic existence" is really aimed at this point: Bultmann has not eliminated the formal structure of "gospel." Edward Farley has also seen clearly the importance of the conceptual framework of the Christian tradition. "Jesus Christ in Historical and Non-historical Schemes," *Perspective* 9 (1968), 61-78.
4. Karen Dovring, *Road of Propaganda* (New York: Philosophical Library, 1959), pp. 5-6.
5. See, for example, Jacques Ellul's distinction between propaganda used for agitation and propaganda used for integration. The former is used to promote revolutions, the latter to build conformity. Ellul observes that the propaganda of integation is a distinctively twentieth century phenomenon. *Propaganda*, trans. Konrad Kellen and Jean Lerner (New York: Knopf, 1965; French ed., 1962), pp. 70-79.
6. Ellul points out that what emerged with Lenin and Hitler was a new relation between propaganda and ideology: "Ideology was of interest to Lenin and Hitler only when it could serve an action or some plan or tactic. Where it could not be used, it did not exist. Or it was used for propaganda. Propaganda then became the major fact; with respect to it, ideologies became mere epiphenomena. . . . Hitler modified National Socialist ideology several times according to the requirements of propaganda. . . . Propaganda's task is less and less to propagate ideologies; it now obeys its own laws and becomes autonomous.

"Propaganda no longer obeys an ideology. The propagandist is not, and cannot be, a 'believer.' . . . He has no more needs to share the political doctrines of the national government. . . . He cannot even share that ideology for which he must use it as

135

an object." *Propaganda*, pp. 195 ff. Even if the ideology shifts for propaganda purposes, it is the changed ideology that is propagandized.

7. For a historical sketch of the use of propaganda in the political sphere, see John B. Whitton and Arthur Larson, *Propaganda: Towards Disarmament in the War of Words*, published for the World Rule of Law Center at Duke University (Dobbs Ferry, N.Y.: Oceana Publications, 1964), Chap. 2.

8. Karen Dovring acutely states that "the communicator becomes the feared Propagandist when he presents the facts in a way that tries to link his own and his public's interest in a certain direction, evoking from his public the particular responses or decisions he wants. This process is one of the most important in the whole communication complex. When the facts are used as instruments for particular purposes the propagandist claims that he merely delivers facts. But he forgets to indicate that he also tells a story. This story is an image of reality, whose degree of fictive character is established by the communicator's and his sponsor's purpose. The world of propaganda is consequently closely related to the world of fiction." *Road of Propaganda*, pp. 13-14.

9. But see note 6. Ellul also reminds us that propaganda also occasions an ideology, pointing out that an entire ideology was created in order to justify action in Algeria which had been sanctioned by propaganda. *Propaganda*, p. 201. On the other hand, Daniel Bell contends that one reason socialism failed in the U.S. was its inflexible ideology, which not only rejected capitalism out of hand but also prevented the movement from relating itself to specific issues. *The End of Ideology* (New York: Free Press, 1960), p. 268.

10. Ellul's paragraphs on the effects of propaganda on the churches (*Propaganda*, pp. 228-32) merit serious reflection. The dangers he sees appear to stem from the church's conscious decision to propagandize the masses.

11. *Propaganda*, pp. 38-39.

12. Ellul shows that propaganda must attach itself to current social myths, which he distinguishes from ideology, but may not challenge them. He sees modern technological civilization dominated by four collective presuppositions: that man's aim is happiness, that man is naturally good, that history develops in endless progress, and that everything is matter. *Ibid*. The way in which these suppositions shape the stance of the church, especially when its main passion is to be "with it," is too obvious to require comment.

13. James Y. Holloway, editor of *Katallagete*, observed (in conversation) that this sanctification of technological society in effect made Cox counter-revolutionary.

14. Ellul points out that propaganda has the effect of creating a new "sphere of the 'sacred,'—'a new zone of the forbidden' in the heart of man. Propaganda makes it impossible to evaluate certain questions or even to discuss them." *The Technological*

Society, trans. by John Wilkinson (New York: Knopf, 1965), p. 370.

15. C. H. Dodd's Apostolic Preaching and Its Developments (London: Hodder & Stoughton, 1936) still repays reading, despite the fact that he does not distinguish sufficiently between what is pre-Paul and what is from the earliest church. One should also read Martin Dibelius, From Tradition to Gospel, trans. Bertram Lee Woolf (New York: Scribner's, 1935; based on 2nd German ed., 1933 [the recent paperback reprint has removed the date!]), Chap. 2.

16. The scholarly literature on the speeches and sermons of Acts is enormous. Thanks to Dr. and Mrs. A. J. Mattill, articles published up to 1962 are listed in A Classified Bibliography of Literature on the Acts of the Apostles (NTTS 7) (Grand Rapids: Eerdmans, 1966). The schematic character of the speeches is clearly presented by Eduard Schweizer, "Concerning the Speeches in Acts," in Studies in Luke-Acts, ed. L. E. Keck and J. L. Martyn (Schubert Festschrift) (Nashville: Abingdon Press, 1966), pp. 208-16. The missionary speeches of Acts have been thoroughly investigated by Ulrich Wilckens, Die Missionsreden der Apostelgeschichte, WMANT 5 (Neukirchen-Vluyn: Neukirchner Verlag, 1961). Wilckens' work supplements that done earlier by Martin Dibelius, "The Speeches in Acts and Ancient Historiography" (1949) and other studies in Studies in the Acts of the Apostles, trans. Mary Ling and Paul Schubert (New York: Scribner's, 1956).

17. Because I Cor. 15:1-11 is pivotal for many questions of New Testament interpretation (e.g., forms of resurrection tradition, early Christian soteriology, status of Peter, James, and Paul in the early church), this passage has generated an extensive critical literature. For our purpose, it would be significant if one could establish not only the Aramaic origin of the tradition Paul received (which must first be recovered from the text) but that it originated in Jerusalem. That Paul received the tradition in Damascus or Antioch is to many scholars more likely than that he received it in Jerusalem, since our knowledge of Paul's early relation to Jerusalem depends largely on Acts, which has special reasons for pointing this out; in contrast, Paul's own words in Galatians 1 appear to assert almost total independence of Jerusalem tradition. Joachim Jeremias has defended the Aramaic origin in The Eucharistic Words of Jesus, trans. A. Ehrhardt (Oxford: Blackwell, 1955), p. 30, 130. Hans Conzelmann has denied the import of Jeremias' evidence in "Zur Analyse der Bekenntnisformel I Kor. 15, 3-5," EvTheol 25 (1965), 1-11 (a translation is found in Interpretation 20 [1966], 15-25), though he does not claim to have disproven the possibility of a Jerusalem origin (since not all Greek texts, or even translations into Greek, must have originated elsewhere). Jeremias defended his position in "Artikelloses Χριστός. Zur Ursprache von I Cor. 15:3b-5," ZNW 57 (1966), 211-15.

18. The issue was not which title is appropriate to Jesus but whether the expected Messiah had come unexpectedly in Jesus. It must

not be inferred, of course, that this was the sole way of understanding Jesus, or necessarily the very earliest. For an analysis of titles, see R. H. Fuller, *The Foundations of New Testament Christology* (New York: Scribner's, 1965), Chap. 6. See also Ferdinand Hahn's important *Titles of Jesus in Christology*, trans. Harold Knight and George Ogg (Cleveland: World, 1969; German ed., 1963).

19. This judgment has been challenged repeatedly ever since H. S. Reimarus' ice-breaking study, which Lessing published posthumously. For an opposite view, which at the same time is sensitive to the Zealotic appeal of Jesus' work, see Oscar Cullmann, *The State in the New Testament* (London: SCM 1963, rev. ed.; 1st German ed., 1957).

20. Even if one is convinced that Jesus believed himself to be the Messiah or the Son of Man, or to be the Messiah-designate, no text (apart from the problematic Mk. 14:62, which must be seen in light of the movement of Mark's portrait of Jesus) allows us to say flatly that Jesus claimed to be the Messiah. To the contrary, it has been argued, with considerable persuasiveness, that "Messiah" is the one category he deliberately avoided (Mk. 8:27-30). Christians commonly forget that "Messiah" had a specific meaning—anointed ruler. This is why the Messiah-question is inseparable from the Zealot-question.

21. Even though occasional Jewish texts can be cited in which the death of the Messiah is indicated, Jesus' death at the hands of the occupation government contradicted what the Messiah's relation to Rome was expected to be.

22. It is sheer assertion impelled by existentialist requirements when James Robinson says, "Easter *was* the revelation of Jesus' transcendent selfhood to his disciples . . . the culmination of their historical encounter with him." *A New Quest of the Historical Jesus*, 107. The statement is, fortunately, deleted from the German edition (1960).

23. Scholars such as Ferdinand Hahn and Reginald Fuller maintain that the title Messiah was applied to Jesus *after* he had already been titled Son of Man. This hypothesis has two advantages: (a) Since it is likely that Jesus himself expected his work to be vindicated by the Son of Man (Mk. 8:38), it was inevitable that the appearances of the resurrected Jesus led to the conclusion that Jesus himself was now Son of Man; hence the title seeped into the tradition of Jesus' words about himself (e.g., Mk. 9:31). Once Jesus was believed to be installed as the heavenly Son of Man who would soon judge mankind as God's regent, it was easy to take the next step and conclude that Jesus was now the Messiah as well. On this basis, one can see that Acts 3:20 means exactly what it says: "[God will] send the Christ [Messiah] appointed for you, Jesus, whom heaven must receive [as Son of Man] until the time for establishing all that God spoke by the mouth of his holy prophets from of old" (RSV). (b) It explains how the title "Messiah," which Jesus had avoided, nevertheless was applied to him. As Fuller puts it: "When it is used

of Jesus by others after his assumption into heaven and in the specific context of his return it is crystal clear that the term Christos-Mašiaḥ is an equivalent for the apocalyptic title, Son of Man. In this context there was no danger of confusing the title with the political type of Messiah. The Palestinian church was forced to use the word which Jesus had avoided, because only so could it proclaim, to Jews, Jesus as the end-time ruler." *The Foundations of New Testament Christology*, p. 159. See also Ferdinand Hahn, *The Titles of Jesus*, pp. 161 ff.

24. C. F. D. Moule puts it aptly: "The Christians began from Jesus—from his known character and mighty deeds and sayings, and his death and resurrection; and with these they went to the scriptures, and found that God's dealings with his People and his intentions for them there reflected did, in fact, leap into into new significance in the light of these recent happenings. Sooner or later this was to lead, through a definition of what God had done, to something like a definition of who Jesus was." *The Birth of the New Testament* (New York: Harper, 1962), pp. 57-58. H. W. Boers has gone even farther: Psalm 16 suggested to the disciples "that Jesus was alive in heaven and so produced in them that state of mind which led to their experiencing the resurrection appearances." "Psalm 16 and the Historical Origin of the Christian Faith," *ZNW* 60 (1969), 105 ff.

25. Martin Dibelius is probably right in his intuition that the "witness of Scripture may have been spoken of before it could really be adduced." *From Tradition to Gospel*, p. 184.

26. Acts 3:17-26, evidently relying on ancient traditions that in all likelihood go back to earliest days, expresses the conviction common to Christianity from that start: "What God foretold by the mouth of all the prophets . . . he thus fulfilled" (RSV).

27. R. V. G. Tasker has suggested the path of development. Inferring that earliest Christian worship included the Eucharist, which inevitably was related to Jesus' death, the community "carried over from the synagogue the practice of reading passages from the Old Testament Scriptures; and the passages which would be the most relevant to their worship, and therefore the ones most frequently used, would be the Passion psalms, and the Suffering Servant passages from Isaiah. When, therefore, they came to shape the material which ultimately found a place in the Gospel stories of the Passion, these could not have failed to be uppermost in their minds." He does not see, unfortunately, that precisely his reconstruction undermines our confidence in his next sentence: "But we have no good reason for supposing that some of them were not also uppermost in Jesus' own mind when He was actually facing the ordeal of His Passion." *The Old Testament in the New Testament* (Philadelphia: Westminster Press, 1957), pp. 41-42. The influence of Old Testament language on sayings in which Jesus speaks of his own mission, especially of his death, is striking. See, e.g., the passion predictions (particularly Mk. 9:31) and the formulations in Mk. 10:45 and Mt. 11:4-6.

In addition to the influence of the Old Testament itself, one must reckon with the Jewish Haggadah—the homiletical interpretation that grew up for instruction in synagogues and scribal circles and in festivals in the home. David Daube has suggested that beneath the present Gospels one can detect this influence not only on individual units but on blocks of material as well. See, e.g., "The Earliest Structure of the Gospels," *NTS* 5 (1959), 174-87. Unfortunately, John Bowman's book, *The Gospel of Mark: The New Christian Jewish Passover Haggadah*, "Studia Post-Biblica 8" (Leiden: Brill, 1965) carries this to the absurd conclusion that the present Gospel of Mark is itself a Passover Haggadah (though ignoring the work of Daube).

28. See, for example, the entry to Jerusalem (Mk. 11:1-10 par.), and above all the passion story itself. See the excellent discussion by Martin Dibelius, *From Tradition to Gospel*, Chap. 7, and his earlier "Die alttestamentliche Motive in der Leidensgeschichte des Petrus-und des Johannes-Evangeliums" (1918), now in *Botschaft und Geschichte* I (Tübingen: J. C. B. Mohr [Paul Siebeck] 1953), pp. 221-47. F. F. Bruce explored the influence of Zechariah, but he contends that it was the events of the passion that suggested the use of the texts rather than the texts generating details of the narrative. "The Book of Zechariah and the Passion Narrative," *BJRL* 43 (1961), 336-53.

29. Despite the rigorous, minute, and in some ways ingenious efforts of Joachim Jeremias to prove the existence of a pre-Christian Jewish belief in the suffering Messiah, the case has not been made. (See his contribution to *Servant of God*, SBT 20 [1957; German original published in Kittel's *Theologisches Wörterbuch* V, 1952], Chaps. 3-4.) Jeremias' evidence was assessed, with negative results, by Martin Rese, "Überprüfung einiger Thesen von Joachim Jeremias zum Thema des Gottesknechtes im Judentum," *ZThK* 60 (1963), 21-41. See also Morna D. Hooker, *Jesus and the Servant* (London: S.P.C.K., 1959). Nor can one show that Jesus applied the Suffering Servant theology to himself. Fuller himself has been forced to admit that the "thesis that Jesus understood himself as the Servant of the Lord" has been "demolished." *The Foundations of New Testament Christology*, p. 119. Moreover, while it is probably true that the Servant Christology is Palestinian, and quite early, it was soon abandoned, surviving explicitly only in occasional fossils embedded in texts such as Acts 3:26; 4:27, 30. This evidently became one of the least viable categories for interpreting Jesus. What, then, is finally gained by maintaining that Jesus himself used it concerning himself? Apparently it is the desire to find a link between Jesus' self-interpretation and that part of the Old Testament which modern scholarship regards as its apex—the Suffering Servant—thereby silently dissociating Jesus from apocalyptic. John Wick Bowman has recently reasserted such a view. *Which Jesus?* (Philadelphia: Westminster Press, 1970), Chap. 7.

30. At times, this reinterpretation included adjusting the text itself in order to make it fit the Jesus-tradition more precisely. An example of this is Mt. 27:9, which relies on two versions of Zech.

11:13 and combines them with Jer. 18:12 and 32:6-9, according to Krister Stendahl, *The School of St. Matthew*. (Uppsala, 1954; reprinted by Fortress Press in 1968), pp. 120-26, 1968-9.

The practice of re-pointing the Hebrew text in order to gain new phrasings was an accepted procedure in Palestinian exegesis, as the Qumran texts have confirmed. See Barnabas Lindars, *New Testament Apologetic* (Philadelphia: Westminster Press, 1961), pp. 24 ff.). See also the detailed analysis by my colleague, Lou H. Silberman, "Unriddling the Riddle. A Study in the Structure and Language of the Habakkuk Pesher," *Revue de Qumran* 11 (1961), 323-64.

31. Ever since Rendell Harris inaugurated the discussion (*Testimonies* I, II, Cambridge, 1916-20), scholars have reckoned with the theory that there was a growing body of "proof texts" which Christian preachers and teachers developed. Harris' work was followed especially by C. H. Dodd, *According to the Scriptures* (London: Nisbet, 1952); by Barnabas Lindars, *New Testament Apologetic* (see foregoing note); and by Jean Danielou, *Études d'exégèse judeo-chretienne* (*Les Testimonia*), "Théologie historique 5" (Paris: Beauchesne et ses fils, 1966). Lindars provides a useful sketch of the development of Scripture use in early Christian apologetic (Chap. 7). The theory of "Testimonies" has received significant external support from Qumran, where the community compiled such texts for its own self-interpretation. Technically called a *Florilegium*, such a text is now available (under the rubric, "A Midrash on the Last Days") in G. Vermes' translation, *The Dead Sea Scrolls in English* (Pelican; Baltimore: Penguin Books, 1962), pp. 245-46.

32. Surely the evidence of the Fourth Gospel (e.g., 7:40-43), as well as Justin's *Dialogue with Trypho*, warrants our inferring that the gospel-interpretation of Jesus to Jews not only relied on Scripture but was met by counter-claims and rebuttals also based on Scripture. In other words, Christian preaching to Jews soon became a hermeneutical struggle over the right understanding of the Scriptures, the Word, and revelation of God. The role of Jewish-Christian exegetical debates in the milieu of the Fourth Gospel is discussed by J. Louis Martyn's important *History and Theology in the Fourth Gospel* (New York: Harper, 1968), esp. Chap. 6.

33. Bultmann is consistent: he condemns this exegetical effort as theologically illegitimate. In his essay, "The Significance of the Old Testament for the Christian Faith," he wrote, "Faith which would believe on the basis of such proofs is not genuine faith at all. The scriptural proofs of the New Testament must be abolished not just on the basis of rational historical criticism, but for the very reason that they only obscure the character of of faith." This essay is the lead article in Bernhard W. Anderson's collection, *The Old Testament and Christian Faith*, New York: Harper, 1963) (unfortunately, this volume conceals the date of the original publication). In "Prophecy and Fulfilment" (1949), he not only insists again that the apostles misused the Old Testa-

ment because what they found in it was what was already known to them, but that this whole enterprise deprives Jesus' life of its offense and transforms it into its opposite—confirmation of salvation. *Essays on Old Testament Hermeneutics,* ed. Claus Westermann, trans. James L. Mays (Richmond: John Knox Press, 1963), pp. 51 ff.

34. Whatever the critical assessment of individual apostolic miracle stories in Acts may be, there is no reason to doubt the general point, for Paul himself reminds the Corinthians that they also received this compound of word and deed as marks of his mission (II Cor. 12:12).

35. C. H. Dodd, *The Apostolic Preaching,* pp. 28, 29, 31.

36. *A New Quest of the Historical Jesus,* p. 49. There appears to be an inconsistency between Robinson's insistence that (p. 41, n. 2) the primitive Christian kerygma included a "recital of past event" (as well as its "recurrence"), and his arguments against Dodd that outside of Acts there is little use of biographical data in kerygmatic texts (p. 49). Moreover, the objection is exactly the sort Robinson castigates: "positivistic." Precisely when one insists on "moving beneath the terminological level" (p. 120) he should desist from counting occurrences. It was such a confusion that led Bultmann and others to use Paul's references to "preaching the cross" as arguments against his interest in the life of Jesus altogether, as if "cross" meant only Jesus' execution.

37. Lindars rightly observes that "the tendency of apologetic is not to choose between various Messianic expectations, but to take them up into the expanding concept of the person of Christ." *New Testament Apologetic,* p. 256.

38. This sermon's long roots in Greek traditions were pointed out long ago by Eduard Norden, who also analyzed the way the traditions were modified in Acts. *Agnostos Theos* (first published in 1913; in 1956 the Wissenschaftliche Buchgesellschaft in Darmstadt reprinted the unrevised edition of 1923). The Anglo-Saxon theological world is the poorer because this important work, dealing also with the history of other religious formulas found in the New Testament, has not been translated. Martin Dibelius' essay remains a landmark in the vast literature about Acts 17. "Paul on the Areopagus" (1939), *Studies in the Acts of the Apostles,* pp. 26-77. The most recent monograph is Bertil Gärtner's *Areopagus Speech and Natural Revelation.* "Acta Seminarii Neotestamentici Upsaliensis 21" (Uppsala: Gleerup, 1955). Gärtner acknowledges the Hellenistic components, but emphasizes the Jewish and biblical roots.

39. This view differs somewhat from that of Günther Bornkamm, "The Missionary Stance of Paul in I Corinthians 9 and in Acts," *Studies in Luke-Acts,* pp. 194-207. Had Bornkamm distinguished between the formal and the material aspect of "gospel" he might not have written that "Paul could not modify the gospel itself according to the particular characteristics of his hearers. The whole of his concern is to make clear that the changeless gospel . . . empowers him to be free to change his stance" (p. 196). However,

as I understand the text, precisely for the sake of the constant formal understanding of the gospel Paul was free not only to change his life-style but to restate its material content as well so that both Jew and gentile were engaged where they were by the call to faith. Bornkamm's discussion of this passage in his excellent *Paulus* (Stuttgart: Kohlhammer, 1969, pp. 181-83), is more in agreement with our interpretation precisely because he does not deny explicitly that Paul could have changed the content of the gospel. He sees that Paul's freedom earned him the reputation of vacillating. He does not, however, take up H. Chadwick's suggestion that "all things to all men" is actually Paul's quotation of the epithet used about him by opponents. " 'All Things to All men (I Cor. ix. 22)," *NTS* 1 (1955), 261-75. C. H. Dodd's discussion of our passage, being concerned with Paul's alleged use of Jesus' sayings, is not germane to our problem. "*Ennomos Christou*," *Studia Paulina* (de Zwaan Festschrift) (Haarlem: Bohn, 1953), pp. 96-110.

The question here eventuates in much broader issues, such as the relation of the "juridical" understanding of salvation (i.e., justification) to the "mystical" understanding. Albert Schweitzer, along with others, understood the former to be only a "subsidiary crater" within the main one, partly because justification is not a major theme in the Corinthian and Thessalonian letters. But all such efforts to see a double track in Paul's theology overlook the fact that (a) Paul never really repeats himself (e.g., the treatment of Abraham in Gal. 3 and in Rom. 4), (b) that each letter is a specially crafted response to particular questions (except for Romans where the relation to the church is elusive for us, but thereby revealing all the more the importance of justification when Paul is more or less free to reflect systematically, (c) that precisely the letters to Corinth reveal how Paul is free to reformulate the material content of justification so as to address the specific problems without making those readers in Corinth depart from their own categories in order to converse with Paul. It is Paul who shows himself free to adopt their categories in order to expose the meaning of the gospel of free grace in a way that the Corinthians cannot miss.

40. The old view of Paul as the "second founder of Christianity" (Wrede), the inaugurator of Hellenistic Christianity, cannot be sustained. Ever since Heitmüller's essay ("Zum Problem Paulus und Jesus," ZNW 13 [1912] 320-37), it has become evident that between Paul and Jerusalem Christianity lay not only pre-Pauline Hellenistic Christianity in Damascus and Antioch (in delineating this Bultmann carries forward the work of his teacher, W. Bousset (see *Kyrios Christos* trans. John Steely [Nashville: Abingdon Press, 1970]) but also a Hellenistic Jewish Christianity whose roots also go back, at least according to Acts 6-7, to Jerusalem. In other words, a Hellenized version of Christian faith was proclaimed among Hellenized Jews who apparently were in the vanguard of preaching to gentiles. At Antioch such a church, founded by Hellenized Jewish Christians who soon drew to their ranks gentile neighbors,

became the locale of Paul's work (according to Acts 13 this church later sent him westward to found other such churches). Given this experience, it is understandable that he gained the capacity to to translate the traditional Jerusalem-based gospel into other modes of thought—that is, to find new material expressions for the formal understanding of gospel. Paul, then, is not the innovator of a new theology, but the traveling preacher of a message that already in his day was the result of a somewhat complex development and reformulation. Taking note of this intricate process, only partially recoverable from the formulations that the New Testament enshrines, is important for our topic mainly at this point: it protects us from assuming that the different pattern of preaching to gentiles emerged programmatically, at one stroke, when Paul (or someone before him) had a "bright idea" or retreated to his study to work out a demythologizing program that was then put into practice. Peter Stuhlmacher has published the first part (the background) of his investigation of Paul's gospel, *Das Paulinische Evangelium I, Vorgeschichte*, FRLANT 95 (Göttingen; Vandenhoeck & Ruprecht, 1968).

41. However one may finally adjudicate the complex questions of the degree of adaptation to common Hellenistic modes of thought among the more sophisticated of the day, it should not be overlooked that the sermon itself is effectively interrupted when the specifically Christian theme is articulated—the resurrection and the judgment by the coming Christ. Luke seems to make clear that the adaptation has been for the sake of a genuine encounter that runs the risk of precisely the sort of failure which the Areopagus speech turned out to be. Yet even this was a gain over Paul's previous effort in Athens in which, implicitly, he "preached Jesus and the resurrection" without the kinds of adaptation the speech represents and hence was not even understood.

42. The qualifier "new" must be understood properly—not that this particular myth was itself new. Rather it was "new" in the Christian tradition, having a long and complex history behind it. Nor did Hellenistic Christianity initiate the use of myth, as if earliest Christian preaching were nonmythological and only subsequently became contaminated with myth. Actually, Christian preaching was mythic from the start. Nor can the presence of of myth material at the earliest stage be seen as a distortion of the pure, a-mythic preaching of Jesus. There never was an a-mythic Christian tradition, preaching, or theology.

43. This myth has been reconstructed many times. A readily available outline is provided by Bultmann, *Primitive Christianity*, trans. R. H. Fuller (New York: Meridian, 1956; German ed. 1949), pp. 163-64. See also the extensive description and discussion by Walter Schmithals, *Die Gnosis in Korinth*, FRLANT 66 (1956). Exursus II, pp. 82-134. Schmithals undertakes to sketch the morphology of the figure of the Redeemer, to show the role of Jewish heterodoxy in its development, and to relate it to particular Gnostic systems. The reconstructed myth, and especially the means by which it was recovered, have been criticized repeatedly, though

little that is more convincing has been proposed in its stead. One must not confuse necessary refinements and movements toward precision with repudiation wholesale. The most thorough and responsible critique is offered by Carsten Colpe, *Die religions-geschichtliche Schule*, FRLANT 78 (1961). See also his article, "Der erlöste Erlöser," *Der Islam* 32 (1957), 195-214.

44. The Christian Gnostic texts found two decades ago in Egypt do not manifest this myth as clearly as we had been led to expect. Thus we need to reckon more seriously with diversity within Christian and non-Christian systems and with multi-speed developments. In any case, Gilles Quispel's hasty judgment is too extreme: "There would appear to be good grounds for supposing that it was from Christianity that the conception of redemption and the figure of the Redeemer were taken over into Gnosticism. A pre-Christian redeemer and an Iranian mystery of redemption perhaps never existed." *The Jung Codex* (London: Mowbray's, 1955), p. 78.

45. A. D. Nock was even more cautious: "In the environment of early Christianity there were materials which could be built into Gnostic systems—but no Gnostic system, . . . there was an appropriate mythopoeic faculty—but no specific myth, . . . a 'Gnostic' state of mind—but no crystallized formulation of that state of mind and no community or communities clinging to the formulation." By this he rightly, but with dubious relevance, points out that there was no Gnostic "church." *Early Gentile Christianity and Its Hellenistic Background* (New York: Harper, 1964), Intro. to Torchbook Ed., p. xiv. The above suggested catalytic function of the Christian message about Jesus comports with Nock's view that it was the figure of Jesus that "caused the raw material of Gnosticism to take definite shapes . . ." (p. xvi). The colloquium on the origins of Gnosticism, convened in Messina in 1966, demonstrated how complex are the issues and the methodological impediments to a scholarly consensus. The papers were published as *Le Origini dello Gnosticismo*, U. Bianchi, ed., "Supplem. to *Numen* XII" (Leiden: Brill, 1967). For a brief survey of the complexities there exposed, see J. W. Drijvers, "The Origins of Gnosticism as a Religious and Historical Problem," *Nederlands Theologisch Tijdschrift* 22 (1968), 321-51.

46. For a brief survey of the texts and ideas, see Heinrich Schlier, *Principalities and Powers in the New Testament*, "Quaestiones disputatae 3" (London: Nelson, 1961; German ed. published in same year). See also G. B. Caird, *Principalities and Powers* (Oxford: The Clarendon Press, 1956). Pioneer work in this area was done by Martin Dibelius, *Die Geisterwelt im Glauben des Paulus* (1909).

47. "Therefore it is said,
'When he ascended on high he led a host of captives and he gives gifts to men.'
(In saying, 'He ascended,' what does it mean but that he had also descended into the lower parts of the earth? He who descended is he who also ascended far above all the heavens, that

he might fill all things.) And his gifts were that some should be apostles, some prophets, . . ." (RSV) This text shows the result of an interpretive process whose steps and rationale must be inferred. The subject matter concerns the gifts of the Spirit which the Christian community enjoys. Whereas Paul had understood them to be various capacities and functions persons have in the life of the church (I Cor. 12), the author of Ephesians sees them as offices of the church. But the point he himself wants to register is that the offices are gifts of *Christ*. For support, he appeals to Ps. 68:18. The Hebrew text is translated by the RSV as follows:

> Thou didst ascend the high mount,
>   leading captives in thy train,
>   and receiving gifts among men,
> even among the rebellious, that the
>   Lord God may dwell there.

The quotation in Ephesians does not follow the LXX. (a) It changes the 2nd singular to 3rd singular, thereby changing the whole from an ascription of praise to a description of an event; (b) it changes "received gifts" to "gave gifts"; (c) the reference to the rebellious was deleted, for obvious reasons once the verb had been changed. The Greek verb used in the LXX can mean either to give or to take; Eph. uses an unambiguous word meaning only "give," thereby establishing an interpretation of the LXX. The LXX itself had changed the image of the Hebrew from leading captives to leading captivity captive. (Interestingly, the Targumim of the Synagogue had made an analogous interpretation by saying that it was Moses who went up to the mountain and received the Torah.) The Psalm originally, evidently, spoke of God the Victor, whose triumphal procession up Mount Zion was accompanied by payment of tribute. Such a text is serviceable to the author of Ephesians only if two things are made clear: that the subject spoken of is Christ, and that the distributed gifts are the offices of the church. The latter can be affirmed easily enough, but the former must be argued. Eph. 4:9 serves precisely this end. The interpretation of Ps. 68 in this passage makes sense *only* if one sees that the author assumes that Christ was a divine being who descended to earth, fulfilled his terrestrial ministry, and ascended to heaven again from whence he distributed the gifts. The very fact that the author does not need to argue this descent/ascent pattern but assumes it as self-evident shows how firmly established the whole point of view was.

48. It is not necessary to review the complexities surrounding Phil. 2:5-11, since the magisterial survey of the problems and critical literature has been provided by R. P. Martin, *Carmen Christi*, "S.N.T.S. Monograph 4" (New York: Cambridge University Press, 1967). My own understanding of the passage is shaped by Ernst Käsemann's essay, "A Critical Analysis of Phil. 2:5-11" (1950), now in *God and Christ*, *JThC* 5 (Torchbook; New York: Harper,

1968), 45-88. It is probably the most significant study of the passage since Lohmeyer's (1928). Even though R. H. Fuller wants to avoid talking about the Gnostic redeemer myth in as firm a fashion as Käsemann, he nevertheless agrees that a descent/ascent pattern is operative here. *Foundations*, pp. 203 ff. Moreover, A. D. Nock's dictum is undoubtedly on target: "Pre-existence involved some sort of descent." *Early Gentile Christianity*, p. 50.

49. The interpretation brings Phil. 2 and Gal. 4 into the same frame of reference.

50. Because Rudolf Schnackenburg struggles against this line of interpretation, his discussion is instructive for methodological questions. He grants that we cannot assert that the Gnostic myth of the descending/ascending Savior is traceable to Christian thought, just as he sees that sources do not permit us to speak of a "ready-made and unified myth of the Savior." Moreover, he sees that many important aspects of the full-orbed Gnostic myth are absent from John. Yet he confuses everything when he concludes that "the Gnostic myth of redemption and Johannine Christology are worlds apart," and yet grants that John "depends on the Gnostic myth of the Savior only for his modes of thought and expression"; moreover, to say (with reference to John 3:13-14) that "John merely develops a manner of speaking that was already used in the early church" clarifies nothing. "Johannine Christology and the Gnostic Myth of the Savior" in *Present and Future*, "Studies and Research in Christian Theology at Notre Dame 30" (Notre Dame, Ind.: University of Notre Dame Press, 1966), Chap. 9.

51. This is what R. H. Fuller has called the "three stage Christology,"

which he diagrams ⁀⁀‿‿ in contrast with

earlier ⁀‿ and still earlier ⁀

patterns. *The Foundations of New Testament Christology*, Chap. 9.

52. Rudolf Schnackenburg's statement expresses a profound misunderstanding: "If the expressions 'descending from heaven' and 'ascending' were proved to be bound to a Gnostic myth of a Savior, the very basis of our Christian faith is then questionable." "Johannine Christology and the Gnostic Myth of the Savior," p. 164. For one thing, he does not see that even if it were "bound to the myth, partly because Gnosis did not invent and patent the myth Christianity's adaptation of such a myth for the sake of its own gospel. Here the "genetic fallacy" is permitted to tyrannize exegesis and theology. Moreover, it is a misstatement of the issue to ask whether the descent/ascent pattern is "bound" to a Gnostic myth, partly because Gnosis did not invent and patent the myth but drew on primordial ideas, myths, and rites which it fused into a new world view, and partly because the validity of the Christian faith does not rest on "untying" the myth from the heretics.

53. See also the foregoing discussion concerning Eph. 4.

54. Misled in part by the foregoing discussion of the Law as tutor (Gal. 3:24-25), which was understood pedagogically (from the Greek *paidagogos*) rather than forensically ("tutor" as trustee, custodian, warden, guardian), previous interpreters commonly understood the *stoicheia* to be rudiments of knowledge (ABC's), a rendering philologically possible. So E. D. Burton's commentary (ICC) and Wilfred Knox, *St. Paul and the Church of Jerusalem* (Cambridge: Cambridge University Press, 1925), p. 114, n. 13. Recently the cosmological interpretation has come to prevail, based in part on the discussion that follows (esp. 4:8) and in part on the overall role principalities and powers are seen to have played in Paul's thought. This interpretation sees the continuity between the problem posed in the Galatian churches and that found in Colossae.

55. This is what Nels F. S. Ferré implies when he writes, "Jesus could not of himself conceive the new level, nor effect it in his own life, but in the fulness of time, when Jesus was ready, God sent forth His own Son." *The Christian Understanding of God* (New York: Harper, 1951), p. 201.

56. Eduard Schweizer has pointed out that while the phrase "God sent" was used in diverse ways in the Hellenistic world so that it does not of itself point directly to the descent/ascent pattern, Paul's unique formulation here ("God sent out"), as well as the adjacent motives of Spirit and of sonship are parallelled in Wis. of Sol. 9:10-17, where Wisdom's role is presented in mythic form. Schweizer rightly infers not only that the descent pattern is taken for granted in Gal. 4 but that it is probably influenced by Hellenistic Jewish theology, which had already appropriated the mythic pattern. (Locating the descent-myth in Hellenized Judaism, of course, does not take it away from Gnosticism, but attests its widespread use.) Also, it is in accord with our argument when Schweizer says that Paul's real interest here was the cross as the center of the saving act; that is, Paul did not simply rename the subject of the myth "Jesus" but, having adopted the myth-pattern to identify Jesus, he modified it precisely by concentrating on the climax of Jesus' life, the cross. "Zum religionsgeschichtliche Hintergrund der 'Sendungsformel' Gal. 4:4 f. Rom. 8:3 f. Joh. 3:16 f. I Joh. 4:9," ZNW 57 (1966), 199-210. See also his "Zur Herkunft der Präexistenzvorstellung bei Paulus" (1959) and "Aufnahme und Korrektur jüdischer Sophiatheologie im Neuen Testament" (1962) in *Neotestamentica* (Zürich-Stuttgart: Zwingli Verlag, 1963).

57. It is not clear to me why Hugh Montefiore insists that in vv. 6-7. the author does not apply the phrase "the Son of Man" to Jesus. Evidently, he is guided by the original Old Testament meaning of "maknind." Montefiore conceivably might have argued that the text views the subjection/mastery assertions about the Son of Man to express the view that he is the prototype of mankind's ultimate mastery over the cosmos, but he does not do this either. *The Epistle to the Hebrews*, "Harper's Commentary" (New York: Harper, 1964), *ad loc.*

58. For uses of this Psalm in I Cor. 15:27; Phil. 3:21; I Peter 3:22 see Lindars, *New Testament Apologetic*, pp. 50, 168.
59. The fundamental importance of the human life of Jesus for the Epistle to the Hebrews has been noted frequently. See, e.g., Erich Grässer's "Der historische Jesus im Hebräerbrief," *ZNW* 56 (1965), 63-91, and the literature cited there. Otto Michel's commentary in the Meyer series (Göttingen: Vandenhoeck & Ruprecht, 12th ed., 1966; Michel is responsible for all editions after the 6th) discusses the way Old Testament exegesis is related to Jesus, especially in our passage (pp. 151 ff.) His skepticism with regard to a "Gnostic" interpretation of Hebrews does not affect the core of our argument, since here the descent/ascent pattern was not borrowed directly from Gnosticism anyway but probably came into Christian thought through Hellenized Judaism's wisdom theology.
60. For a convenient survey to the entire complex of literature and problems, see James M. Robinson, "The Coptic Gnostic Library Today," *NTS* 14 (1966), 356-401.
61. For example, the Gospel of Truth, widely attributed to Valentinus himself, has a rather subtle and subdued relation to characteristic Gnostic teachings; the same is true also of the new Gospel of Thomas. See Kendrick Grobel, "How Gnostic is the Gospel of Thomas?" *NTS* 8 (1962), 367-73.
62. Irenaeus (*adv. haer.* i 24:3, 4) traced Basilides' theology to Menander, the pupil of Simon Magus; Hippolytus saw primarily Aristotle behind the scene. The fragments of Basilides' extensive literary production, which Clement preserved (now available in R. M. Grant, *Gnosticism* [New York: Harper, 1961], are not sufficient to settle the question of which report more accurately reflects Basilides himself. Eugene de Faye suggested that Hippolytus reports the form of Basilidean Gnosis current at the time (early third century). *Gnostiques et gnosticisme* (Paris: Libraire Orientaliste Paul Geuthner, 1925), p. 54. On the other hand, Grant follows those who regard Hippolytus as recording the original system (e.g., Gilles Quispel, "L'homme gnostique. La doctrine de Basilide," in *Eranos-Jahrbuch* 16 [1948], 89-139).
63. Hans Jonas reminds us that Gnostic religion centers in the paradox that the unknown and unknowable God is nonetheless known. "He who according to Valentinus is the Abyss, according to Basilides even 'the non-being God' . . . ; whose acosmic essence negates all object-determinations as they derive from the mundane realm; whose transcendence transcends any sublimity posited by extension from the here, invalidates all symbols of him thus devised; who, in brief, strictly defies description—he is yet enunciated in the gnostic message, communicated in gnostic speech, predicated in gnostic praise. The knowledge of him itself is the *knowledge of his unknowability;* the predication upon him as thus known is by negations: thus arises the *via negationis,* the negative theology, whose melody, here first sounded as a way of confessing what cannot be described, hence swells to a mighty chorus in Western piety." *The Gnostic Religion* (Boston: Beacon Press, 1958), p. 288 (his italics).

64. Origen, too, could speak of God as beyond "being," for he insisted that "God does not even participate in being. For he is participated in rather than participates." (*C. Cel.* vi. 64.) Richard A. Norris has recently related this view to both Platonism and Middle Platonism. *God and World in Early Christian Theology* (London: A. & C. Black, 1966), p. 127. The perennial character of this problem is exhibited in Tillich's discussion of "God as Being" in which he shows why "it is as wrong to speak of God as the universal essence as it is to speak to him as existing." *Systematic Theology* I, 236.

65. Consubstantiality (*homoousios*) is basic to Basilidean and many other forms of Gnostic theologies. This material basis of salvation is a corollary of the view that the soul of man is essentially divine; on this view its sojourn in matter is tragic, at the same time this view states the ontic ground for salvation.

66. Hippolytus writes, "Jesus, therefore, became the firstfruits of the distinction of the various orders of created objects, and his Passion took place for not any other reason than the distinction which was thereby brought about in the various orders of created objects that had been confounded together. For in this manner . . . the entire Sonship . . . was divided into its component elements, according to the manner in which also the distinction of natures had taken place in Jesus." *Ref.* vii. 15 (quoted from *Ante-Nicene Fathers*, V, 109).

67. Even though the exegetical works of Basilides have been lost, from reading Hippolytus one can gain a vivid picture of his concern to reinterpret Christian literature. It is evident that Basilides was a brilliant exegete; again and again he interprets biblical language in ways appropriate to his understanding of man and his salvation.

68. The most extensive narratives of the Son's descent are to be found in the Gnostic Pistis Sophia (whose roots go back to the second century), the Ascension of Isaiah (whose chaps. 6–11 may go to the second century), and the Epistle of the Apostles (slightly later than Basilides). The latter shows how Gnostic modes of understanding were used by those who opposed Gnostic sects.

69. Commonly it is said that the Son of God was sent into the world, or that he came, appeared; Irenaeus likes to say that the Son of God was made the Son of man (thereby showing that he is unaware that originally the cosmic Son of Man was virtually the Son of God!).

70. Origen, of course, is an exception, but an exceedingly instructive one. He held that the souls of men did exist prior to birth, yet refused to regard them as eternal. In this way, he combined a Hellenistic view of the soul's pre-existence with a biblical conviction that only God is uncreated and eternal. For a comparison of post-canonical and early Christian views of the soul, see Jaroslav Pelikan, *The Shape of Death* (Nashville: Abingdon Press, 1961). A recent study by Luise Schottroff, concentrating on the Apocalypse of Adam, indicates that one must be more cautious in contrasting absolutely the Gnostic and the Christian understand-

ings of salvation. "Animae naturaliter salvandae," in *Christentum und Gnosis*, Walther Eltester, ed., "Beiheft 37 of ZNW" (Berlin: Töpelmann, 1969), pp. 65-97.

71. Helmut Köster rightly speaks of a "power-struggle between the non- (or pre-) Christian connotations and implications of such mythical language and particular Christian insights . . . derived from the . . . claim that the decisive revelation took place in the history of Jesus of Nazareth." "The Role of Myth in the New Testament," *Andover Newton Quarterly*, January, 1968, p. 186.

72. In this connection, Samual Laeuchli's analysis of the struggle between Christian and Gnostic language is useful. *The Language of Faith* (Nashville: Abingdon Press, 1962).

73. That the process of telling such stories in Hellenistic churches caused them to take on the character of Hellenistic miracle stories in general is natural; for precisely this reason, however, one should not draw premature conclusions concerning the origin of all the stories.

74. This is what S. Schulz does not see: "Precisely because the contemporary orient made propaganda for numerous superlative miracle-workers, in the Markan miracle stories the absoluteness and exclusiveness of Jesus is to be set forth through the fact that repeatedly special power is emphasized." *Die Stunde der Botschaft*, p. 70.

75. These paragraphs draw on my article, "Mark 3:7-12 and Mark's Christology," *JBL* 84 (1965), 341-58. (See also H. D. Betz' article mentioned in Chap. 1, n. 32. Betz ventures a list of all materials with "divine-man" motifs. Betz, however, does not interpret Mark's intent quite as I do.) Ulrich Luz takes a generally parallel line to that advocated here, but diverges in denying that Mark checked the divine-man theology; rather he is said to have interpreted it in light of the cross. 'Das Geheimnismotiv und die markinsche Christologie," *ZNW* 56 (1965), 9-30.

76. This colloquial phrase is often used by older Christians in Appalachia to refer to the Old Testament. Far from being merely quaint, it calls attention to the fact that the first part of the Christian Bible was, and remains, a complete Bible for a community faith.

77. In this connection, it is good to recall Tillich's rejoinder to certain critics: "But I cannot accept criticism as valuable which merely insinuates that I have surrendered the substance of the Christian message because I have used a terminology which consciously deviates from the biblical or ecclesiastical language. Without such deviation, I would not have deemed it worthwhile to develop a theological system for our period." *Systematic Theology* II, Preface, p. vi.

78. Interestingly, from quite opposite ends of the theological spectrum comes the same criticism of Bultmann: because his Jesus is essentially one who calls for obedience he is effectively reduced to law rather than grace. Paul Althaus, *Fact and Faith in the Kerygma*, trans. David Cairns (London: Oliver & Boyd, 1959), p. 46.

See also Paul Tillich, *Systematic Theology* II, 106: "The situation of having to decide remains one of being under the law." Bultmann responded to Althaus by saying that the demand for faith "is basically different from the demand of the law which puts a man on his own. That faith which the kerygma demands is openness to the new possibility of existence. . . . It is not that a man *must*, but rather that he *may* believe." "The Primitive Christian Kerygma and the Historical Jesus," p. 41, n. 79. But does not the law also imply that a man may obey?

79. As we shall see in the next chapter, this has been a common error.

80. E.g., James M. Robinson: "The historical Jesus does not legitimize the *kerygma* with a proven divine fact. . . . The historical Jesus confronts us with existential decision, just as the *kerygma* does. Consequently it is anachronistic to oppose the quest today on the assumption that such a quest is designed to avoid the commitment of faith." *A New Quest . . .* , p. 77. The reason the new quest does not make this prominent is that it is so dominated by the concern to show how the kerygma continues what was already present in the situation of Jesus with the disciples that it minimizes Easter: "Easter only confirmed" the significance of Jesus (p. 78). Consequently Fuchs never tires of insisting that Good Friday did not plunge the disciples into doubt or despair. It is a rule of thumb that the more ambiguous and offensive Jesus' life was (either during his lifetime or especially after Good Friday) the more pivotal the resurrection; conversely, the more the disciples already in Jesus' lifetime laid hold of the kingdom, the less important is Easter as simply the continuation of Jesus. Willi Marxsen (wrongly) insists that the former view makes Jesus' life a mere prelude. "The Resurrection of Jesus as a Historical and Theological Problem," trans. Dorothea Barton in *The Significance of the Message of the Resurrection for Faith in Jesus Christ,* ed. C. F. D. Moule, *SBT* 8; 2nd series (1968), pp. 45-46.

81. It may be observed that this definition of Docetism is more functional than substantial. That is, the accent is not on the actual denial of Jesus' humanity but on the fact that in Docetism Jesus loses his integrity and "over-againstness" vis-a-vis the church so as to become the embodiment of its theology. This way of seeing the matter nullifies the objection registered by Georg Strecker that Docetism and historicizing do not go together. "Die historische und theologische Problematik der Jesusfrage," *EvTheol* 29 (1969), 470-71.

82. It is well known that Bultmann appeals especially to II Cor. 5:16-17, and construes the text to have Paul speak of a "Christ according to the flesh" (i.e., a historical Jesus), and not of "knowing according to the flesh." For a careful exegesis that is critical of Bultmann's interpretation, see J. Louis Martyn, "Epistemology at the turn of the Ages: 2 Corinthians 5:16" in *Christian History and Interpretation* (John Knox Festschrift), ed. W. R. Farmer, C. F. D. Moule, R. R. Niebuhr (New York: Cambridge University Press, 1967), pp. 269-88.

83. Suggestive as Ulrich Wilckens' hypothesis of the two major streams of early Christianity (earliest Jerusalem church with a Jesus tradition, Hellenists and Paul in Antioch without one) may be in some regards, I balk at his statement that in the latter "virtually nothing was preached or known about the teaching and acts of Jesus for a long time, but only about his death, his resurrection and his function as savior and Judge in the last days." It is incredible that one could say all this about a figure named "Jesus" and neither know nor care to know anything more. Moreover, since the Hellenists were originally in Jerusalem and came to faith in Jesus through the witness of the earliest church, Wilckens has himself undercut his thesis, for this was the group that made the Jesus-tradition central! "The Tradition-History of the Resurrection of Jesus" in *The Significance of the Message of the Resurrection*, pp. 55-56. On p. 74 he hedges, and so becomes more accurate, in saying that the Hellenist wing did not make the Jesus-tradition central.

84. Gordon D. Kaufman has emphasized this point in *A Systematic Theology* (New York: Scribner's, 1969), pp. 9 ff.

85. *A New Quest of the Historical Jesus*, pp. 85, 90, 94.

4

THE
HISTORICAL
JESUS
AND
SALVATION

"A theology which makes this [the expected fruits of the Holy Spirit] its starting point will end up as an ideology."

DIETRICH RITSCHL

"Hence all our righteousness has been infected with anxiety . . . and hidden rebellion against the One.
This is the . . . network of interactions ruled by fear of God the enemy. For salvation now appears to us as deliverance from that deep distrust of the One in all the many that causes us to interpret everything that happens to us as issuing ultimately from animosity. . . . Redemption appears as the liberty to interpret in trust all that happens as contained within . . . a total activity that includes death within the domain of life. . . . [This transition from God the enemy to God the friend] is inseparably connected with an action in our past that was the response of trust by a man who was sent into life and sent into death and to whom answer was made in his resurrection from the dead."

H. RICHARD NIEBUHR

I. Toward a Rehabilitation of the Issue

Our age either finds salvation irrelevant (because it is assumed to be otherworldly) or it trivializes it as sanctions for middle-class life, or perverts it into ideology for radical change. Until some clarity is gained here we can scarcely probe the relation of trusting Jesus to man's salvation. In this context, only pivotal points can be noted, and but tersely.

A. *The Rationale of Salvation.* The noun "salvation" refers either to an act of saving or to the state of having been (or being) saved. It has a negative as well as a positive moment: salvation *from* (e.g., death) and salvation *for* (e.g., life). In existentialist jargon, salvation is the movement from in-

154

authentic to authentic existence. These are coordinates logically and experientially. Though most metaphors disclose but certain facets of the matter, an adequate grasp of salvation includes both elements.

While each metaphor for salvation has its own rationale, constitutive of them all is a tension between our perception of man as he is and our image of man as he ought to be and is destined to be. An awareness of this hiatus, however explained and overcome, belongs to the primordial experience of man—at least Indo-European man. This is not to be equated with a sense that man is not yet as good as he might be—a technological understanding of man as improvable product. Rather, here is a root awareness that what man is, he ought not to be. Apart from this awareness of tension between the empirically accurate and the normatively true, philosophers would not advocate, prophets preach, or revolutionists plot. Even the perception of the absurdity of the human situation, as developed by Camus's *Myth of Sisyphus* for example, does not escape this fact, for the absurd is recognizable as the absurd only vis-a-vis a norm of meaning, whether perceived clearly or not. This underlying perception of man is the first thing to be seen in our reflection on salvation.

Philosophies and religions take on distinctive character in part by the way they perceive this contradiction, account for it, and deal with it. Behind the almost infinite variety stands a fundamental alternative: either the situation of man is understood as given with his existence as such, or it is seen as the result of a tragic event, a "fall." If one thinks God and man together with regard to the origin of the human situation,[1] one either (a) makes man the innocent victim of the created order, thereby indicting creation and its Ground, or (b) he affirms the integrity of the Creator by speaking of a primordially good creation that experienced a tragic event from whose consequences man has not extricated himself, or (c) he tries to work out a way of conceiving of man as the unfinished product, in which case the tragic element recedes because the bastardy of men tends to be taken in

155

stride as the by-product of human progress. If the latter view was sired by the Enlightenment and reared by post-Darwinian theology, the second represents the biblical and classical Christian view, while the first expresses the Gnostic and Manichean stance.

The classical Christian view, so strange to us today,[2] is nothing less (and much more) than an attempt to illumine and account for the perceived contradiction between what is and what ought to be, and to do so in light of the character of God. Not only does a particular understanding of man's situation underlie every mode of speaking about salvation (and vice versa), but each perception of man has consequences for the understanding of God and world as well. Thinking about man's salvation—his attainment of what he is destined to be— is not an optional consideration wherever one thinks through consistently the nature of man, his relation to the world and to its Ground, God. This is the second thing we must see.

It is important to reflect farther on the implications of Fall theology. The event can be understood in more than one way. It can be traced to man's own disobedience, as in the myth of Genesis 3, or to supramundane powers who usurped authority over the created order and victimized man and creation, as in the myth of the fallen angels.[3] In either case, the myth functions to preserve the moral integrity to God by refusing to make him the author of man's plight. Interestingly, Genesis 3 also refuses to make man the mere victim of malign power; therefore, the serpent appears not as man's sovereign but as his seducer, so that man is an accomplice in his Fall.

Moreover, the Fall (Gen. 3) does not have in view a Golden Age, the first historical period. That would make the Fall a tragic historical, cultural event. Rather, by locating the Fall prior to all history and culture, one affirms that the whole human experience is "Fall-affected." The Bible knows no history of paradise. Paradise lies on the yonder side of history. This is why paradise and Fall are spoken of as myth, indeed must be. The Fall accounts for the character of history and for the conviction that its tragic quality cannot be traced to the structure or the nature of the physical world. The Fall myth asserts that man is not necessarily a sinner because he exists but that he is inescapably one because he is the son of Adam, who now lives east of Eden where all history takes place.[4]

In this light, salvation requires that the effects of the Fall be undone and man restored, if not advanced beyond Adam. If the Redeemer is not the Creator (as for Marcion and certain Gnostics), then the Redeemer deals with a situation for which he has no responsibility. But if the Creator is also the Redeemer (as monotheism requires), redemption (or salvation) is the restoration of creation, the achievement of the Creator's primal purpose, so that origins and ends, alpha and omega, must be thought together. This is why the doctrine of creation and the doctrine of salvation are developed as coordinates.

The third consideration is now in view. If ends and origins are coordinates, it follows that redemption can be spoken of only in mythic terms as well. Salvation-talk, therefore, no more is a direct empirical analysis of Christian life as presently lived than the character of creation can be inferred directly from a phenomenological analysis of the world and of man as we know them empirically. Hence the word "creation" as used by physical science is not identical with the word's use in theology.

Our point has important theological consequences. For one thing, one cannot simply analyze the human situation in its own light in order to define the problem to which salvation is the answer. Rather, it is in light of the answer that the real character of the problem is seen. Otherwise, one merely exhibits his bondage to the present by projecting its opposite as the norm, thereby selling the alternative short. For instance, when "eternal life" is understood as immortality, it has been trivialized into mere deathlessness because the negation of present morality has controlled the alternative. Another consequence is that salvation is still to be expected; only its foretastes can be savored now. This is why there is no real description of salvation in the New Testament. What is described, analyzed, and required is the hallmarks of present

157

anticipation. This leaning into the future will be a major concern of the next chapter.

B. *A Critique of Alternative Views.* While one may recognize the classical motifs of soteriology in the foregoing sketch, it is abundantly clear that they do not resonate with much of the contemporary mind. They may be intelligible, but they are not yet justifiable. From the multiple factors involved, we take note of the following as specially significant. (a) In rejecting the Fall myth and its logical coordinates, we see the problem of man as that of his unrealized potential—not a potential primordially given and subsequently violated, but an ever-enlarging capacity, though repeatedly frustrated. The fundamental thing to say about man is not that he is a creature now fallen, but that he is on the way up. (b) Not surprisingly, sin and salvation—if still in our vocabulary—concern man himself and man alone, whether the sin is against his personality, his capacity, his self-understanding, or his societal potential. It is not "against God" save in an attenuated sense. Salvation, accordingly, tends to be self-fulfillment, Socratically achieved, or fulfillment of a culture's potential. The former has relied heavily on psychological categories, the latter on technological and Marxian ones. With the Fall myth out of the way, God is now the patron of the process we know and manage; sin and guilt have to do with the frustration of man's potential. God's wrath, if such a term is still legal tender at all, is directed against man the actor, against what he does (sc. fail), not against man the self who is sin-shaped before he becomes an operational sinner. Salvation, then, concerns the eradication of manageable problems and impediments, not the root mystery of man's self as rebel. The saved man is the achiever, whether of psychological wholeness or as a contributor to socioeconomic development.[5] Religion is functional in this world and is prized when it contributes, despised as a vestigium when it does not.

This prevailing outlook is quite inadequate. For one thing, that this is a middle-class theology (ideology) is increasingly clear the more the Blacks protest against its manifold results. It is increasingly evident that no civilization has yet been built apart from exploitation of man by man. Our own rests on genocide against the Indians as much as on the Mayflower Compact, on the slavery of the Blacks and the exploitation of immigrants who came for freedom and found themselves in sweatshops. These crimes against humanity affected not only the victims but enslaved the successful to illusions as well: the Indians were declared to be savages, the Blacks were given the opportunity to become Christian niggers, and the immigrants were fed the myth of the self-made man while markets were manipulated and resources exploited in the name of "building up the country." This story is no American monopoly but has been repeated in every civilization known; that no alternative is available is shown by the failure of Rousseauism, on the one hand, and the success of totalitarian states on the other. That civilizations have at the same time contributed science, art, philosophy, literature, and technologically based comforts including health itself is not gainsaid in the least. The point is that these have been purchased at prices so dear that the buyers have preferred not to reckon the cost at all until revolutions compel them to.

Still, Genesis said this is what history is right from the start: it begins with envy and murder and is built ever after with these stones and others quarried from the same perverted heart. Man's history, like the person himself, is this enigmatic compound of majestic achievement and malicious exploitation of his fellows. And over against all modern evolutionary plans of salvation in which all these horrors are redeemed as necessary to progress, the Bible announces the wrath of God against every exploitation of man by man no less than it does against man's defiance of the Creator. The biblical myth and its subsequent historical narrative jar the optimistic view that the achievements of man are surely worth the exploitation of man, and invite us to ponder whether the root problem is man himself and not merely his works, whether he is the innocent he thinks he is.

It is not simply that every person has incurred guilt, for this is far too atomistic an understanding; rather, man's interdependence points to irreducible solidarity through which one participates in a guilt-laden situation whether or not he is a "responsible" actor. For example, many whites today know themselves culpable for the racial turmoil even though their forebears were still in Europe when slavers imported Africans to the New World. Protests of historical innocence ("My fathers never owned any salves and scarcely saw a Negro except on a train") are intuitively judged as self-justifying attempts to extricate oneself from complicity. This perceived solidarity is but a latter-day rediscovery of the primordal soldarity of man in guilt—a situation aptly symbolized in the Bible as Adam.

Adam has two roles: he embodies the Fall myth [6] of the *origin* of man's plight, and as primal man, he symbolizes the *solidarity* of man in history set in motion by the Fall.[7] Adam is the mythical author of man's situation and a symbol of man's solidarity in it at the same time. Because man's plight stems not from externally imposed bondage (e.g., from fallen angels) but from his disobedience, every attempt to restrict salvation to the breaking of tyrannous external structures turns out to be superficial because these structures tyrannize not an innocent victim but an accomplice, whether one has in view racism, the technological reduction of man,[8] or systems of government and economies. It is not merely the Pentagon, for example, which resists disarmament but the civilian populace as well because its economic security is geared to the widely dispersed production of arms.

Paul Ricoeur observed astutely that concepts and myths function to clarify this primordial awareness by symbolizing it, whether as stain, missing the mark, trespass, or others. In Israelite tradition, it is the "confession of sins" in the cultus and the prophetic appeal for justice which furnish the explanatory myth (Adam) with its meaning-substratum.[9] The Adam story did not introduce the view of man, but clarified an awareness already present. The classical understanding of

Adam remains, I believe, the most penetrating and realistic mode of thinking theologically about man. If one ignores it in order to emphasize the glory and potential of man, it is the historic experience of man with man (whether at Auschwitz or in personal guilt) which repeatedly calls for a more profound understanding and a more adequate symbol of who we are.

But why is man the willing accomplice in the process, and why does he delude himself en route? Understanding adequately man's situation requires us to deal with the character of the self, not only with its deeds. This consideration leads us to the next area of reflection.

C. *The Question Reformulated.* When traditional Christian theology, then, speaks of salvation, it has in view not merely the amelioration of symptoms, but the resolution of man's situation at its deepest level. It intends to deal not only with man the doer but with man the self, since the human situation is not merely a network of problems which man *has* but concerns who man *is*, what is constitutive and pivotal for man's life.[10]

We have already spoken of "trust" as the *Leitmotiv.* Pursuant to this, our objective now is to inquire whether trusting Jesus redeems man from his deepest malaise. Concretely, we will explore the potential of "trust in Jesus" as we probe the mystery of man's fault as well as the promise of his redemption. In other words, concentrating on trust requires us to ask whether the root problem is distrust. By exploring the phenomenon of trust beyond what was staked off in Chapter 2, we expect to discern the depth of man's plight and the salvific potential of putting one's trust in Jesus. We are not contending that trust in the historical Jesus is the only way to speak of redemption. Rather, in a theologically pluralistic setting, we are inquiring whether trust in the historical Jesus is redemptive at all, at what level and in what way. We are not the first to engage in these reflections. Therefore, we will next take note of important precedents.

II. Models of Salvation Through Jesus

In dealing with Bultmann, we explored the decisive kerygmatic model of salvation in which the historical Jesus is not the ground but the presupposition of salvation, understood as authentic existence made possible by obedience to the kerygma. Here we turn in other directions to note several attempts to make the historical Jesus paramount for salvation. Wilhelm Herrmann concentrated on the power of Jesus' inner life—an emphasis that anticipates the Ebeling-Fuchs emphasis on his faith. Paul van Buren and Dorothee Sölle, both striving to be theologians *post mortem dei*, make Jesus pivotal while avoiding "God-talk" as much as possible. Paul Tillich emphasized Jesus as the actual bearer of the New Being. Each in his own way is instructive for our theme. In order not to arrest the argument, however, we will be content to draw bold lines of the argumentation.

A. Wilhelm Herrmann,[11] the teacher of both Barth and Bultmann,[12] enjoyed the reputation of being a major dogmatician of liberal Protestant theology. His influential book, *The Communion of the Christian with God*,[13] insists not merely that only God can elicit faith, but that apart from personal communion with God, dogmas about him are useless.[14] Dogmas about Christ (e.g., two natures, atonement) are no exception, for what is decisive for salvation is the relation to God effected by Jesus.[15] For our purpose, we limit the discussion of Herrmann to this classic book.

Whereas Luther's central problem was, How can I find a gracious God? Herrmann's was, How may I be certain that God communes with me? This personal communion, which can also be called faith, is primary because for him faith is not a means to salvation but its mode: "For a fundamental proposition of Protestantism is that faith, this new attitude of man towards God, itself signifies salvation." (P. 309)

Herrmann found the answer to his question in the inner life of the historical Jesus. "God makes Himself known to us, so that we may recognize Him, through a fact, *on the strength of which we are able to believe on Him*." (P. 59, his italics.)

162

Why is it the *historical* Jesus who is important? Because "it is only out of life in history that God can come to meet us" (p. 65); furthermore, in our own matrix "there is no fact more important for each individual than Jesus Christ" (*ibid.*). Implicitly, then, Herrmann suggests that Jesus' history makes contact with our own in a redemptive way. How does this occur? For Herrmann, it is within the church that one is grasped by Jesus' inner life, for in the church we not only learn about Jesus but "are led into his presence and receive a picture of his inner life (pp. 74, 72 resp.). Ultimately, however, this picture stems from "the power of Jesus Himself," not from the authority of Scripture or from historiography. Anticipating Fuchs and Robinson, Herrmann argues that the New Testament is the witness to the power of Jesus' inner life (or as they would say, to his selfhood).[16] Therefore, in contact with the biblical witness and the Christian church, Jesus makes a sovereign impression on us so that "there arises in our heart the certainty that God Himself is turning towards us in this experience" (p. 83).[17] Actually, Herrmann appeals to a double fact: the fact of the moral grandeur of Jesus, which compels our submission, and the fact that "we hear within ourselves the demand of the moral law" (pp. 102-3) awakened by him. In other words, Jesus' inner life operates like a Kantian categorical imperative.

Herrmann is aware that he cannot merely assert this about Jesus, and so undertakes to delineate Jesus' inner life and to analyze its impact on the consciousness of the beholder. Herrmann's Jesus believed himself to be the Messiah in a sense that transcended Judaism's understanding of this office, for he saw the kingdom of God as "God's true lordship over personal life, especially in men's souls, and in their communion with one another" (p. 87; see also p. 95).[18] Though colliding with Judaism, Jesus "shows us the portrait of a man who is conscious that He Himself is not inferior to the ideals for which he sacrifices Himself"; indeed, He knew Himself to be sinless. Furthermore, "the Jesus who thinks thus of Himself and who looks on humanity with such a confidence in His power to redeem them . . . stands as a fact before us, a fact

163

that has no equal!" (P. 92) For Herrmann, it was not Jesus' words alone which were important but his whole life. "Jesus did not write the story of the Prodigal Son on a sheet of paper for men who knew nothing of Himself. He told it rather to men who knew Him, and who, because of His own personal life, were to be sure of the Father in Heaven." (P. 132) Here Herrmann anticipates Fuchs's insistence that the demeanor of Jesus is the interpretive context of his words.[19]

Seeing the moral grandeur of Jesus and taking note of his inner life makes us conscious of our sinfulness, for "as soon as the law of duty is set forth and expounded to us as Jesus does it, we recognize its unassailable right" (p. 100)—like a categorical imperative. But at the same time, Jesus' attitude toward sinners assures us that "His God is our God and thereby it uplifts us into the Kingdom of God's love," thereby making us certain that God communes with us.

Herrmann is sensitive to Lessing's problem and tries to deal with it. He too insists that historiography gives us "nothing more than probability," and that this does "not give us facts on which our religious faith could be based" (p. 69). He responds by saying that "the content of these narratives may also become a fact for us" when we ourselves establish its reality (p. 67). The first step is to extend "the confidence we place in the trustworthiness of the narrator to that which he narrates." [20] But even this is ambiguous. Hence the second is to discern "those elements in Jesus, which, beyond all doubt, are with us today" (that is, the moral impact of Jesus on one's conscience), confident that "every reasonable man will hold the more general features of the common story of this life to be correct" (pp. 70-71), and that Jesus' present impact is just as much a fact as the result of historical investation. After this step has been taken, the third follows: once we are grasped by this power of Jesus' inner life, attested by the texts and tested by our consciousness, we no longer need the records, for now we depend on Jesus himself. In this way, Herrmann says that he who through the Gospels comes to be grasped by Jesus' inner life can "allow historical criticism . . . to have full play" (pp. 75-76), just as Bultmann

164

could calmly "let it burn" because he looked to the kerygma.

Herrmann rightly saw the importance of Jesus himself for faith because life responds to life; he also saw the place of faith as the mode of salvation and not simply as a means to a greater end, just as he perceived in his own way the unavoidable role of the witness of the Christian community. Still, precisely in order to honor what he saw rightly we must rebuild his position and for several reasons.

First of all, critical study has made it impossible to speak so confidently about what Jesus thought of himself, for the very passages that are most conducive to Herrmann's argument are under the suspicion of reflecting more the faith of the early church than Jesus himself. Herrmann sought to overcome this with a *theological* point: if the narratives were traced only as far as the church they would show us only ourselves and what we already know. But this cannot be turned into a *critical* move toward historical validation of Jesus himself.

Second, even if one could demonstrate that the confession-impregnated materials comport with hard-core evidence about Jesus himself and so can be understood to arise from him, one still would not have an unambiguous, self-validating Jesus, one who compels our allegiance like a categorical imperative. Here Herrmann simply manifests his dependence on Christendom in which one might assume that the gospel's picture of Jesus "compels us to simple reverence," or that in confronting Jesus himself we confront God.

Finally, one must ask whether Herrmann's perception of the root issue is adequate. Also his problem is shaped by Christendom: how to vitalize personal faith within a folk-church in which many baptized citizens assent to the Christian beliefs but lack personal faith. Herrmann's theological program was aimed more against the Christian right than the left,[21] more against orthodoxy's insistence on right beliefs than against radical challenges to Christian faith or against the erosion set in motion by radical criticism itself.[22] Hence, he could assume that the key question is one's confidence in God's manward stance—the problem is, how can I *believe* in God? But what

165

will happen when the problem of faith (and salvation) can no longer be isolated from the question of *the God to be believed in?* That is, whereas for Herrmann the problem was that belief in God could not be derived from assent to beliefs about God, today the beliefs about God cannot be assumed; hence the act of trusting and the act of understanding occur together or not at all.

B. Whereas Herrmann's problem was the rise of personal faith, Paul van Buren's book, *The Secular Meaning of the Gospel*,[23] concerns Christian understanding: "How may a Christian who is himself a secular man understand the Gospel in a secular way?" (p. xiv). He intends to do justice to three considerations: "the conservative concern for Christology, the 'liberal' concern with a contemporary way of thinking, and the logical analysis of theological statements" (p. 18).[24] The last consideration has the final word: "a careful, functional analysis of the language of the New Testament, the Fathers, and con-temporary believers will reveal the secular meaning of the Gospel" (p. 19).[25] That is, language analysis allows him to honor the conservative right without accepting at face value the irreducible mythological dimensions of the tradition, while it also allows him to correct the liberal left, which unavoidably diminishes the centrality of Christ (he has especially Schubert Ogden in view). In this program, Jesus is central.

He accuses the left of displacing Jesus with the response of the believer to the kerygma and insists that "the Gospel . . . concerns Jesus of Nazareth . . . [and] that the language of Christian faith has always to do with a particular man who lived and died in Palestine" (p. 109), and that the resurrection is the reason this is the case (pp. 89, 171). He sees Christology as language about Jesus which is used by those for whom he has become the occasion and determinant for their "blik" (p. 91)—a term derived from Hare and understood in terms of Ian Ramsay: a nonverifiable perspective that entails commit-ment.[26] Drawing on Collingwood,[27] he concludes that to find meaning in history is to have a "blik" (p. 113)—that is, meaning is neither "in" history nor "in the beholder" but arises from the process in which the self ponders the past. Meaning points to *"the way in which he sees history"* (his italics). This is why christological statements must be understood in terms of their function among believers, not their content.[28]

How can Jesus be central in such a view of Christology? Whereas Herrmann emphasized Jesus' confidence in God, van Buren concentrates on Jesus' freedom—freedom from tradition and from personal anxiety as well as freedom for others. He prefers to understand Jesus in terms of freedom rather than of his faith in God, because freedom avoids "the slippery ground of the nonempirical." That is, one can talk about Jesus' freedom without talking about God. He makes the resurrection more important than do Fuchs and Ebeling by insisting that "Jesus did not cause his disciples to share in his freedom" (p. 125). It was Easter, which he treats as a discernment situation in which the disciples suddenly saw Jesus in a new way, which marked the beginning of the Christian faith. "On Easter the freedom of Jesus began to be *contagious.*" (P. 133, his italics.) In this way, the New Testament faith is based on Jesus himself.

The christological statements that emerge from this situation of having caught Jesus freedom after Easter are then interpreted in such a way as to expose their real "meaning." For example, the confession that Jesus is Lord "means" that Jesus became their point of orientation (p. 142) and that talk of his lordship expresses and commends this blik.[29] In fact, all kerygmatic statements are bliks that grasp the believer but are not chosen by him (p. 140). Similarly, statements about what God achieved in and through Jesus are interpreted in ways that delete the reference to God completely.[30] But what happens to the "objective" character of the New Testament statements, to the *extra nos* dimension of the gospel? "It belongs to the language of a discernment situation that we speak of that situation as containing ('objectively'), prior to its becoming the occasion of a discernment, what was only 'seen' at a later time" (p. 153). Hence Christians speak of what was accomplished by God for them prior to their faith not because this is objectively true but because this way of talking inheres

167

by nature in bliks. On the other hand, there are "objective" external factors to which one responds, for there is no "sheer discernment" without reference to elements in the situation. This is why "conversion to the Christian historical perspective depends in part upon some acquaintance with the history of Jesus" (p. 144). Moreover, we continue to depend on this history after we are grasped by our blik since "it is the context in which the light dawns anew and in which that freedom proves again to be contagious for us" (p. 145).

It has already become evident that we are prepared to ride with van Buren for some distance because he not only tries to make the historical Jesus central but intends to deal responsibly with the Christian tradition. Nevertheless, we soon want out of the car because his chosen route will not take us where we want to go.

In the first place, he must be faulted in his historiography. On the one hand, his Jesus may have been a free man, but he is not free to have been a first-century Jew grasped by the radical impact of God's rule on human life, a reign that is on the verge of overturning the present. Van Buren's Jesus is disabused of the eschatological factor that was his decisive horizon. The irony is that although he is willing to grant that Christian faith may indeed be contingent on historical work (p. 126) while Herrmann was not, neither man makes a serious effort to ascertain through historiography what was constitutive for Jesus. On the other hand, just as Herrmann knows that what counts is Jesus' inner life before he goes to the Gospels, so van Buren determined, on *a priori* grounds, what may and may not be "found" in Jesus. In fact, van Buren's empiricism is precisely what bars the door to the possibility of knowing historically that Jesus was a free man. How can empirically verifiable data verify that Jesus was free from anxiety? The new questers, it will be recalled, insist on perceiving Jesus' faith (or understanding of existence) by maintaining that since selfhood is actualized in word and deed, one may reverse the flow in order to infer the selfhood from its expression. If there are hidden dogmatic shoals there (e.g., the sinless perfection of Jesus is presumed throughout but nowhere stated—in con-

168

trast with Schleiermacher's candor), there is a methodological waterfall here which cannot be navigated at all.[31]

In the second place, just as Herrmann sought the inner life of Jesus because he believed its intrinsic grandeur evoked confidence in us, so van Buren aligns evidence to speak of Jesus' freedom because this is secular salvation without the transcendent. But because *theology* and *anthropology* are correlates, this disavowal of the transcendent leads to fatal results. On the one hand, this discussion of salvation is not persuasive because it is not grounded in an analysis of man. He agrees with his erstwhile teacher, Barth, that "the language about sin is for the Christian a language concerning a problem answered" (p. 179) and that the understanding of sin is evolved in light of the true man, Jesus. Had he taken these formal observations seriously enough to develop an understanding of sin as bondage, then it might have become evident whether man's bondage is effectively dealt with by Jesus' freedom or not. His view of freedom tends to be that of the middle-class intellectual. It is not enough to say, concerning justification, that the believer is "free to accept himself, convinced that he is acceptable, for he has been set free by Jesus of Nazareth" (p. 181), so long as it is not clear from what we are liberated and at what level of existence. Van Buren, then, illustrates in a negative way our observations about the correlative character of soteriology, anthropology, and Christology.

Third, van Buren has a faulty view of theological language. Since we can neither specify nor verify empirically what we mean by "God" we are forbidden to use the word at all (p. 84), or even to reckon with transcendence. It did not occur to him, apparently, to ask whether the word "God" could be applied to what is verifiable and still mean what believers affirm when they use the word. Ought not his own concern for the function of language to have alerted him to ascertain just what Christians do and do not mean by the word, and attend to that? He seems to assume that they have always been empirical literalists, whose language has been rigorously denotative and descriptive, instead of being connotative, imaginative, suggestive, and metaphorical.[32] But who has ever claimed that

169

Christian language was "straightforward empirical assertions about the world" (p. 199) save perhaps a defensive orthodox Protestant who overshot the mark? There is another side of the language problem which ought not to be neglected. Unless one sees that what Christians say about Jesus (he is Lord, Savior, etc.) always exceeds its empirical function in Christian lives, there remains no possibility that Christians understand themselves to be judged by what they affirm. Van Buren's argument, in effect, turns theology into ideology, for if one obliterates the difference between what one confesses to be true over against him and what is true *of* him, there remains no way for the confession to judge him. Has not the church steadily, though not constantly, seen that its confession is eschatological, that it confesses more than it can show empirically about itself or about God? [33] Strange that he goes on to judge American Protestantism, for his method surrendered the basis for doing so. What reason remains for not taking the meaning of Christian statements to be precisely those functions which they actually have in acculturated Americanized Christianity? [34]

Whereas Herrmann probed the question of what made the Christian confident of God's communing with him in order to clarify salvation as personal faith in God, and while van Buren saw salvation as a more or less unspecified freedom engendered by Jesus, Dorothee Sölle[35] sees salvation as identity affirmed in a technological world in which persons are dissolved into mere duplicate integers in mass society. After the death of God we need "to find other names for Christ which may be better suited to define Christ's work in the world" (p. 12). This work is best spoken of as representation, a theme developed in sharp contrast with substitution. The same reasons that prompt van Buren to speak of freedom led her to speak of representation—it is "more abstract"—that is, less mythological and metaphysical. Relentlessly she insists that only as a representative, not as substitute, does Christ assure the identity of the self. With equal resolve, she refuses to understand Christ on the basis of God—to appeal to the character of God in order to interpret the "work of Christ" as his agent.

170

The representative, she insists, takes the place of another temporarily;[36] he never displaces him as does the substitute. She then reviews the history of the Christian theology of the atonement to argue that every form of substitutionary atonement depersonalizes man by making him irrelevant.[37] But Christ does not substitute himself for us so that we are now left out; rather he represents us for a time.

Christ does not replace our life, making us superfluous, not counted on by anyone any longer. . . . Any doctrine of representation which treats us, our sins, our history, as "over and done with" not only destroys the irreplaceable individual but also abandons the God for whom men are not interchangeable. God . . . is still not content with the representative, continues to count on us . . . to wait for us . . . God is *not* content with our representative. Our representative speaks for us, but we ourselves have to learn to speak." (Pp. 103-4)

Consequently, Christ is the provisional forerunner who enables us to live without fulfillment;[38] he is the teacher who identifies with us and suffers with us who must live without God as something discrete; he is the forerunner of God to us who keeps the way open for God's future with men. In a way reminiscent of Herrmann, the last point is developed in a way that appeals to Jesus as the one who makes confidence in God possible—though in a radically different way:

For the time being, Christ takes God's place, stands in for the God who no longer presents himself to us directly and who no longer brings us into his presence in the manner claimed by earlier religious experience. Christ holds the place of this now absent God open for him in our midst. For without him, we should have to "sack" the God who does not show up. . . . We would have no reason to wait for him, no reason not to write him off as dead. . . . What Nietzsche called the "death of God" . . . is in fact only the death of God's immediacy. . . . But Christ is not a replacement for the dead God. He is the representative of the living God, of the God who like man is irreplaceable yet representable. (Pp. 13 ff.)[39]

Here is a far more subtle and suggestive statement of the "secular meaning of the gospel" than van Buren's, for the

171

central role of Christ is related to the irradicable need to be an authentic self. Here anthropology and Christology are coordinated. Further, against kerygmatic theology, Sölle declares, "God is not just proclaimed . . . he is also represented in the world" (p. 148) by Christ and his present disciples. Like Herrmann, she is after a way of perceiving the centrality of Christ in such a way as to make vital personal life in the world possible, a way of grasping the work of Christ which elicits deep response from the whole man.

Still, important questions are provoked with respect to our problem. (a) The historiographic question has already been noted. Here we may simply rephrase it: Is this really a Christ-figure who has been attached to Jesus without due warrant? If not, can all she says about Christ be said of the historical Jesus? Is it accidental that she speaks regularly of Christ rather than of Jesus? (b) Despite the powerful, and welcome, resurgence of the "not yet," can one really show that for Jesus the coming of God's kingdom meant the establishment of the self and its capacity to participate constructively in this world? Or did he not have in view the transformation of this age (not merely this epoch!), and thus presuppose a judgment on it as a whole? Moreover, it appears to be a long step from the New Testament view of the incompleteness of the work of Jesus Christ to Sölle's view of the transitional role of Christ—especially when one asks, Transitional to what? (c) Can we no longer speak of guilt and shame, of the tyranny of death? [40] How does the Representative deal with our guilt? Or does her silence mean she deems this an unreal question because she sees Jesus merely as the remover of impediments to self-actualization? Having no place, apparently, for the Fall (unless it be the emergence of technological society!), she assumes that it is an innocent self who is victimized by impediments to self-fulfillment. Despite the pathos that surpasses that of van Buren, she too has a middle-class intellectual's view of man and his root problem. (d) Precisely because the quest for identity is prevailing and self-evident today, one must ask whether this is to be accepted as *the* legitimate question to which the entire answer must be shaped and by which the whole history of

172

theology can be judged.[41] Surely this would turn Christology, and theology as a whole, into mere ideology.

C. This criticism does not apply to Paul Tillich,[42] in whose theology the theme of salvation is constant.[43] Tillich is concerned to understand salvation in a genuinely evangelical way—one that does not impose a law or a requirement that men do something in order to be saved. He wants Jesus and his salvation to be a genuine gift, and the gospel to be truly *good* news.[44] At the same time, he wants to speak of the *extra nos*, of the ground of salvation in Jesus.[45] To do so, he casts the discussion in terms of being, the Ground of being and of the New Being who appeared in Jesus. He sees the human predicament in ontological terms: since the human predicament is ontic (man is estranged from his being and from the Ground of his being), salvation in Jesus must be couched in ontic terms as well—participation in the New Being who himself overcomes this estrangement and thereby has healing power for those who participate in him. Because he insists on participation in the New Being, he is critical of Bultmann's concentration on the words of Jesus as call to decision, arguing that "the situation of having to decide remains one of being under the law." [46]

Nor does Tillich have in mind a Christ-figure, for he has no doubt about the pivotal significance of the actual historical Jesus:

If there were no personal life in which existential estrangement had been overcome, the New Being would have remained a quest and an expectation and would not be a reality in time and space. Only if the existence is conquered in *one* point—a personal life, representing existence as a whole—is it conquered in principle. . . . This is the reason that Christian theology must insist on the actual fact to which the name Jesus of Nazareth refers. (II, 98)[47]

Tillich clearly emphasizes the incarnation in his view of salvation. Tillich's debt to Greek thought and his affinity with Greek Christianity are evident in his critique of Anselm, who regarded the incarnation as the necessary step for the atonement on the cross rather than the salvific event itself (II, 123);

173

that is, for Tillich it is the appearing of the New Being which is decisive, not his historical career.[48] Furthermore, in contrast with classical Christology, Tillich shifts the subject of the incarnation from God to man. This is why he formulates the matter in ways like these: "essential man appearing in a personal life under the conditions of existential estrangement" (II, 95); or "it is the eternal relation of God to man which is manifest in the Christ" (II, 96); or, "in Christ the eternal God-Man unity has appeared under the conditions of existence" (II, 169). Such statements intend to interpret John 1:14, but it is doubtful whether the Fourth Evangelist understood Jesus to be the *bearer* of a reality, on the one hand, or as incarnating archetypal man and not the divine Logos himself, on the other. Given such a reinterpretation of the incarnation, it is but natural that the history of Jesus becomes the illustration for a reality discerned independently.

Tillich, then, emphasizes the reality and role of the New Being, but has no significant interest in the particulars of the one in whom the New Being appeared. The quest of the historical Jesus is declared to be a failure because it "could not provide a safe foundation for the Christian faith" (II, 105)— a consideration that has by now become a cliché. Nor will he grant the possibility that one works with a Gestalt of Jesus which exceeds the sum of particular facts.[49] Like Bultmann, he insists that the lives of Jesus are "more like novels than biographies. . . . Christianity is not based on the acceptance of a historical novel" (II, 105). At the same time, he speaks repeatedly of the biblical "picture" of Jesus.[50] Just as Herrmann argued that the picture of the inner life of Jesus was created not by the church but by Jesus himself, so Tillich insists that the picture of the New Being is the product not of Christian experience or of faith, but of the New Being himself.[51]

Clearly, for Tillich faith is not dependent on facts about Jesus. It cannot even guarantee that the name of the bearer of the New Being was Jesus.[52] "But faith does guarantee the factual transformation of reality in that personal life which the New Testament expresses in its picture of Jesus as the Christ" (II, 107), because faith can guarantee its foundation—in this case, the appearing of the New Being who heals estrangement. Thus Tillich comes close, formally, to Bultmann. If the latter needs only the fact of Jesus for the kerygma, Tillich needs only the fact that the New Being appeared. He affirms that the New Being appeared in Jesus because, as a result of believing this, estrangement was (and continues to be) overcome.[53]

Tillich does not rely on sheer assertion, but considers two other factors—the picture of Jesus and the experience of the church (both being the receptive aspect of the Christ event:[54] "The Christ is not the Christ without the church,"[55] [II, 180]). Similarly, he affirms that "the New Being has power to transform those who are transformed by it" (II, 114)—which is but the restatement of Herrmann's point that the basis of faith and the object of faith are identical. Like Herrmann, too, he distinguishes between an imaginary and a real picture. "A picture imagined by . . . the contemporaries of Jesus would have expressed their untransformed existence and their quest for a New Being. But it would not have been the New Being itself. That is tested by its transforming power." (II, 115) But one might well ask whether it is not also the case that illusions transform persons in accord with their content.

Tillich himself provides perspective on his aims. He admits that, like Schleiermacher, he emphasizes Jesus as the relation to God but instead of concentrating on his God-consciousness, he pursues the ontological motif (II, 150). Likewise he refuses to separate Christology from soteriology because he sees the category "New Being" as holding together the person of Christ and the work of Christ (II, 168). But he does insist on separating Christology from historiography, even though liberal Jesus-research has affected his Christology.[56] Still, it is odd that, as David Kelsey puts it, "a great deal of Tillich's discussion of Christology consists in arguments that are, at least covertly, designed to show that the biblical picture of Jesus the Christ does correspond with historical fact."[57]

Our main criticism of Tillich stems from this equivocation

about the concrete historical life of Jesus. Inevitably, he knows by definition (that is, on the basis of his ontology) everything he needs to know about Jesus. The historical figure of Jesus adds nothing but concreteness to what is known in advance, out of the system. Tillich has the answer in hand before he turns to the Gospels or to what can be learned there about Jesus. Actually, this is a characteristic weakness of most forms of incarnation Christology—everything decisive about the incarnate one is known from an analysis of that which is incarnated and why it must be. Hence it is only to be expected that Tillich writes that "in all its concrete details the biblical picture of Jesus as the Christ confirms his character as the bearer of the New Being" (II, 125), and that he should be more interested in the legendary story[58] of Jesus' temptations than in other aspects of the tradition because this story exhibits Jesus' struggle with the conditions of existence to which he does not succumb.

D. *The Issue Sharpened.* Taking note of certain predecessors, terse as it was, has helped us to sharpen the assignment in several ways. First, it has underscored the necessity of seeing the understanding of salvation and the understanding of man together, and of seeing both on a sufficiently deep level to deal with man himself, not merely with certain symptoms of his situation. Moreover, fidelity to the Christian tradition forbids our seeing this situation apart from its resolution in Jesus. Otherwise he takes us no further than the questions we already have and so becomes an ideological construct. Our questions at hand are by no means to be repudiated, but they are not to be taken as the last word or as the necessary norm, as in Sölle for example.

Second, concentrating on Jesus as the locus of the answer requires us to deal more significantly with historical inquiry. While each of the four theologians has affirmed the centrality of Jesus, none was prepared to depend on the Jesus who could be ascertained by historical work. Rather, each in his own way prescribed the sort of Jesus who had to be found. Historical study appears to be valued as a way of circumventing certain unacceptable elements in the Gospels (e.g., Virgin Birth or miracles) but disallowed as a determinant for ascertaining the content of the name "Jesus." But one cannot say that it is Jesus who saves and refuse to be contingent on inquiry as to who he was and what he was about.

Third, it is neither an aspect of Jesus (van Buren's freedom), nor an ontic reality that appeared in him (Tillich), nor a message that he proclaimed (Bultmann and others), nor the confidence within him (Herrmann) which is decisive but the whole configuration of word, deed, and career capped by death, which is decisive. No aspect of Jesus saves us, but the whole life touches our life as a whole. The atonement did not occur when Jesus became a free man, or when he preached the parables, or when the New Being appeared, or when he developed his inner life and shared it, just as it is not to be reduced to his dying. It occurred rather in the whole event, for it is Jesus as a whole who was vindicated in the resurrection and so made trustworthy. It is the life of the whole man that is trustworthy, just as it is his life as a whole that is offense and question. Trusting Jesus is a way of overcoming this reductionism which concentrates either on Jesus' inwardness, his articulations, or on a reality greater than he, for in each of these cases Jesus is validated by that aspect of him which is taken up into the theological system.

III. Salvation by Trust in Jesus

A. *On Trusting Jesus.* Is it possible to trust a person not immediately present? We noted earlier how Lessing's perception of the problem dominated the entire discussion until now: only what is immediately present is trustworthy. Because we are not driven by this passion for certitude through the immediate, we can affirm that one can trust a person not immediately present, one whom we know by historical study and reconstruction of traditions.

To begin, trust in persons not immediately present to us is not peculiar with regard to Jesus. We trust many persons whom we never met, and whom we know only indirectly. Even on TV, where preachers, politicians, and artists are "present" on the screen so that the man comes across (or fails to), the programs are planned and often edited so that, insofar as possible, a desired image is projected. Responding to a candidate or an ad is possible only through the medium, not by direct confrontation. Also with regard to persons we know directly and intimately we are partly dependent also on reports of others for our image of them and confidence in them. A person who refuses such dependence lacks perspective, we say ("I know *my* boy would never do such a thing!"). As noted in the analysis of trust, reports of others play an inescapable role in the emergence of trust.

But can we trust persons not contemporary with us, persons whom we can never meet directly because historical time separates us? Here too the answer is affirmative because the character of mediated knowledge of persons in general permits it.

Many persons today trust Martin Luther King, Mohandas K. Gandhi, or Dietrich Bonhoeffer because through reports they perceive a man's life and what he stood for. Here we introduce an important factor in all mediated knowledge of persons—a discernment of what that person was "really all about." The same factor operates when one distrusts or hates another: one responds to what is seen in him, to what one perceives the man to be and to be about.

We commonly distinguish between accurate facts and the larger, more important reality that makes them significant, and do so without splitting them apart. If someone asks me, "What is going on at Vanderbilt?" and I report the appointments made, buildings erected, budgetary and enrollment figures, etc., he will probably counter, "But what is *really* going on?" He wants to know what these data represent because he knows intuitively that "what is going on" cannot be learned simply by compiling facts. He wants perceptive knowledge that gives perspective to the data. If I then tell him that the faculty are developing political power, that the administration is nervous about finances, that shifts of power balance between students and administration are under way, he may understand

178

what is going on in a way that no set of data alone can give, though he will neither understand it nor believe it if no data are adduced. That is, this "second level" report (and the reporter) is untrustworthy as soon as it becomes evident that it is unsupportable by a representative[59] body of data. This discernment of the whole is greater than the sum of the parts. In dealing with a person, it is important to see that more is involved than generalizations about him (e.g., He does not understand finances); it is the perception of the man as a whole that is decisive (e.g., He is a man of his word). In the same way, when perceiving a figure in the past, one discerns the man as a whole through his commitments, words, deeds, etc., which are ascertainable through evidence. The evidences adduced do not verify the discernment the way the reported weight of a bunch of bananas is verified, but the discernment is supportable by the data.[60] At the same time, because others may read the person differently, the task of discerning another person is never complete, and the image of him always subject to correction. Moreover, there is no single true discernment of a person because the standpoint of the discerner cannot be, and should not be, ignored. But such tentativeness does not preclude one's trusting a person in the past any more than lack of absolute and total knowledge prevents trusting a contemporary. In fact, it is often the case that the evidence is ambiguous for persons we know very well and that we still say, "But I trust him anyway." Distrust begins when the balance of evidence shifts enough to require the discernment to be fundamentally different. Either way, the individual not only makes a judgment about Jesus but manifests something of himself. The level of this reciprocal act depends on the character of the issue.

These observations are relevant to the problem of trusting the historical Jesus. The Gospels do not compile trivia about him (Why was he a bachelor? Just how was each day spent?), but present material in the service of perceptions of what was really going on in his life as a whole. Neither the categories they used (e.g., Son of Man, Son of God) nor the legends they reported (e.g., baptism, transfiguration) are to be seen as

179

theology imposed on his life. Rather, they were ways of bringing to expression what early Christians believed was going on in him,[61] whether they did so by titles or stories.[62] Whether the titles and categories were arbitrarily employed or not depends on whether the evidence is such as to permit them; no historical evidence can be such as to show that the titles were necessary or inevitable.

If our reflections are in order, it is clear that there can be no sharp demarcation between "the picture of Jesus in the New Testament" (Kähler, Tillich) and the lives of Jesus which are commonly dismissed as novels. Such language may be effective theological rhetoric, but it will not survive careful scrutiny because it obscures the fact that the New Testament, no less than the modern interpreter, develops an image of Jesus as a whole within which ascertained data (in the New Testament, traditions) are significant. The important differences between the New Testament pictures and those of the historian ought not to obliterate the continuity between their functions. When one studies a figure in the past, be it Socrates or Jesus, the image he has formed of the man as a whole clarifies that life by putting information about it into perspective,[63] and thereby facilitates a response to the person, whether trust or distrust. He who trusts believes that his picture can be substantiated by data. If the image is unsubstantiable, one cannot entrust himself to the person, or appropriate him as his model. This is why one cannot really believe the kerygma, to return to this terminology, and be indifferent to the historical Jesus. That would be believing a sheer assertion.

At the same time, because neither the image nor the reliability of any person can be proved the way Euclid proved the laws of triangles, the trustworthiness of Jesus cannot be proved by historiography. The reliability of a person, whether Jesus or my neighbor, can be affirmed only by the confluence of evidence, witness, and experience. The latter, at the same time, confirms the reliability of the evidence and of the testimony of others. Moreover, because trust does not enjoy freedom from risk, the vulnerability of the man who trusts cannot be eliminated; in fact, it is in affirming it that the vitality of trust becomes manifest.

Accordingly, one trusts a figure in the past when he trusts his integrity and the validity of what he stood for. That is, he risks making the trusted person a model for his own life. He seeks to appropriate what gave the trusted life its integrity and to participate in that integrity. The trusted person—as a person—becomes the warrant for one's own mode of life and its commitments. He also becomes the lens through which one understands his own experiences and questions, so that the trusted life acquires capacity to interpret him who trusts. In this process, distance in time simply does not play the inhibiting role Lessing assigned to it. Therefore, the process we have noted here occurs with regard to Jesus as well, and its traditional name is discipleship.[64] The disciple is one who trusts the model and who does not expect to make him superfluous by his own attainments. In other words, becoming a disciple of Jesus is appropriating his life as the model and warrant for one's own; it is making him the stack-pole around which life is organized and lived. It is this process which inaugurates salvation. Explicit theological reflection commences when one begins to probe the relation of this process to the understanding of God; but, as Herrmann saw, theological analysis does not set the experience in motion, and cannot be required to do so. In any case, a contemporary person can trust Jesus because Jesus was about God and his reign, and that subject matter, by definition, touches the trusts of every man.[65]

What makes trust possible? Kerygmatic theologians reply that it is Christ's presence in the preached word. Classical theology has appealed to the Holy Spirit as the cause of one's faith-response, or to divine revelation. In declining to appeal to any of these, we have not denied their legitimacy; we have, rather, affirmed that appealing to the Holy Spirit, to revelation, or to the presence of the living Christ is to *confess* the source of one's trust but not to *explain* it at all. Explanations have to do with causes that one can assess and adjudicate; confessions move on a quite different level. Ultimately, why one trusts another person remains a mystery, despite the number or the variety of psychological, biographical, and sociological factors one might compile. None of these factors competes with the confession that God himself called one to trust, because God is not a factor. The language system of Christian dogmatics does not need to have a place made for it in descriptive analysis such as we have undertaken here. Rather it is another mode of reflecting on precisely the same matters. Hence one might say, in dogmatic terms, that the work of God's Spirit in relating the believer to Jesus is precisely what we have been talking about. We also said, moreover, that it is our avowed intent to explore the potential of working with the historical (the historian's) Jesus in as fruitful a way as possible by beginning there and allowing theological and confessional matters to emerge, rather than beginning with theological axioms and confessional statements and then moving to the historical Jesus.

Still, perhaps the old liberals were not completely wrong when they pointed to the evocative power of Jesus' life, though they sometimes wrongly assumed that his life, as they saw it, invariably had compelling power to evoke faith. Any strong figure evokes a response, whether it be attraction or repulsion. No less is true of Jesus. Above all, a life with commitments such as his which nonetheless ends in execution requires a response, a perception of what it was all about and a decision whether it is trustworthy.

Someone else might object that one may not compare trust in Jesus (a religious act) with other trusts in other figures. Before one hastens with his objections, however, he ought to reflect on the fact that what makes a given trust "religious" is its degree of ultimacy (to speak with Tillich), its capacity to give life coherence, direction, and meaning. It has often been observed that what one trusts ultimately is one's God. If this trust could not be misplaced, there could be no idolatry. The difference between idolatry and worship of the true God is not in the phenomenology of trust but in what is trusted, what accompanies this trust and flows from it. Moreover, consciously or unconsciously, most persons have a model or a norm, historical or conceptual, which they appropriate and which warrants the quality and direction of their lives. The real question, then, concerns not whether trust in Jesus is phenomenologically comparable with other trusts, but the effects of trusting Jesus on the network of trusts which constitutes life, and whether trusting Jesus coincides with trusting God. Far too much discussion of faith and trust seems to assume that one is poised at zero-point, deciding whether or not to trust, whether or not to live by a model. In fact, however, life is constituted by trusts and models, so that news of Jesus calls these into question and perhaps causes a realignment. With these questions, we are at the threshold of the last section of this chapter, and have touched the theme of the next as well.

B. *The Scope of Salvation.* As the sketch of movement from non-trust to distrust implied, trust is the antidote to the entire range of estranged relationships. More precisely, *trust in Jesus overcomes the past history of the self.* Hence it is now incumbent upon us to speak directly to the matter of trust in Jesus as a way of healing our relationship to God and to one another. The holistic perception of Jesus implies that trust in him is reliance on the man seen as a whole, an entrusting of the self to a self because one is persuaded that what he was is valid ultimately, and because the quality of his life elicits a response from our life-center.

Jesus' whole career has to do with the trustworthiness of God and with the trusting response of man. He did not use this terminology, of course, but this is what his proclamation of the kingdom and the summons to repent (turn Godward), his deeds of mercy and his acceptance of death centrally mean.[66] For Jesus to announce that the kingdom is at hand, to undertake to make it operational through his exorcisms, which expelled the demonic anti-God, and through the texture of his own career, whose consequences he did not flee,[67] was to undertake the task of showing the sort of reality God is and that precisely this God is trustworthy. To trust Jesus is to appropriate him as the index of God.

If Jesus restructures our understanding of who God is (to be explored in the next chapter) and so remodels the quality of our trust, then we see our previous trusts and conceptions in a new light. Jesus concentrates on the One whose integrity means faithfulness to what he has made; those upon whom this light dawns see that they once sat in darkness and deemed it light. H. Richard Niebuhr can write of faith as "trust in that which gives value to life; on the other hand it is loyalty to what the self values." [68] Accordingly, standing with Jesus we see that apart from him our ultimate trusts, whatever Sunday verbalizations we might muster, may have been marked by an ideological *use* of God rather than by allegiance to him who is loyal to all men. In the wake of Jesus who insists that the kingdom is not the supremacy of Essene or Pharisee, we find ourselves slowly liberated from making God the almighty guarantor of those structures of power congenial to ourselves. And so on. The point is that because theology and anthropology are coordinates, it is not simply a matter of coordinate ideas but of the reciprocity between the trusted center and the trusting self. By refocusing our trust in his God, Jesus saves us not only from spurious theology but from allegiance to alternatives to which our previous life was beholden. For life is composed of the multiple trusts and allegiances that are the seedbed of concepts. This is why Jesus does not simply set another idea of God alongside those we already have, but summons us to trust the God whose rule restores the right order of all things according to his integrity (or righteousness), not according to our expectations and values. In the healing of our trust at its deepest level the life history of him who trusts Jesus is redeemed.

He who in the face of life and death remains loyal to Jesus in his life and death and thereby persists in trusting his God's integrity, who trusts Jesus to be the valid model for his own life, discovers that he stands in right relation to God no less than Jesus did. That is, he knows himself to be reconciled to God and to life and death. This is a fair restatement of what Paul meant by his argument that it is by faith that we are "justified"—set in right relation to God who is righteous because the integrity (righteousness) of God is revealed in the gospel in such a way as to pass judgment on what was previously thought to be God's (and man's) righteousness. Trust, then, affords release (this is what forgiveness means) from bondage to no-gods, and from alienation from the God of integrity who is trustworthy in precisely the way disclosed by the career and death of Jesus. By trusting Jesus not to mislead us we are reconciled to the only God who in the face of enigmatic life and absurd death is morally credible and trustworthy at the same time. (The next chapter continues this theme.)

When one undertakes to align his life with that of Jesus as model or paradigm, he restructures his life—that is, he repents. Immediately, it is apparent that Jesus revolutionizes repentance itself, for whereas John the Baptist required repentance as readiness for the coming of the Judge, Jesus summoned men to repent as a response to God's kingdom. Accordingly, in realigning the contours of one's life by trusting Jesus, one appropriates the central thrust of Jesus' own message: repentance as response.[69] Since repentance is neither regret for not being religious sooner, nor remorse requisite for forgiveness, but the steady lifelong process of appropriating Jesus as one's paradigm, repentance holds together faith and ethics, religious trust and moral action. Repentance, so conceived, is not the prelude to Christian existence but the name of the game itself. To repent and to become a disciple (or become a Christian) are the same thing—appropriating Jesus as trustworthy.

Because trusting Jesus is not an instantaneous solution but a lifelong process (contrast Bultmann's repeatedly instantaneous Christian), repentance is a continuum in which trust in Jesus becomes paramount among all other trusts. In this way, the "lordship" of Jesus is effected. "Decision" does not yet make Jesus operational as lordly paradigm. We are beholden to too many lords, too many idolatries, imprisoned by networks of allegiance and values which compete with Jesus' claim upon him who trusts him. Hence repentance and discipleship are to be understood as the struggle of the self to follow the lead of Jesus, to assimilate him as the model.[70] The decision to trust Jesus does not so much settle things as unsettle them; it sets in motion a struggle more than it achieves an equipose (Christian existence in the world). The longer

185

one lives in Jesus' wake, the more he discovers aspects of his own life which have not yet been remodeled by the impact of Jesus' life upon it. In this way, trust and repentance overcome the anomie that stems from the heteronomous and idolatrous trusts that otherwise shape our lives. When man cannot give himself to life because he cannot trust that the good is ultimate or that what is ultimate is good, he mortgages his self to what is less than good and ultimate and develops defensive postures against his brother. Paul saw this when he wrote the devastating yet simple phenomenology of sin: "whatever does not come from trust (faith) is sin" (Rom. 14:23). This is why trust, on the other hand, redeems life at the center, or as the Bible says, in the heart.

Trust not only heals the past but *keeps the future open*. It is in the nature of trust to lean into the future with expectation, as well as to rely on the past, for trust is not only a present reliance on evidence and attestation from the past but a future-oriented stance. So trust merges with expectation and waiting; we do not wait for one we do not expect, and we do not expect one who is untrustworthy. But if we trust one who is trustworthy, we are prepared to wait and to expect —despite inconveniences and distress—because our reliance on his integrity outweighs the present. Expectation and waiting need not be passive, of course, for one frequently acts in expectation and trust that his activity will be vindicated. One need only think of such simple acts as cashing a check, or writing one in the hope that funds will have been paid into the account by the time the check is cashed.

These reflections on the forward movement of trusting are all the more germane when the one trusted is himself determinded by trust in the future, as was Jesus. His entire career was predicated on trust in the kingdom's coming, so that he set in motion the kingdom's impact ahead of time, and called disciples to share in a restructuring of life on the basis of the not yet.[71] By living out of the future into the present, instead of living into the future out of the past, he appropriated the freedom of the future and made repentance possible. This is why those who share his mode of existence by appropriating

186

him as the model find themselves out of step with the past-controlled present, though not yet entirely free from it. They live on the borderline where the freedom of the future constitutively challenges the stability of the present. Preserving this dialectic which keeps the future open is what constitutes the continual struggle to repent in the face of the habituated present; at the same time one continues this agony precisely to the extent to which he trusts Jesus as the forerunner or the preview of the kingdom. For God's kingship manifests itself in making men free.[72]

Because one relies on Jesus, whom God has disclosed to be trustworthy through the resurrection, one is not anxious about the future even though it is not yet verified publicly. The dread of the future, whether as the unknown ravager of the present or as the unpredictable shaper of destiny, is overcome even though the future remains unknown and unpredictable, because through Jesus one trusts the character of the One whose power is exercised in bringing the future forward into the present sufficiently to be trusted. One expects God to be the consummator of what by present trust is anticipated or grasped ahead of time.[73] The epitome of the dreaded future is death, that impenetrable curtain. He who trusts Jesus—the Jesus whose death rattle is interpreted as a cry of dereliction[74] hurled into the face of the God he trusted—faces the mystery of his own dying with expectation because this Jesus with whom he identified came into his own only beyond death. In death, as in life, the disciple is not above his master. Contrary to all jejeune optimism about this-worldly fulfillment—advocated regularly, it seems, by the achievers or by those who expect to be—Jesus is the trusted reminder of the incompleteness, the frustration, the disastrousness of history, and so he redeems those who trust him from false expectations grounded in a future projected out of the past. Resurrection is a way of asserting the freedom of the future to meet death-bound history in order to transform it into fulfillment.

Another dimension of the future granted by trust concerns responsibility and accountability. In trusting another one holds himself responsible to him who is trusted while at the same

187

time he evokes responsibility from the one trusted. We need to comment briefly on this interrelated responsibility. In trusting another, I make myself responsible for being loyal to him, to a course of action which does not deny this trust or its object, for one acts in the name of and for the sake of him who is trusted. Another way of saying this is to observe that trust makes one contingent on one who is trusted, and therefore accountable to him for his life (one thinks of the patient who trusts the doctor and commits himself to follow instructions). Accountability, moreover, is future-oriented since one expects a response to his trusting because the trustworthiness of the other precludes his indifference. The obverse is now in view: being trusted also makes one responsible for those who trust him. The officer in battle is made responsible for his men not merely by military organization but also by the confidence that his men have in him. If he is a trustworthy officer, their trust evokes responsibility for them and to them more than does the manual; because he cannot let them down without denying his integrity, their trust establishes his accountability to them. Similarly, a son's trust evokes trustworthiness and accountability from his father, for the father—if he has integrity—cannot be indifferent to his son's trust. In this case, the future is not the mere extension of the present but new freedom for it. The point is that trust leads to mutual accountability, and accountability for trust keeps the future open.

It is not difficult to see that he who trusts Jesus is accountable to him—that is, that he knows himself judged by that in Jesus which evokes his trust. To grasp Jesus as "the man for others" (to use the new cliché), for instance, and to trust him is to know oneself accountable for his own "being for others." How trust in Jesus evokes accountability *from* him is not obvious, especially if we ask, Can one speak of the historical Jesus' accountability to those who trust him now?

One way to explore this is to appeal to the category of myth, specifically to the resurrection and the Coming. One of the functions of these myths is to express the continuity of Jesus across time.[75] One might also explore a more abstract

188

consideration: because the God whom Jesus trusted proved trustworthy beyond death, the responsibility of the historical Jesus to his original disciples is extended to all who trust him subsequently, for through him they trust the same God.[76] One's life-experience brought about by trust in Jesus enters a moral claim on Jesus (and on God) not to let him down. In this light we can understand that the resurrection and the Coming are modes of affirming that his responsibility for man's trust-engendered life will not be shirked.

In the third place, trusting Jesus produces a *community of trust*. This would be true even if Jesus had not called disciples and so inaugurated a community centered in him, for those who trust a life in common begin to trust one another. Thereby the manifold distrusts among persons are healed by their individual—and concerted—trust in Jesus.[77]

The indivisibility of trust in Jesus and trust in others who trust him is consonant with the Great Commandment, which Jesus made central: one cannot love God without loving what God loves, one's neighbor and the world. I John registers the same point in a different vocabulary: "If we walk in the light, as he is in the light, we have fellowship one with another" (I John 1:7). Precisely because Jesus was determined by the God who was faithful to all his creatures, one cannot trust Jesus and erect walls against another person or ravage the physical world carelessly.

Those who trust one another because they trust Jesus also begin to dismantle the barriers that they, as sons of Adam, erected and sustain. In New Testament times, the key barrier was understood as that which separates Jew from gentile; today, it is not only Jews and Christians who are alienated, but gentiles are pitted against gentiles as well—blacks and whites, rich and poor, East and West. The historical Jesus is paradigmatically redemptive also for our situation, for he did not interpret the kingdom of God as the divine sanction and fulfillment for any of the conflicting groups of his day but moved among both outcasts and Pharisees, and called insurrectionists as well as others to his circle. In other words, just as God ignored moral achievements in providing sun

189

and rain, so Jesus ignored hostilities among men and claims on God as he undertook to effectuate this God's kingship. The community that comes into existence by trusting such a man will inevitably be a motley one that must struggle to sustain its allegiance to Jesus because each element in it wants to reduce him to the bulwark of its own ideology. The history of the church includes the panorama of the pressures to evade the import of trusting Jesus no less than the struggles—undertaken from time to time—to follow him in dismantling our walls and structures. Because the fulfillment of what is inaugurated in Jesus lies in the future, there never was a paradisical church that was free from this struggle. Hence every exhortation to return to the New Testament church, as if *that* were the golden age, is misplaced and diversionary. The church is summoned to the future, not to its own past. In this sense, the historical church is always the New Testament church.

The extent to which the trusting community struggles to be loyal to Jesus is at the same time the extent to which it is estranged from the world, for the world is constituted and tyrannized not only by bondage to distrust and hostility but by a sense of futility and of false optimism. The more one is conscious of the power and pervasiveness of mistrust, the more one is inclined to futility, so that distrust becomes our fate and we are its witting accomplices. Thereby we nurture the demonic. Not even revolutions succeed in escaping the past, since revolution is predicated on distrust and alienation and its leaders are not exempt from the "law of Adam," as the history of revolutions shows. (Was there ever a revolution which, in retrospect, is not seen to have been betrayed? Does power not corrupt those who come to power through power, whatever their original intent?) When the community gives paramount trust to Jesus it cannot confer equal trust to any class or status, revolution or movement, race or nation. The more persistently these require full allegiance, the more the trusting community is estranged from the world.

What preserves the trusting community from being ghettoized is its preception that it is estranged from the world for the sake of the world, not simply for the sake of its own purity. The community can exist in Jesus' name only if it shares his way—that is, if it undertakes to make clear what the kingdom of Jesus' God is all about. It is in the name of the integrity of God with respect to all creation that the church goes to work, constantly open to seduction to do so for reasons that buttress this or that party and class. Hence while it may say Yes to a given struggle for justice or peace, it must never forget to say No as well, the more so because all historical movements absolutized their claims and demand an unequivocal Yes. But it is precisely in saying both Yes and No that the church seeks to hold the future open for the world, for this No is a protest against self-absolutization and tyranny over the future. This is how the community that trusts Jesus takes up its cross and stays with it. Like the Jesus it follows, its task is to be a forerunner of God's kingdom, not the bulwark for any man's. Trust in Jesus is a central way of resisting the lure of even "Christian" ideology.

One aspect of the church's life has peculiar poignancy because of the church's actual betrayal—the relation to Judaism. Precisely when it is the historical Jesus whom the community trusts it must not forget that it trusts a loyal Jew. We gentiles cannot trust this Jesus and be anti-Semitic. Every form of anti-Semitism is a betrayal of trust in the historical Jesus, on the one hand, and the erection of a Jesus-cult for paganism on the other. Trusting Jesus can only bring us closer to Judaism, not farther from it, for it was in Israel's God that he trusted and to whom he committed those who trust him. If today Jew and Christian will not agree in their stance toward Jesus it is less because of Jesus than because of the Christian betrayal of him. The tragedy of the original, and repeated, Jewish refusal of Jesus has long since been overshadowed by the Christian betrayal of him as a Jew. Full exploration of the way in which, by trusting Jesus, we gentiles become co-heirs with Judaism of God's kingdom exceeds the bounds of this discussion. It must suffice to say that whoever entrusts his life to Jesus becomes a son of Abraham without being a convert to Judaism, and that the community that lives by trust in this man renounces every form of pagan tribalism—whether to race or to nation or to class—in order to enter the one people of God and to stand with Judaism in relying on God to be faithful to himself by redeeming the world he made.

It might be objected that because the foregoing sketch concentrates on trust, we have seriously eroded the classical Christian emphasis on salvation by grace, or have unwittingly replaced the understanding of faith as a gift with a synergistic view in which man's own faith saves him. We cannot deal adequately with such charges here. We must be content to register several observations in the hope that they may suffice, momentarily, to allow ruffled feathers to lie down again.

First, trust is not self-generated from zero-point, but is elicited. Not only do we learn to trust in the process of becoming human, but trust is response to another. Consequently, trusting Jesus does not put the initiative with man. Second, we speak of divine grace to confess that what we have found in Jesus (and elsewhere) is not divine compensation, that it is grounded in God's freedom and integrity; it is a way of relating our joyous surprise to the character of God. Nothing we have said about trust in Jesus vitiates this proper insight; to the contrary, it confirms it because that complex of word, deed, and death called "Jesus" is not the construct of the mind, nor a carefully nurtured product of a religious society determined to produce a perfect model. Precisely as a historical event, Jesus is a surprise to mankind; for though he was understood to be the expected one, he was not what was expected. To put it mythologically, God manifested his grace when he brought on the scene Jesus, above all when he ratified him. Third, then, trust in Jesus is not man's own "work" but his lifelong response, his lifelong "Yes" to what God has done in this life.

Because Jesus understood himself to be dependent on God, trusting Jesus cannot intervene in our relation to God; it can only concentrate and clarify it. How this is the case is the topic of the final chapter.

NOTES TO CHAPTER FOUR

1. The logical and theological problems here are fantastically intricate, as the history of Christian theology shows. Christian theology rejected the view that God is only the shaper of the "given" because it implies that matter is independent of God, and implicitly co-eternal—basically a dualistic view. Instead, it argued for *creatio ex nihilo* because this makes clear the utter contingence of everything on God. In doing so, it also rejected an emanationist view according to which God emitted a Son, who in turn began a whole series of downward emissions (a devolution) in the course of which the emitted grew ever more material until at last the cosmos came into being. Once popular in certain Gnostic circles, this view was rejected because it implied an ontic continuity between matter and God. Even so, from New Testament times onward, Christian theology has regularly asserted that it was through the Son (Logos) that God created the world, thereby admitting the principle of mediation but limiting it to one mediator. The Nicene theological controversies therefore centered on the question whether the Son was himself a creature (Arius) or not ("begotten, not made"—Athanasius). The central problem, then, was how to affirm a rigorously monotheist view of God as sole cause of the world while at the same time not involving him directly in time-space, for this would obscure the fundamental difference between God and world. Greek Logos theology was the means, following Hellenized Judaism, for holding these two concerns together. For a helpful recent discussion of the way the early church drew upon classical philosophy in order to deal with problems emerging from holding the biblical view in a Greek world, see Richard A. Norris, *God and World in Early Christian Theology* (London: A. & C. Black, 1965). For a general treatment of the doctrine of creation, see Langdon Gilkey, *Maker of Heaven and Earth* (New York: Scribner's, 1959).

2. Helmut Gollwitzer makes an analogous point: the biblical understanding of sin presents a greater difficulty to modern man's thought than the much-heralded problem of "theism." *Von der Stellvertretung Gottes* (Munich: Chr. Kaiser Verlag, 1967), p. 118. So already Reinhold Niebuhr, *The Nature and Destiny of Man* (New York: Scribner's, 1941), pp. 93 ff.

3. A trace of the fallen angels myth appears in Gen. 6:1-6. It is found chiefly in certain Jewish apocalyptic texts such as Enoch. The most thorough discussion of the entire Fall tradition in the early church remains that of N. P. Williams, *The Ideas of the Fall and of Original Sin*, Bampton Lectures for 1924 (London: Longmans, Green & Co., 1927).

4. The influence of Reinhold Niebuhr on this formulation is evident. Gordon D. Kaufman has recently interpreted the Fall in radically historical terms as referring to the process in which man acquired language and criteria for morality. While he sees that this occurred prior to all known culture, he also insists that it was a historical

development. The view sketched above is consonant with the intent of Kaufman's interpretation, but calls the Fall mythological in order to avoid confusing the matter by a subtle shift in the meaning of the word "historical." *Systematic Theology: A Historicist Perspective* (New York: Scribner's, 1968), Chap. 24.

5. Gerhard Ebeling has seen this and observed that the apparent lack of interest in salvation is but the obverse of the fact that salvation has become equated with man's achievements so that our era is actually preoccupied with "salvation" in this sense. "Das Verständnis von Heil in sekularisierter Zeit," *Kontexte* IV (Stuttgart-Berlin: Kreuz-Verlag, 1967), 10-11.

6. I am aware that the term Fall does not appear in Genesis 3, that the term Fall itself may have come into Christian vocabulary from Gnostics who spoke of the fall of the souls into bodies, etc. I wish to call attention to the fact that it is being used in a symbolic way to refer to the tragic event that befell creation, an event traditionally understood to be what is reported in Gen. 3. I have, further, deliberately avoided speaking of original sin and total depravity.

7. The use of Adam to symbolize the solidarity of man comes into Christian thought through Paul (Rom. 5; I Cor. 15), who surely did not invent it. Paul does not identify what Adam's sin was or concern himself with explaining how it was transmitted or with similar questions that interested Augustine. Paul was interested in Adam as the symbol of the "old man" in contrast with the "new man" in Christ. For Jewish interpretations of Adam, see Robin Scroggs, *The Last Adam* (Philadelphia: Fortress Press, 1966), chaps. 1-3.

8. See Herbert Marcuse, *One-Dimensional Man* (Boston: Beacon Press, 1964).

9. Paul Ricoeur, *The Symbolism of Evil*, trans. Emerson Buchanan (New York: Harper, 1967), pp. 6 ff.

10. Ebeling formulated this aptly: "Sin is the illusion of being primarily and finally only doer." "Das Verständnis von Heil," p. 13. Here one should engage theologically a current fad of speaking of salvation almost solely as social revolution; much of this enraged literature views salvation only as deliverance from the misdeeds of others (oppressors, variously named). That the Christian news of Jesus pertains to the worldwide struggles for human dignity in freedom is clear. Milan Opocensky stated it well: "The Gospel is related to every effort aimed at humanizing man's situation. Of course, the Gospel puts question marks over our goals and means . . . but it never dissociates itself from man with his hopes, aspirations and troubles." "The Message of Salvation for a Secular World," *International Review of Missions* 57 (1968), 437 (the whole issue is devoted to salvation). The difficulty in the statement lies in what it neglects to say—that the gospel pertains to all men as men, not simply to oppressed strivers and doers, that guilt is not simply a class problem.

11. Herrmann (1846-1922) was professor of theology at Marburg

from 1879 until his retirement in 1917; from 1907 until 1916 he was co-editor of ZThK.

12. Barth shares an interesting reflection on Herrmann in the classroom. "There was a ring in Herrmann's voice—those who heard him lecture hear it today in his writings—the ring of prophetic utterance which pointed to a content, hidden indeed but to be evaded by no one without penalty, the recognition of which demanded a scientific *theology*." Quoted from "The Principles of Dogmatics According to Wilhelm Herrmann" (1925), in *Theology and Church*, trans. Louise Pettibone Smith (New York: Harper, 1962), p. 257. Barth also observed that "in Herrmann's lectures each listener felt himself individually addressed." (P. 262; see also p. 261, n. 4.)

Barth comments on his own relation to Herrmann. "Herrmann was *the* theological teacher of my student years. The day twenty years ago in Berlin when I first read his *Ethik* . . . I remember as if it were today. . . . I can say that on that day I believe my own deep interest in theology began. I came to Marburg as a convinced 'Marburger.' And when on the day I began my ministry the mail brought me, five minutes before I was to go to the pulpit, the new, fourth edition of the *Ethik* as a gift from the author, I accepted this coincidence as a dedication of my whole future. . . . I cannot deny that through the years I have become a somewhat surprising disciple of Herrmann. 'Much is altered here, the dishes differ and the wine is changed.' But I could never inwardly agree that I had really turned away from my teacher. Nor can I so agree today." At the same time, he says that what he learned from Herrmann "later forced me to say almost everything else quite differently and finally led me even to an interpretation of the fundamental truth itself which was entirely different from his. And yet it was *he* who showed me that truth." (P. 238-39)

13. The translations of Herrmann's works have long been out of print. *The Communion of the Christian with God*, first published in 1886, was revised and republished repeatedly. All references here are to the second English translation by J. S. Stanyon, revised by R. W. Stewart in accord with the fourth German ed. of 1903. This will be included in the "Lives of Jesus" series and will be introduced by Robert Voelkel. Voelkel's book, *The Shape of the Theological Task* (Philadelphia: Westminster Press, 1968) uses Herrmann appreciatively but neither summarizes nor converses with him. Fortunately, Peter Fischer-Appelt has undertaken republication of important works, one volume of which has appeared. *Wilhelm Herrmann. Schriften zur Grundlegung der Theologie*, Teil I. "Theologische Bücherei" (Munich: Chr. Kaiser Verlag, 1966). Fischer-Appelt provides a 51-page introduction in which he puts the Herrmann literature in context. Neither this nor the projected second volume, however, will include a critical edition of the *Communion*.

14. To the question, "Whereby shall we know that God makes Himself known to us, so that we may know that a living God is communing with us?" Herrmann replies, "God makes Himself

195

known to us, so that we may recognize Him, through a *fact, on the strength of which we are able to believe in Him*." (*The Communion of the Christian with God*, p. 59; his italics.) In this same context, he insists that "no doctrine of any kind can do more than tell us how we ought to represent God to ourselves. No doctrine can bring it about that there shall arise in our hearts the full certainty that God actually exists for us; only a fact can inspire such confidence within us."

Herrmann insists that "we must regard as revelation only that which brings us into actual communion with God; and we can regard as the thoughts of our own faith only what comes home to us as truth within the sphere of our actual communion with God. Thus all that can be the object of Christian doctrine is summed up in religious experience, and first gains satisfactory definition in that connection. But, on the other hand, we can describe as religious experience only that turning toward God which takes place under the influence of the revelation of God within us, and can be expressed in doctrines of faith." (P. 37-38.) See also p. 128 and "The Moral Teachings of Jesus" in *Essays on the Social Gospel*, by Adolf Harnack and Wilhelm Herrmann, trans. G. M. Craik and M. A. Canney (New York: Putnam's, 1907), pp. 145-46.

15. "We must get past the old dogma of the Deity of Christ to a higher conception of Christ, one which does not compel us to leave Him outside when we take religion, that is the communion of the soul with God, in all earnestness and truth." (P. 34) See also p. 164, where under the tutelage of Luther, Herrmann says, "The Deity of Christ means more to a believer than the mere presence of divine substance in Jesus." It means "that the personal God Himself turns towards sinners and opens His heart to them in that human life, . . . belief in Christ's Deity can only arise out of that which the Man Jesus brings about within us." Fischer-Appelt calls attention to the lifelong opposition in Herrmann to metaphysics in theology.

16. "And the one thing which the Gospels will give us as an overpowering reality which allows no doubt is just the most tender part of all: it is the inner life of Jesus himself." (P. 75) The course of critical investigation since Herrmann has led to the opposite conclusion—that the inner life of Jesus is precisely what cannot be known. As we saw, the allegedly new quest claims it *can* ascertain Jesus' selfhood or understanding of existence.

17. "We are Christians because, in the human Jesus, we have met with a fact whose content is incomparably richer than that of any feelings which arise within ourselves—a fact, moreover, which makes us so certain of God that our conviction of being in communion with Him can justify itself at the bar of reason and of conscience." (Pp. 36-37)

18. In "The Moral Teachings of Jesus" (see note 14) Herrmann takes note of the work of Johannes Weiss, who insisted that Jesus must be understood as preaching an apocalyptic kingdom of God. Yet he cannot really absorb Weiss's point. He recognizes that

Jesus' demands on the disciples were "coloured by this expectation" of the end (p. 177); while he admits that "this expectation had a certain amount of influence" he is quick to add that "the characteristic note in the words of Jesus is due above all to His intentness upon the eternal goal" (p. 202). Above all, Jesus' teachings about love are not dependent on his expectation of the end. Here Herrmann pioneers a solution that became rather popular, especially through works of Hans Windisch in Germany and Amos Wilder in this country: some of Jesus' teaching is eschatologically derived, some is not. For a convenient survey of responses to Weiss's point, see Norman Perrin, The Kingdom of God in the Teaching of Jesus (Philadelphia: Westminster Press, 1968). Weiss's Jesus' Proclamation of the Kingdom of God, tr. and ed. R. H. Hiers and D. L. Holland, is included in "The Lives of Jesus" series (Philadelphia: Fortress Press, 1971).

Still, Herrmann did not try to reject Weiss's conclusions but tried valiantly to see their positive import. (a) "The one great benefit . . . is the way they (studies espousing Weiss's point of view) help us to get rid of such longings and regrets"—longings for specific guidance from Jesus for our particular questions, and regrets that Jesus does not supply them (p. 176). (b) Seeing Jesus' eschatology is really a gain because it "prevents us from following Jesus in the same way that those who aim at perfection in the Church of Rome try to do. . . . Endeavors to imitate Jesus in point inseparable from His especial mission in the world, and His position . . . towards that world . . . have so long injured the cause of Jesus, that our joy will be unalloyed when scientific study at last reveals to everyone the impossibility of all such attempts." ("The Moral Teachings of Jesus," pp. 180-81.) Reliance on Jesus as portrayed in The Communion having been eroded, he now puts the brunt of Jesus' work this way: "Jesus aimed . . . at proving that by no word coming to us from without can we come to know what is good; the undeviating direction of our will must receive its impulse from within. For this purpose He employed a two-fold method: in the first place, as against mere piety, He vindicated the claims of moral righteousness, and in the second place He explained the meaning of love." (P. 192) Here the hand is Herrmann's, but the voice is Immanuel Kant's. Herrmann has shifted ground so as to become less vulnerable to the barrage laid down by Weiss. In contrast with the bold assertions of The Communion, the opening section of "The Moral Teachings of Jesus," which deals with "the sense in which the gospel becomes a real power," is vague and without power.

19. See also his comments in "The Moral Teachings of Jesus" included in Essays on the Social Gospel, p. 150. I fail to see how Robinson could say that Herrmann was indifferent to whether the inner life of Jesus was historical or only an idea. Das Problem des Heiligen Geistes bei Wilhelm Herrmann (Marburg: Universitäts-Buchdruckerei, 1952), p. 70. See Ernst Fuchs, "The Quest of the

Historical Jesus" (1956) in *Studies of the Historical Jesus, SBT* 42 (1964), pp. 21-22.

20. As if speaking to Lessing, Herrmann writes, "No one is ever awakened to true religion by allowing himself to be persuaded that religion in the heart must *begin* with an absolutely unhesitating confidence in narrators" (*The Communion of the Christian with God*, p. 79, my italics).

21. Barth wrote, "The enemy front towards which Herrmann's concept of religion and revelation faced is not the anti-Christian position of modern philosophy and of natural and historical science. . . . The real enemy's position is on the right, within Christian theology itself." He also pointed out that of the three enemies against which Herrmann battled—traditionalism, rationalism, mysticism— the chief was the first. "There is scarcely any other idea which Herrmann presented so frequently and so passionately. . . . What he could cite against superintendent-generals, Consistories, 'positive' theologians, etc., is beyond telling. 'Roman Christianity' was for him embodied in the error 'revelation is doctrine.' 'Dishonesty,' 'immorality,' 'sin,' 'seductive evil'—no terms were too severe for him to use as a label." "The Principles of Dogmatics According to Wilhelm Herrmann," p. 248.

22. "The traditional record may appear doubtful; but the essential content of that record, namely, the inner life of Jesus, has the power to mainfest itself to the conscience as an undeniable fact. That means everything." (*The Communion of the Christian with God*, pp. 235-36)

23. We refer to *The Secular Meaning of the Gospel* (New York: Macmillan, 1963). Page numbers in parentheses refer to this book. The essays in *Theological Explorations* (Macmillan, 1968) are generally peripheral to our questions and are far less stimulating than the book of 1963.

24. For Harmon Holcomb the combination of these aims made the book *prima facie* implausible. "Christology Without God. A Critical Review of 'The Secular Meaning of the Gospel' " in *Foundations* (1965), p. 50.

25. That is, reveal it to the Christian ill at ease in the modern world. Van Buren clearly disavows any apologetic interest in recasting the gospel so as to make it more available to "secular man"; it is an analysis for worried "believers" that he undertakes (p. 20).

26. It is not necessary for our purposes to inquire whether van Buren has understood "blik" rightly or used it appropriately. Harmon Holcomb, however, points out that van Buren follows Antony Flew in misconstruing Hare, for whom a blik is a non-testable assertion that makes it possible to test other assertions. This is something different from a basic attitude, stance, perspective. "Christology Without God," p. 61, n. 3.

27. Holcomb is also sensitive to this appeal to Collingwood, pointing out that Collingwood and those he influenced—the new questers and Bultmann himself—despise what van Buren attempts to honor: empiricism. "Christology Without God," p. 54. Van Buren does not succeed in making the wolf lie down with the lamb.

28. I fail to see why van Buren criticizes the Bultmannians for shifting from the content of the faith to the act of believing, for his own "translation" makes the same move in allegedly functional terms rather than existential ones.

29. Holcomb chides van Buren for not analyzing the function of New Testament language in its own context. Having repudiated that conceptual context, "he is in the awkward position of having to hold that he knows the true intention of the Gospel writers, although they, being blinded by a meaningless belief system, were unable to state what they meant. But how could he know their hidden intent? . . . Furthermore, the verification principle is not a principle for getting at intentions, it is a device for locating sentences which are subject to observational tests, another matter altogether." "Christology Without God," p. 57.

   In his review Langdon Gilkey asks what van Buren is really saying: "that the actual historical meaning of Chalcedon is the same as his own meaning? Or that this is what they *should* have meant, all they validly *could* have meant, or what? . . . Surely an intention hidden beyond what is said is as mysterious and elusive as the old ontological substance!" *JR* 44 (1964), 242.

30. Gilkey scores this on two related counts. (a) It would have been better to say that this is not the religion of Paul or John, but that they were wrong. (b) By refusing to do this, the faces of Wittgenstein and Flew "beam at us from the pages of Acts and Paul, and strangest of all, they keep popping out from behind the pillars of fifth century Alexandria and Chalcedon!" See the review cited in n. 30, p. 241. Though not mentioning Gilkey, van Buren appears to respond affirmatively to this criticism when he writes, "Even the Church Fathers of the fifth century have no peace from us but must be pushed and shoved around to fit into our current conversation as though they too had been products of our times, not of their own. Is nothing sacred to us 'new theologians'?" See "Is Transcendence the Word We Want?" in *Theological Explorations* (New York: Macmillan, 1968), pp. 165-66.

31. Holcomb sees this also. "Christology Without God," p. 55.

32. For example, van Buren says the doctrine of justification, "if it is understood empirically . . . puts us in a cosmological courtroom which is logically meaningless and morally doubtful" (pp. 180-81). But did not Paul know that he was using language metaphorically, struggling to say the unsayable?

33. See also Helmut Gollwitzer, *Von der Stellvertretung Gottes* (Munich: Chr. Kaiser Verlag, 1967), p. 61.

34. In "Is Transcendence the Word We Want?" he identifies this as the central problem: "sorting out the ways in which we justify for ourselves and to each other our ways of seeing, our perspectives, our (to give them a more honorific title) metaphysical beliefs" (pp. 172-73).

35. *Christ the Representative*, trans. David Lewis (London: SCM Press, 1967; German ed., 1965). All page numbers refer to this translation. Gollwitzer devoted a short book to a debate with

Sölle and questions she raises (see note 33); so did Otto Reidinger, under the dramatic title *Gottes Tod and Hegels Auferstehung* (God's Death and Hegel's Resurrection!) (Berlin and Hamburg: Lutherisches Verlagshaus, 1969). In her suggestive tract *Phantasie und Gehorsam* (Stuttgart and Berlin: Kreuz-Verlag, 1968) she deals with freedom engendered by imagination (*Phantasie*). A collection of essays was published as *Atheistisch an Gott glauben* (Olten and Freiburg im Breisgau: Walter-Verlag, 1968). Friedrich Delekat critized the material in "Zur Theologie von Dorothee Sölle," *KuD* 16 (1970), 130-43. We restrict ourselves to *Christ the Representative*.

36. "Representation regards man from the standpoint of time. It gains time for the man who is for the moment incapacitated. Substitution, on the contrary, is a spatial concept. In space, one thing can be replaced by another thing; in time, it is possible for one person to be represented by another person . . . the chief thing which Christ does for us—that is to give us time, new and real time for living, time which his representation makes available for us." (P. 91) This rigid separation of time from space is denied at the outset by Gollwitzer, *Von der Stellvertretung Gottes*, p. 7.

37. Anselm's Christ "stands where we shall never stand . . . his action creates salvation independently of those he represents" (p. 79). Luther's Christ, on the other hand, emphasizes what is missing in Anselm—Christ's relation to us. Hence she draws out the meaning of imputed righteousness as total dependence on how God regards man: salvation is not a new being or essence but a new relationship and a new relation only: "God believes in man" (p. 77). Barth's equating representation with substitution, she says, simply advances the depersonalization of man (pp. 88-89). She is also critical of Bonhoeffer because he interprets the church as representing the world solely in terms of responsibility to it, so that the world needs the church without the church needing the world. This de-eschatologizes the situation because it no longer looks forward to the end of serving (pp. 96-97). In all these "the irreplaceable individual became a mere pawn in God's chess game" (p. 101).

38. "In representation, God's kingdom is attested, but as one which has not been built here. The reminder Christ gives us of identity is the consciousness of the kingdom which has not yet appeared, a consciousness kept awake in the form of pain. . . . The man who participates in the 'sufferings of God' will go on waiting for God's identity, or as it was called in the older terminology, the kingdom of God." (P. 148) On p. 110 she wrote: "In the provisional Christ, the kingdom of God is at the same time present and still not present. In the pure and limited representation of the One, who is now already where we have not yet arrived and who waits for us as the forerunner, there cannot possibly be any ground for the brash and confident Messianism which makes *pogroms* and courts of inquisition possible. The still invisible kingdom of God remains open as something future rather

than as something which already exists and has to be defended by all available means."

39. She works with the unstated axiom that God and man are co-ordinates. Hence she writes: No one can make himself irreplaceable—the subject suffers" (p. 45). In other words, consciousness of one's irreplaceableness is what points to the reality called "God." This is why she refuses to say flatly that God is dead. "For what does is mean to assert that God is dead if, and so long as, there is still something which concerns us unconditionally? Is not atheism merely a different mode of speech from theism? Does not everything depend on anthropology, that is to say, on the problem of the irreplaceable man who is seeking personal identity and can never be free from this search? For if we regard 'God' as the One who by his 'interest' guarantees the infinite value of the subject, by the same token we can also say that this infinite value appears in the consciousness of the individual as an irradicable claim. To realize his true identity is an essential element of man's longing." (P. 44) This appears to be a reformulation of Augustine's "restless heart," though without clarity with respect to the question: Can the "longing" be escalated into evidence that there is someone longed for?

40. Gollwitzer raises this question too. Von der Stellvertretung Gottes, pp. 65, 75, resp.

41. Gollwitzer, ibid., p. 65, points out that in Sölle's method, the gospel brings nothing but an answer to a question already in hand, whereas, he observes, the gospel helps us not only in our questions but in our needs.

42. We concentrate on his Systematic Theology, Vol. II: Existence and the Christ (Chicago: University of Chicago Press, 1957; the entire three-volume work is available in a single volume published in 1967).

43. Tillich himself points this out (Systematic Theology, II, 150).

44. Neither "legalistic liberalism," which emphasized the moral teachings of Jesus, nor "existential liberalism" answered the question, "wherein lies the power to obey the teachings of Jesus or to make the decision for the Kingdom of God. . . . The answer must come from a new reality . . . the New Being in Jesus as the Christ" (II, 106). This is why Tillich insists on the factuality of the appearing of the New Being.

45. Tillich deeply resented the accusation that he interpreted Christ in a Gnostic way. See his comment in his response to Smith's article in JR 46 (1966), 192. One such accusation was made by Robert E. Cushman, "The Christology of Paul Tillich," in The Heritage of Christian Thought (Calhoun Festschrift), R. E. Cushman and E. Grislis, eds. (New York: Harper, 1965), p. 181.

46. II, 106 ff. Paul Althaus saw this too (see p. 151, n. 78).

47. It is suggestive to compare Tillich's insistence on the historical appearance of the New Being with D. F. Strauss' contention that this is precisely what is not necessary. Strauss observed that for Schleiermacher everything "depended on this—that this ideal once lived on earth as a real man." For Strauss himself, on the

other hand, this ideal which actualizes itself evermore, yet never prefectly, in the course of history is a reality more true than any historical embodiment of it, even in Jesus. "The picture of man without sin, of the soul united with God, is the ideal of humanity which has its origin in human nature and its moral-religious foundations; it is developed, clarified and enriched with it, and was especially clarified and enriched through Jesus, but has experienced further development also after him and will continue to do so." This is precisely what Tillich rejects as an aspiration. Like Schleiermacher, Tillich undertakes to wed idealism to the Christian theology of the incarnation by insisting that the ideal man (i.e., the New Being) actually appeared in history. See D. F. Strauss, *Der Christus des Glaubens und der Jesus der Geschichte* (Berlin: Franz Duncker, 1865), pp. 218 ff. This book will be included in "The Lives of Jesus" series (published by Fortress Press), and will be translated and edited by L. E. Keck.

48. D. Moody Smith, Jr., also sees the irony of the fact that while Tillich intends to preserve the historical basis of salvation he actually calls it into question by insisting that "only faith can guarantee its ground." "The Historical Jesus in Paul Tillich's Christology," *JR* 46 (1966), 139.

49. He argues that "historical research cannot paint an essential picture of Jesus after all the particular traits have been eliminated because they are questionable" (*Systematic Theology*, II, 103).

50. Tillich is clearly influenced by his teacher, Martin Kähler. Tillich expressed his debt to Kähler in the Foreword to Carl Braaten's edition of Kähler's *The So-called Historical Jesus and the Historic Biblical Christ* (Philadelphia: Fortress Press, 1964).

51. "The religious picture resulting from it [the incarnation of the New Being] has proved to be the power of transforming existence. This is our primary requirement; and in saying this, I may express the hope that one false view is excluded by everything I have tried to say: namely, the mistake of supposing that the picture of the New Being in Jesus as the Christ is the creation of existential thought or experience. If this were the case, it would be as distorted, tragic and sinful as existence itself, and would not be able to overcome existence. The religious picture of the New Being in Jesus is a result of a new being: it represents the victory over existence which has taken place, and thus created the picture." "A reinterpretation of the Doctrine of the Incarnation," in *Church Quarterly Review* (Jan.-Mar., 1949), quoted by A. T. Mollegen's article, "Christology and Biblical Criticism in Paul Tillich," in *The Theology of Paul Tillich*, C. W. Kegley and R. W. Bretall, eds. (New York: Macmillan, 1952), p. 232.

52. In order to avoid Lessing's problem, Tillich separates completely the factuality of the New Being from the contingency of the historical Jesus. The New Being "might have had another name. . . . Whatever his name, the New Being was and is actual in this man" (*Systematic Theology*, II, 114).

53. David Kelsey rightly observed that this judgment is warranted not by historical research but by "analysis of the dynamics of

revelatory events. Faith is the receiving side in a revelatory event; something objective and finite has to be the giving side. If a man has faith, it follows analytically that he is correlated in revelatory constellation with some holy object." *The Fabric of Paul Tillich's Theology* (New Haven: Yale University Press, 1967), p. 94. Kelsey points out also the reason why the New Being must have appeared in a *personal* life: Tillich's insistence that only man can embody what the New Being is (II, 120)—an illustration of Tillich's use of ontology to provide warrants (but not proofs).

54. Actually, Tillich's view is somewhat more complex. In the original Christian revelation, Jesus himself was the bearer of the New Being, and the picture of him as the Christ by which the disciples responded was the receptive side. Subsequently, this picture becomes the giving side when the gospel is preached; when it is believed, a new receptive side is present. Therefore, the picture does for us what Jesus himself did; the picture, however, has its ground in Jesus as bearer of the New Being. See the analysis by Kelsey, *The Fabric of Paul Tillich's Theology*, pp. 25 ff. But one must ask whether Kelsey has not made Tillich say something different when he concludes that "the disjunction between event given in history and event at least in part *derived* [my italics] from experience is illicit" (p. 34). Tillich is walking a tightrope between two unacceptable alternatives—making Christ a Kantian *Ding an sich* and making revelation a Feuerbachian projection of man's act. In walking this rope, Tillich insists that revelation occurs when both the given and the perception coincide. Instead of insisting on a disjunction, as Kelsey says, Tillich insists on distinction. (See following note.)

55. Tillich insists that the factual side and the receptive side belong together, that they are equally important, and that "only their unity creates the event upon which Christianity is based" (*Systematic Theology*, II, 99). Cushman, however, accuses Tillich of making the receptive side more important because "the faith of the community is the sole datum of knowledge we have of Jesus as the Christ," since the "*event of faith*, the New Being in Christ is all we have to deal with in Christology." "The Christology of Paul Tillich," pp. 175-77. But this surely misses Tillich's intent, because Tillich insists that existence is participation *in* the New Being— that is, Christian existence has a Ground outside itself.

56. As Smith rightly sees ("The Historical Jesus in Paul Tillich's Christology," p. 40). Tillich speaks of the attempt to "liberate Christian faith in its very center from the bondage to scholarship," though theology is very much in it. What is decisive is being personally grasped by the New Being through its picture, and this is invulnerable to scholarship and its probabilities. Tillich sees the risk of historical knowledge and the risk of faith as being on two levels; the former has to do with the mind (and its doubts), the latter with the "character of my ultimate concern" (and its decisions). See his response to Smith, *JR* 46 (1966), 192-93. But is this not too neat a bifurcation?

57. *The Fabric of Paul Tillich's Theology*, p. 98.

58. For Tillich, of the three ways of presenting Jesus in the New Testament (historical anecdote, legends, and mythical meanings), myth is the most important because it speaks directly of the New Being (*Systematic Theology*, II, 151).

59. The word "representative" calls attention to the fact that by careful filtering and selection, accepted data can be compiled in various ways; what matters is whether the data are a fair sampling. This consideration is one of the major factors in persuasive historical writing.

60. The term "warrant" is used more generally here in the sense of "legitimate" or "justify" than in Van Harvey's book (drawing on Toulmin), where he points out that warrants are usually assumed reasons for moving from data to conclusions. Van A. Harvey, *The Historian and the Believer* (New York: Macmillan, 1966), p. 52.

61. See Van Harvey's discussion of the "perspectival image" of Jesus in the Gospels (*ibid.*, pp. 268 ff.). He speaks of the Gospels as "bas reliefs" in which details deemed unimportant by the artist are eliminated in order to expose what is held vital.

62. It is useful to draw some distinctions between Tillich's symbol (which Kelsey rightly terms a "verbal icon") and what we have said about "perception." For one thing, our historically induced perception of Jesus is not a symbol in Tillich's sense because we do not ascribe to it power to mediate the Holy or the New Being or even Jesus' existential selfhood. We are speaking more of a *Gestalt* image of the man. Further, it is unlike Tillich's symbol because the latter disavows any historical fact claims, whereas our image is a way of grasping the historical data in a holistic configuration. Therefore, it is subject to critical judgment about its appropriateness in a way not permitted of his symbol. In addition, his symbol (or the biblical picture of Jesus as the Christ) must be a universal, while ours is not. On the other hand, there are certain similarities. Like the symbol, our picture points beyond itself to Jesus because it is a response to information about him (though for Tillich it is a response to his power as bearer of the New Being). Further, both can be shared by groups. Finally, because the picture of Jesus is not simply "read off" the data but involves the beholder, like the symbol it relates the contemporary to Jesus and thereby manifests his sense of who he himself is as well as who Jesus is.

63. The necessity of such a working model of Jesus for historical inquiry is equally clear, for otherwise the historian merely analyzes pieces; the same is true for the study of the early church, monarchic Israel, or any other historical event. I am pleased to find that Richard R. Niebuhr has published similar observations in "Archegos. An Essay on the Relation between the Biblical Jesus Christ and the Present-day Reader" in *Christian History and Interpretation: Studies Presented to John Knox*, W. R. Farmer, C. F. D. Moule, and R. R. Niebuhr, eds. (London: Cambridge University Press, 1967), p. 80 ff.

64. The theme of discipleship and its relation to the *imitatio* motif in the New Testament (and its milieu) has been investigated

recently by Hans Dieter Betz, *Nachfolge und Nachahmung Jesu Christi im Neuen Testament, BhTh* 37 (Tübingen: J. C. B. Mohr [Paul Siebeck], 1967). Our delineation of discipleship neither presumes nor requires repristination of earliest understanding. That would violate discipleship itself, which is open-ended, not slavish copying.

65. Richard R. Niebuhr, I discover, formulated this aptly: "men belong to God before Christ belongs to them through the Church." This is why he can call attention to the fact that John Knox's emphasis on the "remembered" Jesus in the church is too restrictive, and that Knox has not really concerned himself with how Jesus is apprehended outside this remembering community. "Archegos," pp. 83-84.

66. It will be recalled that Gerhard Ebeling insisted that Jesus sought but one thing—faith (see Chap. 2). Our view is formally parallel to Ebeling's, but materially different because (a) we have not found it possible or necessary to disabuse Jesus of apocalyptic and hence of his concern for the kingdom of God as the manifestation of God's integrity; (b) this entire essay is not set in motion by the need to reduce Jesus to "word" so that the preached word can be shown to grow organically out of Jesus himself. In a word, the faith Jesus himself sought was at least as Jewish as it was Lutheran.

67. This statement should not be read as if it presumed Dodd's "realized eschatology" to be the definitive solution. There is a broad consensus today that for Jesus God's kingdom was manifest and accessible through his work and that at the same time he expected it to "come." But in no case should it be inferred that Jesus believed God would *become* king, as if he were but heir apparent now, a sort of heavenly Prince of Wales. In other words, Jesus grasped the kingdom as foretaste in a way quite parallel to Paul's understanding of the Spirit as "down payment." This tension between the "already" and the "not yet" should not be reduced to "personal experience," as Norman Perrin (and many others influenced by existentialism) appears to do. *The Kingdom of God in the Teaching of Jesus* (Philadelphia: Westminster Press, 1963), p. 191. One can agree with his formulation in his subsequent book: "In the teaching of Jesus the emphasis is not upon a future for which men must prepare, even with the help of God; the emphasis is upon a present which carries with it the guarantee of the future. The present that has become God's present guarantees that all futures will be God's future." *Recovering the Teaching of Jesus* (New York: Harper, 1967), p. 205. But the point is that this future is oriented to creation as a whole, not simply to selves.

68. *Radical Monotheism and Western Culture* (New York: Harper, 1940; quoted from 1960 ed.), p. 16.

69. Ernst Fuchs is skeptical about this, and for somewhat strange reasons. Though he is concerned to make Jesus the bringer of the kingdom in such a way as to preclude his being its herald, he argues that thinking of the kingdom as near raises the problem

of the delay of the parousia, and says Jesus had no such problem! Nor does he want to grant any form of continuation between beginning and consummation, because this would erode the full presence of the kingdom in Jesus. Hence he concludes that neither the kingdom nor repentance made up the content of Jesus' message. "Jesus' Understanding of Time," in *Studies of Historical Jesus*, trans. Andrew Scobie, *SBT* 42 (1964), 116 ff.; 143. Here historiography is made the slave of existential theology. Stranger still is the way in which it occurs: by word count, a rather "positivistic" approach to Jesus' message, he shows that "repentance" was not part of Jesus' vocabulary. One would have thought that existential analysis would show that repentance is what Jesus was all about whether he used the word or not.

70. It ought to be evident that assimilating Jesus as the model, as sketched here, is not to be confused with emulating him as a moral ideal; that would be a strenuous striving for perfection which would deny the central quality of Jesus' own life. For further reflections on such a mode of discipleship, see James Gustafson, *Christ and the Moral Life* (New York: Harper, 1968), pp. 154 ff.

71. Walter Hartmann formulated it well: "Jesus assumes the place of the first citizen of the Kingdom of God. Not that he claims this place, but he actually assumes it in that he proclaims the irruption of the kingdom and lives his life in the reality of the kingdom. Jesus is temporally the first who lives in the reality of the irrupting kingdom." "Reich Gottes," *Kontexte* IV (Stuttgart and Berlin: Kreuz Verlag, 1967), p. 43.

72. Gordon Kaufman formulated it aptly: "God's kingship, his actual sovereignty over man, is precisely man's free and obedient response to God's loving will." *Systematic Theology*, p. 384. Van Buren's interest in the freedom motif was not misplaced; it was simply not grounded in the kingdom of God.

73. Paul put it well: "Of one thing I am certain: the One who started the good work in you will bring it to completion by the Day of Christ Jesus." (Phil. 1:7; NEB)

74. For an analysis of the role of Ps. 22 in the story of Jesus' death, see Hartmut Gese, "Psalm 22 in das Neue Testament," *ZThK* 65 (1968), 1-22.

75. Also, the inseparability of the risen Lord from the Spirit (whatever one makes in detail of II Cor. 3:17-18) means that the presence of the Spirit as down payment or firstfruits is a pledge for consummation of what is now inaugurated in trust, a consummation pledged by the one who is continuous with the Jesus of history but no longer restricted to the past. In various ways, other New Testament writings make the same point. The Johannine Jesus promises that he will not leave the disciples "orphans'" but will return as Paraclete (or will send the Paraclete—John 14:15-18, 26; 15:26; 16:7); I John speaks of Jesus as the "advocate" with the Father (I John 2:1); Hebrews emphasizes Jesus as the High Priest representing us before God; and the Apocalypse shows

visually how the once-slain Jesus, now Lord, will keep faith with his saints who face martyrdom.

76. See also H. Richard Niebuhr, *The Responsible Self*, p. 83.

77. I am keenly aware that more has been said concretely here about salvation *from* than about salvation *for*, that more attention has been given to justification (right relation to God) than to sanctification (development of Christomorphic life). Restoration of balance by exploring the positive effects of trusting Jesus must remain, therefore, a self-assignment with high priority.

5

"When we reason as depersonalized public minds we look for recurrent patterns and laws in events so that we can say in the midst of initially novel experiences, 'There it is again'; but reasoning faith looks for the presence of one faithful person in the multiplicity of events that happen to the self and learns to say, 'There he is again.' "

H. RICHARD NIEBUHR

THE HISTORICAL JESUS AND THE CHARACTER OF GOD

"The difference between Jesus' present and the Father's future was ever and again actualized in the surrender of the man Jesus to the coming Reign of God that he proclaimed, insofar as it was the future of another. . . . Jesus pointed away from himself; therefore, the interpretation of that which appeared in him must go beyond the appearance of Jesus, to God. . . ."

WOLFHART PANNENBERG

I. The Legitimacy of the Question

We have argued that the historical Jesus is central to Christian faith, that in preaching he functions as a question before he is affirmed to be the answer, and that trusting him is salvific. We must now address the question central to the entire discussion: How is the historical Jesus related to the understanding of God? This question is critical, first, because he is central for Christian believing in God as well as for "the Christian faith"; [1] second, because the question he himself raises is the question of God (not as an object of thought alone); third, because paramount trust in him is ingressive trust in God.

This central theological complex has been the traditional

point of departure for Christology. Commonly, one begins with themes such as the revelation of God in Jesus Christ, initiating the discussion by analyzing revelation and its various media and then moving to show how these are to be coordinated with Jesus Christ. Or one can divide the christological map into the Person and the Work of Christ, dealing first with matters such as the incarnation, deity of Christ or two natures, and second with his threefold office of prophet, priest, and king. In such procedures, one has in view the farthest reaches of "Jesus as the Christ," and is especially attentive to the post-historical Jesus—to Jesus as he is contemporary to the church and its understanding of God, world, and man— and to the pre-existent Word. As we said at the outset, however, we have been concerned here with exploring the potential of the historical Jesus for faith and theology, and that in so doing we hope to lead into larger theological questions, not away from them.[2] Now it is incumbent on us to suggest ways of making good this promise. Not that we expect simply to flip the page over to show that the whole christological discourse still stands unaffected on the other side. Rather, our aim is to suggest how one can move from the role of the historical Jesus as sketched here to a more explicit *theo*logical discussion. Before we can do that, of course, we must show that we are neither arbitrary nor encapsulated traditionalists when we relate Jesus to the understanding of God.

The very fact that we must lay out in elemental form the legitimacy and necessity of exploring the relation of the historical Jesus to God attests the relatively new situation in which we live and reflect theologically.[3] Two observations make this clear: the first is that we can no longer move from God to Jesus; the second is that it is not self-evident to many that we can move from Jesus to God. In establishing the viability of relating Jesus to God (Christology), we must first take account of these two sides of the problem.

A. *From God to Jesus?* We cannot begin with the understanding of God in order to understand Jesus because "God"

209

himself has become a root problem,[4] at least for many. State-ments such as "God's love is revealed in Jesus" no longer clarify Jesus because "God's love" is precisely what we know less about than Jesus. Such statements are not invalid, or untrue, or lacking the possibility of becoming meaningful. The point is, rather, that before they can have meaning their referent—Jesus—must have content. Arguments about the "divinity of Christ" appear as museum pieces because not enough is known about divinity for the predication of this to say anything about Jesus.

As we reflect on our relatively new situation, two observa-tions will help us from going astray. First, we do not intend to suggest that in the past "God" was fixed point to which Jesus was related, as in a surveyor's work. Actually, the under-standing of God was modified and revolutionized by faith in Jesus, as the whole dogmatic tradition attests in various ways. Just as in the process of interpreting Jesus by means of the Old Testament, the Bible itself was reinterpreted and made new (see Chapter 3), so the conception of God was recast in light of Jesus and what was affirmed through one's trust in him. That, in fact, is precisely the hallmark of a revelatory event.[5] Still, in those days it was probably easier to move from God to Jesus than it is today.[6] Second, we do not view our context as a tragedy that has befallen theology. Without in any way inpugning the past, we can say that our situation may well be more appropriate to the core Christian insight in the long run. Our predecessors may, after all, have overextended themselves with regard to what they knew about God with the result that their Christology had to come out in predetermined forms. By contrast, the contingency on Jesus for which we have been contending may turn out to be more congenial to the deep-running Christian intuition that not only the act of trust but the process of thinking about God is Christomorphic.

It may be helpful to recall our earlier observation about the character of incarnational Christology. We remarked that it is characteristic of incarnational theology to know what is necessary about Jesus before one studies him. This is because in incarnation Christology, the decisive factor is always that which was incarnated, which pre-existed, as Tillich's New Being shows. Tillich does not really learn anything from the event of Jesus because he uses it to document and to exhibit what he already knew on other grounds. Jesus embodies the previously ascertained reality and illumines aspects of it in his lifework; but thereby one nullifies the radical dependence on Jesus[7] for which we have been pressing and which we believe is foundational in the New Testament itself. One can appreciate the reasons why incarnation Christology became the most viable mode of relating God to Jesus without foregoing a critical estimate of its long-term effects and without foreclosing the validity of attempting an adequate Christology in a different mode. After all, neither the Synoptics nor Acts knows anything of incarnation theology, and Paul's understanding of the "person" of Christ ought not be read through the eyes of John (more precisely, through the way John was understood in light of subsequent creeds and the more recent preoccupation with revelation in Christian theology).[8]

Our reflections do not disallow categorically the possibility of speaking of the self-movement of God in Jesus, of God's manward act in Christ (not limited to incarnation, of course). Logically, of course, it makes sense to begin just here. But the logical ordering of thought already worked out must not be confused with finding the starting point in thinking. For example, logically the doctrine of creation stands before the discussion of redemption; yet every theologian knows that the Christian understanding of creation is developed in light of redemption, so that one might well begin with the new creation in Christ and as a result of Christ. In other words, in starting with the historical Jesus to reflect on God, we are beginning at the point which for Christians has always been pivotal [9] and where contemporary persons can more readily commence, not denying the logical priority of God-talk over Christology, even less rejecting categorically incarnation Christology. In affirming that incarnation is not the most appropriate place to begin because it too commonly vitiates the historical, we leave open the question whether it may

211

be a proper place to end [10]—as one way of stating the ontic basis for what has occurred in and through Jesus.

B. *From Jesus to God?* We also take cognizance of our situation in saying that it is not self-evident that we can move from Jesus to God. On the one hand, some, like van Buren, deliberately eschew God-talk and refuse to move beyond Jesus to God because such a move is declared to be out of bounds. On the other hand, others may deem such a move otiose. Because Jesus, they might argue, can be adequately grasped as the man for others there is no need to raise the God question at all. Despite the meteoric career of the death of God theology, it did succeed in exposing sharply the inflation that eroded the purchasing power of language about God. Consequently there is undeniable appeal in the resistance to opening the question once more. Still, the question of God cannot be avoided when one takes with utmost seriousness precisely the historical Jesus.

In the first place, one simply cannot subtract God from Jesus and have Jesus left. (That this statement has nothing to do with the two-natures doctrine should be clear.) The assumption that one can describe Jesus accurately and interpret him adequately without getting into the God-question is simply a retrojection of certain forms of modernity onto Jesus. In principle this process is identical with earlier efforts to make him the prototype of preferred theology, whether Schleiermacher's paragon of God-consciousness or Renan's anti-institutional hero of pure religion. Some might wish Jesus had replied to the wealthy seeker, "Love your neighbor as yourself, and if the question of God is still of interest to you, you will find the meaning of 'God' in your neighbor." But the fact is that Jesus said the primal obligation of man is to love God, and he made the obligation to the neighbor indivisible from the primal one. It would be more honest to say that he erred in doing so or that our historical situation makes his contention untenable for us than to subvert what he did say in the name of interpretation. That would reduce interpretation to the craft of locating what is appropriable.

212

Historiography is by no means invulnerable to distortion and subversion, but it remains our major defense against absorbing Jesus into modern secular piety. Not least among the roles of historical study for theological work is its capacity to keep us honest. The point is that no one can deal with Jesus of Nazareth without confronting the question of God, because his concentration on God and his kingdom is what was constitutive of Jesus. Consequently, the Jesus who remains after God-talk has been nullified is simply unrecognizable. We have not yet indicated, of course, just how God and Jesus are related; we have insisted only that their correlation is not optional for the interpreter.

In the second place, the question of God, in a rudimentary way, is virtually unavoidable as soon as one asks van Buren (and others) to account for his blik. He attempts to circumvent this, to be sure, by his canons of interpretation according to which the apostles' statement, "God raised Jesus" is declared to mean that "what happened to them was fundamental to their life and thought." [11] But one cannot give unequivocal allegiance to Jesus without raising the question whether this has any basis beyond habit or coincidence, whether this is simply the lingering smile after the cat has disappeared. When van Buren is content to say, "This is how it is with Christians because this their 'blik,'" he overlooks two things: one is that Christians have always been committed to Jesus because they related him to God (or as many would have insisted, God related himself to them through Jesus) so that it has yet to be shown that on van Buren's basis anyone would commit himself to the Christian blik about Jesus; the other is that without any reference to God the Christian blik is reduced to a henotheistic religion [12] like that of the pre-monotheist Israelite era in which Yahweh was affirmed to be the God of Israel, while Baal, Marduk, *et al.* were conceded to be the gods of other peoples. While it is true that Christianity is but one of man's religions (and a shrinking minority religion at that) it has always understood itself as a universal religion not primarily for imperialist reasons but because no monotheist religion can ignore the implication that is insight pertains to all men.

In short, if one takes the historical Jesus seriously he must confront the question of God because passionate trust in God was constitutive for Jesus; further, he who trusts Jesus discovers that the question is acute.

But it is one thing to be persuaded that trusting Jesus obligates us to deal with the question of God, and another to perceive just how Jesus clarifies our understanding of God and makes trust in God—Jesus' God—possible. And with this issue we are at the heart of the matter.

II. The God of Jesus

A. *The Task.* Since we are contending for our contingency on Jesus for our perception of God, and for our relationship to him as well, we must outline briefly what it means to understand God through Jesus and how it is possible to do so. Otherwise we are in danger of attributing our ideas to him and then claiming to have derived them from the Christ-event simply because we are Christians. Before we enter the discussion itself, it is necessary to get the scope of the discussion clearly in view. Accordingly, we shall indicate what we intend to avoid and what we intend to pursue. Briefly, we intend to avoid appealing to those aspects of Jesus which are most problematic for the critic (his mind and inner life), and we shall pursue what is so self-evident that it is neglected or neutralized—the Jewishness of Jesus. Both merit further comment before their import is clear.

First, we are not sounding a call to reproduce in ourselves Jesus' ideas of God or his personal piety, or his understanding of existence—though these are not excluded categorically. But what we shall attempt to do is to engage in our own theologizing with respect to Jesus; concretely, he shall be the focal material that shapes our understanding of God. This means that we shall have in view the whole Jesus (root perceptions and assumptions no less than words, deeds, career, and death). Only when we perceive God through the prism of the event of Jesus can we justly speak of God's revealing himself in Jesus.

In undertaking this task, we are not so naïve as to assume that Jesus is accessible to us as a *Ding an sich* or to forget that our own questions about God and the operational understanding of him sensitize us to dimensions of Jesus which might remain unattended had we other questions and conceptions of God. *The role of Jesus in our understanding of God is not that of initiator*—as if we were at zero-point until we learned of him. Rather, *Jesus intersects with those understandings of God and with questions about him which we already have.* Jesus intersects us as we are under way, already involved in a network of trusts and understandings. This is why Jesus does not bring an understanding of God the way a truck delivers fuel to an empty barrel; rather, he calls into question what we think we know about God (including what we "know" about his death!) and compels us to rethink and reorder our conceptions by arresting their present flow. Actually then, nothing is gained, and much impeded, by denying our "interest" in the subject precisely because our interest and "pre-understanding" will be called into question at the intersecting point. The primacy of Jesus as revealer of God manifests itself in his actual capacity to redirect our understanding of God. We hope to show that it is the contour of the whole Jesus which does this, not his ideas or his selfhood alone.

Nor should it be concluded that this function of Jesus in our own theologizing is an arbitrary Christian *use* of Jesus. Actually, this role for Jesus extends his original role. In his own situation Jesus himself intersected those understandings of God which he encountered. In other words, Jesus calls into question both those understandings of God which prevent trust and the Christian understandings that repeatedly pull theology into ideology.

The crucial question is whether such a mode of theological understanding as we have called for can be carried out. In affirming that it can, we must circumnavigate three shoals, each of which might prove disastrous.

(a) The first is the tendency to appropriate Jesus' ideas of God, the danger of holding that Jesus reveals God truly because he conceptualized him accurately. This assumption errs in two ways. On the one hand, it makes Jesus a rationalist, a theologian who first had an insight and then sought for ways to communicate and illustrate it for farmers and fisherfolk. It would not only make Jesus a theologian who was concerned to impart precise concepts, but would make him a propagandist for a theology as well. On the other hand, such an approach would make rationalists (or romantics) of us as well, because it would commit us to ascertaining and appropriating those insights and concepts. That would be but a reformulation of the old liberal view that it is Jesus' own religion which is to be appropriated. Furthermore, it would restrict our own theologizing to that of Jesus.[13] But on that basis, Jesus would be not the material about which we think theologically but the magister of our theological thoughts; biblicism would be replaced with Jesusism. This is why we move in a different direction. Instead of recovering and re-pristinating Jesus' concepts about God, we are seeking a way to expose the implications for *theology* of Jesus' mode of interpreting and effectuating in advance the kingdom of God. Just as one speaks of a Christology implicit in his work, so one can—and must—speak of a theology implicit in it as a whole.

(b) The second shoal to be avoided is that of the new quest's premium on the selfhood of Jesus which came to expression in his work. In Robinson's terms, "history is the act of intention, the commitment, the meaning for the participants, behind the external occurrence. In such intention and commitment the self of the participant actualizes itself, and in this act of self-actualization the self is revealed." [14] This is an amazing statement. As a definition of history, it simply will not do; it reads like absolute idealism, only that instead of speaking of ideas or *Geist* manifesting itself in externals it is selfhood that is actualized in externalizing itself. Moreover, it produces an ideological history because just as Tillich's Jesus was always illustrating the New Being, so this one is always

216

expressing a selfhood cut to *our* specifications. But the fact is that we have no access at all to the inner life of Jesus, to the private self, save by logic. We recall that it is precisely at this point that Ogden and Harvey criticized the new quest for assuming that one can infer selfhood from what is public, as if there were a clear and constant one-to-one relation between the inner man and his public life, as if in Jesus' case the articulation of selfhood were unimpeded by finitude or frustration, as if at every point his selfhood "came to speech" perfectly.[15] But we are moving in a different direction, because we do not quietly presuppose "sinless perfection" (to speak with Schleiermacher) in the event of Jesus. Just as preoccupation with Jesus' ideas binds us to concepts that he held, so concern for Jesus' selfhood or intention commits us once again to a theology of his inner life. But the soul of Jesus, to use classical terminology for the same thing, is not what reveals God or saves man; it is the total Jesus through whom God is known. Consequently, we shall concentrate on the public life of Jesus. That is, in relating the historical Jesus to the understanding of God, we are appropriating the consequences of thoroughgoing criticism: instead of complaining that Jesus has been reduced to a pitifully small pile of data, we hope to show that the data are quite sufficient to be decisive for our understanding of God. This is why we are reflecting theologically about what can be known of the public life of Jesus which was set into motion by the kingdom of God, and are not requiring our understanding of God to be traceable to Jesus' inferred selfhood.

In avoiding these two shoals, it must be emphasized, we are not denying that Jesus had an understanding of God, or that his self-understanding is relevant. That would be absurd. What we are seeking to do, however, is to avoid limiting the material for our theologizing to the one or the other. Here too we proceed in accord with Jesus and the New Testament. Jesus did not make his self-interpretation the content of his mission as is assumed repeatedly. Moreover, he could scarcely have made his work as a whole the datum of theological reflection so long as that work was still in process.

217

That could begin only when his mission was accomplished. This is why Paul and the early church were impelled to reflect theologically about the whole event of Jesus. The Synoptics tell the forward movement of Jesus' career from the standpoint of the result of the whole, and John's daring achievement is to make this viewpoint, implicit in the Synoptics, explicit even on the lips of Jesus.

(c) The third shoal is of a somewhat different sort. It concerns the fact that nineteen centuries have rolled by since Jesus expected the kingdom. Does the fact that the kingdom did not come *when* he expected it nullify *what* he expected and above all, *whom* he expected? The question concerns not simply the viability of Jesus' own ideas or calculations. Jesus does not qualify as the revelatory event when his ideas about the End can be proved right, nor does his calendrical miscalculation disqualify him as the lens through which we see God sharply. What matters for our reflection is not dodging the fact *that* Jesus' life was shaped by his expectation and by the God he expected. It is the contour of his kingdom-shaped life which is decisive here.

Elementary reflections may help us see what is implied by this. Not only does perceiving a life holistically require us to use images to grasp it as a whole, as we saw, but a life functions as a symbol when it becomes the medium for further reflection or disclosure. This is what it means, in this context, to speak of a revelatory event. In the case of Jesus, the event as a whole was shaped as it was because of the expectation of the kingdom. (Because Jesus did not make this point explicitly, the historian arrives at this judgment by probing for the hub that held the diverse spokes together in a single wheel. See also Chap. 1. The whole network of words, deeds, and death which we call "Jesus" was pulled into a pattern by the magnetic power of the kingdom and hence reflected the impingement of that kingdom on his life and work. This was not simply a matter of Jesus working out the implications of a root idea. Rather, it was a matter of being grasped by a perception in such a way that the whole career became a celebration of the kingdom's coming and

218

thereby became its vanguard as well. This is why we cannot simply ferret out that root idea and work with that. As we shall see later, it was this mode of grasping the future which is decisive for what we reflect about theologically. This configuration of Jesus' life has revelatory potential for whoever is prepared to engage his own with it, to look Godward through that pattern. This is why one can say that Jesus' life reveals God in a way that his ideas do not; more precisely, his life continues to disclose God, not merely that his concepts once did. In ongoing reflection on what is implicit in the coordinates of Jesus' pattern, one's understanding of God can be realigned by what one is permitted to see, and compelled to see, by looking at God through Jesus.[16]

The second aspect of our task is pressing the Jewishness of Jesus. It was as a Jew that Jesus trusted God, not as man in general believing in the divine in general. Jesus perceived God through the way the Hebrew Bible was understood in his time. It was present to him not the way it is present to us who have learned about J and P, or about the three Isaiahs; rather the Hebrew Bible was present to him in the exegetical tradition that was part of his milieu just as the Letters of Paul are present to us only in the matrix of our Protestant, Catholic, or Jewish stance toward Paul. While we cannot, and will not, repristinate Jesus' Jewish way of hearing the Bible and of trusting God, we are not free to emancipate him from Judaism either, as if his Jewishness had to be overcome before he could have disciples among us multicolored gentiles. Nevertheless, by trusting Jesus, who is coordinated with the kingdom of God as he was, we are Judaized in our root perceptions and trusts, but without becoming Jews. This is to say that Jesus' Jewishness was not the husk around the kernel of truth as Harnack thought, but belongs to the man constitutively. If on occasion he is critical of his tradition, he is so from within, not as an "emancipated Jew." [17] This is why Christian theology cannot treat Jesus' Jewishness as a mere framework or background and still be loyal to this particular man from Nazareth.[18] In anticipation of what we shall say later, it is the Jewishness of Jesus which saves us from a gentile cult in the name of Jesus.

B. *The God of the Kingdom.* In the foregoing chapter we sketched the import of Jesus' perception of God's kingdom for human redemption. Our aim now is to take note of its import on Jesus' public life and to reflect on that for our understanding of God. In this way, we shall seek an explicitly *theological* understanding of the God of the kingdom.

Despite the fact that the kingdom was made paramount in Protestant theology more than a century ago, this still remains a major task.[19] Up till now, dominant concerns have been of a different sort. (1) The Ritschlian and idealistic interpretation of the kingdom had to be replaced by a truly historical one; through the work of Johannes Weiss and Albert Schweitzer it became inescapably clear that the kingdom that Jesus preached was grounded in apocalyptic theology. (2) As a result of this shock, it seemed necessary to overcome the apocalyptic interpretation of the kingdom. One strategy relied on existential hermeneutics, which, by shifting the discussion from "future" to "futurity" as a mode of the present, attempted to rescue the message of Jesus from the discard pile of untenable chiliasms.[20] Another relied on the presentness of the kingdom in Jesus' own work (Dodd's "realized eschatology") to neutralize the future expectation in the tradition of Jesus' words. (In the work of Fuchs and Ebeling, this presentness is given an existential interpretation as well.) Today, the consensus is that both futuristic and present dimensions must be granted to Jesus' understanding of the kingdom. In any case, the dominant concern for many New Testament critics has been the temporal question: kingdom future or present, kingdom future and present, kingdom as pure future (futurity), etc. (3) Theologians influenced by Barth and Reinhold Niebuhr, on the other hand, were more concerned to deny the Ritschlian (and vulgarized social gospel) contention that the kingdom is a moral task and to insist that it is *God's* kingdom in a radical and consistent sense. Recently, however, with the emergence of Wolfhart Pannenberg and Jürgen Moltmann we see a renewed interest in the *theo*logical concern with the kingdom of God. These men shift away from the individualistic understanding of the kingdom which has dominated existential interpretation and recover the social and universal scope of God's future. While these horizons are important also for our own pursuit, we concentrate here on the impact of Jesus' perception and proclamation of the kingdom for our understanding of God.

Ascertaining the God of the kingdom—the perception of God inherent in the message of the kingdom—means that we do what Jesus did not do; that is, we theologize. Jesus himself was not a theologian. Consequently, we must penetrate his work to those convictions and perceptions which surface in his words and deeds. In this sense one might speak, with Fuchs and Ebeling, of "what came to expression in Jesus" (*was in Jesus zur Sprache gekommen ist*).

We begin with the established philological fact that the kingdom means the kingship, the kingly rule of God more than it means a realm.[21] The kingship of God is the effectuation of God in his role as sovereign creator—as effective king he is redeemer of what he has caused to be. The kingdom's coming, then, is God's coming into actual, operational kingship without challenge. Pannenberg has rightly observed that "God's being and existence cannot be conceived apart from his rule. . . . The deity of God is his rule." [22] Given the human situation, the effectuation of God's rule means overturning those aspects of the present which defy God's godhood and fulfilling those aspects of the present which affirm it and reflect it in anticipation grounded in trust.[23]

The situation of God's rule over the natural world is more difficult to discern and discuss partly because we are not accustomed to thinking theologically about death and the "law of the fang." Arguments for the existence of God based on nature characteristically have rested on design and direction (the cosmological and teleological arguments), and have chosen to gloss over the question of why all living things die and why the animal world is predatory. Though commonly treated in connection with the problem of evil, this aspect of nature has not been seen sufficiently as questioning radically the character of God. Instead of using the balance of nature as an item in the argument from design, one could just as easily grasp it as an argument against the character of God.

221

(Man, of course, is scarcely less predatory than the cougar.)[24] Certain apocalyptic theologies, on the other hand, were sensitive to the bondage of the mortal world to death and perceived it as mocking the affirmation that God is the author of life and that he is rightly perceived as the living God. If God be the author of life, why is everything created subject not only to death but to predatory life? [25] Hence apocalyptic theology— the matrix of Jesus' understanding of the kingdom—developed the view that redemption in the kingdom would include the end of death and a restoration of "peace" in nature—the wolf shall lie down with the lamb.[26] This mythic vision implies a transmutation of the world as we know it;[27] yet, by definition, the content of that transformed world cannot be discerned now since every description is but the projected obverse of the known.[28] But one can trust the One in whose hands it lies and rely on his integrity to make good his deity as author of life, by his defeating the ultimate enemy, death.[29] In other words, the kingship of God is that state of affairs in which the entire creation adequately reflects the will of God.

With these observations in mind, we can explore the theological import of the kingdom's role in the public career of Jesus.

In the first place, Jesus understood the kingdom as an event in which grace and judgment are the obverse of each other, for he announced that God's kingship was at hand, as nearing in such a way as to make possible one's response to it ahead of time, before one can say, "Lo, here!" or "Lo, there!" [30] This means that God functions as king, not when the culture achieves its optimum potential, but when God himself determines to act decisively. This is an anthropomorphic way of saying that the kingdom of God is not the fulfillment of the present but a rectifying alternative to it. Consequently, the word "God" does not refer undialectically to the Ground of what is, but to the Ground of what ought to be and will be, and refers only dialectically to the Ground of the present. Hence the God of the kingdom is not the ideological bulwark of the status quo but a threat to it; hence the kingdom's coming in God's own time implies the judgment of God upon the present. The news that the kingdom is accessible now is good news because it offers proleptic participation in it for those who trust the news and its herald. Since the coming of the kingdom is set in motion by God's freedom and not by man's attainments, it is an event of grace; likewise, since news of its coming intersects with the present, response to it now is also an event of grace. Consequently, had Jesus theologized he would have been a theologian of grace no less than Paul. Failure to see this accounts for the fact that so much of the Jesus-Paul debate is misplaced.[31]

We must now restate this somewhat formal point in relation to Jesus' public career. When Jesus is seen holistically, it is evident that his deeds, demeanor, and career are all shaped by this perception as well as his words. He lived and worked out of the future into the present, and by so doing reconstituted it as the beachhead of the future. We recall that Fuchs pointed out that it was hardly possible for Jesus to make the *idea* of God's judgment more radical than that held by John the Baptist; "all that Jesus could do was to grasp the *time* of the rule of God in a new way; i.e., he could attempt to make the time of the rule of God his own." [32] That is, he could venture to live now out of the kingdom. This means that from Jesus' style, no less than from his words, one infers the conception of God's kingship of which it is the reflex. It remains, of course, our theological inference, not Jesus' big idea.

Although Jesus celebrated and announced the impingement of the kingdom on the present, he evidently did not have a program, an ideological commitment to a plan of action for which he evolved strategies. Apparently, he was impelled by the coming of the kingdom in such a way that he acted with a surprising spontaneity and with a seeming inconsistency (when measured by an ideology) as well. He observed the Sabbath and yet on occasion did so in ways that perplexed the scrupulous; he galvanized a community around himself and yet moved freely among those not part of it; he accepted at least one Zealot to this circle yet was fundamentally critical of Zealotism, saying that if compelled to carry the Roman trooper's pack one mile one should volunteer the second as well.[33] This multi-faceted pattern discloses his freedom from an ideological understanding of God as the bulwark of a given group or program already in existence. It will be recalled that in Chapter 1 we preferred to speak of what was characteristic rather than pressing what is distinctive. Since none of the above polarities can be eliminated on critical grounds, it is apparent that holding all these dimensions of his career together was precisely what was characteristic of Jesus. Our task, therefore, is to reflect theologically on this characteristic contour of Jesus.

We have already seen (Chapter 4) that the motif of Jesus' mission can be understood as the trustworthiness of God. In light of what we just noted, this motif takes on particular significance: no group or party is simply confirmed in its conception of God. This is surely not a sign of disengagement from his people. Just the opposite. Given the intense rivalry among groups and parties in his day, not to mention the secularized and Hellenized Jews who doubtless had little patience with much of the debate, the truly remarkable thing is that Jesus committed himself to "the lost sheep of the house of Israel" without appropriating the viewpoint of any group. He had a passion for his people—Amos Wilder aptly called him a patriot[34]—but refused to let any extant interpretation of that loyalty determine what he said and did. Because he saw the whole Israel as "lost" and not merely those segments which from one group's point of view needed redemption, he identified with all in such a way as to be claimed by none. Instead of ascribing this mode of action to Jesus' equivocation or ambivalence—a psychological interpretation—or to a series of unsuccessful efforts to recruit followers from a broad socioeconomic spectrum—a sociological view—our task is to ask for the theological import of such a career, and to do so on the premise that this pattern is derived from the center, the constraint that the kingdom placed upon him. That is one way of reflecting theologically about the event called Jesus.

By depriving each group or person of his right to appeal to God as the bulwark of his settled convictions, and by doing so in the name of the kingdom, Jesus implies that God's trustworthiness is his fidelity to himself, that God can be counted on to keep faith with his own integrity, and that this is the starting point for the proper understanding of God. Furthermore, this means that God's integrity stems from his freedom to be himself and is not to be measured by the extent to which he fulfills any group's ideology. Jesus' career exemplifies the words, "My ways are not your ways." This is why the kingdom of God is not simply the extension of anyone's present into the future where it is consummated, but is rather the future's claim to restructure everyone's present, including present understandings of God. Consequently every person whom Jesus meets is tacitly or openly called to repent, not only those whom one group might deem sinners. Jesus does not have a doctrine of original sin; but he sees that no one can assume that he stands in right relation to the God of the kingdom and that each must reorder his life if he trusts the God who comes. In this light, the demands of the Sermon on the Mount, for example, are concrete instances of how life is restructured in response to the effectuating kingship of the God who is faithful to himself.

It is not only Jesus' actions which seem to lack consistency from a point of view, but his teachings as well. Jesus' word includes both stern threat and calm reassurance in the name of God, both apocalyptic disaster and continuing providence implicit in existing nature and society.[35] Rather than eliminate one or the other from the "authentic Jesus," [36] or subordinate one to the other, here too we must ask for the *the*ological significance of this seeming incoherence. We may approach it this way: a radically apocalyptic theology is in danger of unwittingly shortchanging the doctrine of creation; on the other hand, a strictly wisdom theology might easily shortchange the doctrine of sin (and Fall). If the former tends to despise the present world in the name of the coming one, the latter tends to extend the present into the future by minimizing the radical resistance to God which characterizes the present.[37] By affirming both, Jesus implies that the God who comes is the Creator upon whom the world depends when it is truly world and that his coming as judge and redeemer is the bringing to fullness that which is built into the world but presently denied. The effectuation of God's kingship does not obliterate creation but actualizes it *as* creation, as world contingent upon the Creator alone. In other words, Jesus perceived God to be faithful not only to himself but to the world as well; more precisely, his fidelity to himself manifests itself *as* fidelity to the world because the existence of the world is grounded in his love. This is why the processes of nature (growth of seed, action of leaven) and of human life in the world (buying and baking) can be used as appropriate metaphors for the rule of God in the world. Only when both sides are seen do we perceive the basis for calling the trustworthy God "Father." [38] This is why a rigorously dualistic Christianity (whether a daulism based on spirit and flesh or on God and Satan) falls out of step with Jesus. As we already noted, the "otherworldliness" of Christianity, if it is to breed true to itself, must be for the sake of the world.[39] Moreover, the God of the kingdom is committed to societal man, not to solitary man, for societal structures are part of creation.[40] Every attempt to individualize the kingdom of God is part of a move to understand God's rule to be truly effective when the self is distanced from the world (*entweltlicht*).[41] Jesus, however, knows nothing of such a kingship over monads, because for him the king who comes is the Creator.

In the second place, the available kingdom was not simply and flatly here, but also coming. It called for *anticipatory* celebration and repentance, not for joyous appropriation of the present alone. Moreover, because fulfillment did not occur as expected, we must draw out the consequences for the understanding of God and man of precisely this unfulfilled Jesus who is the lens through which we see God truly. Concretely, just as in the foregoing paragraphs we dealt with the God of the kingdom as the One who restructures present trusts and concepts of God, so we now comment briefly on the God who keeps the future open and to whom we therefore pray, "Thy kingdom come."

It is at this point that the Jewishness of Jesus is of special importance, because central to this tradition, and characteristic of it, is its refusal to think of God as the inferable One. Instead, it sees God as the impending and impinging One—the One who can most aptly be thought as "coming" and whose coming conditions morally those to whom he comes. (One thinks of foundational texts such as Exod. 3: "I will be [there] as I will be [there]" or Isa. 42:9: "Behold, the former things have come to pass, and new things I now declare; before they spring forth I tell you of them." RSV) To those in disarray he comes as saving power (to Hebrews in Egypt, to oppressed Israelites in Canaan, to Exiles in Babylon); to those who misconstrue the covenant into security he comes as judge (as announced by Amos at the shrine or by Jeremiah at the temple). God can be counted on to come in order to keep faith with his word and his people. At no crucial point in Israel's history is the character of God simply to be inferred as the Ground of the present, the status quo, but consistently he is to be understood as the One who reconstitutes the present by his coming. Always he stands over against the present so as to be the impending One whose coming impinges on the present as summons to respond to his integrity. The appropriate response is therefore moral, and its mode is venture, for it is ventured doing set in motion by expected vindication. That eminently Jewish prayer, the Lord's Prayer, formulates this inner connection: when the kingdom comes the king's will is done on earth as it is in heaven.

Because the Jewish Jesus stands in this tradition and concentrates it on himself by anticipating the kingdom,[42] we cannot look Godward through Jesus and refuse to have our understanding of God to be open-ended; faith merges with hope. To trust this God is to expect him. To expect God is the opposite of inferring him, for the inferred God is bound to the present evidence from which he is inferred and contingent on the inferrer. By allowing the future-leaning, future-grasping, expectant Jesus to be the model by which we think of God we are led away from understanding God to be only the Ground of what is and what is presently experienced, and we are brought to understand God to be the One who is free to restructure the present by impinging upon it. Only a gentile can survey the

227

culture and infer God's death. The God of Israel, the Father of our Lord Jesus Christ, on the other hand, repeatedly comes through and manifests himself into such situations as the impending God who is not here. This God is not only Source of the present but the Initiator of the future. Such a God is perceptible only by promise and expectation.[43]

The fact that the Jesus-event was constituted by this expectation of the impending One and that this expectation was not fulfilled as expected is not a surd to be negated but a coordinate to be grasped affirmatively: the impending God retains his freedom even vis-a-vis Jesus. But does this disallow Jesus as paradigm and prism?

This expectation is constitutive for the whole Jesus (his entire public career), but the whole historical Jesus cannot be seen until he is dead.[44] This means that the whole Jesus must be viewed from the cross, for he cannot come into view in the Galilean fields and boats alone. Moreover, Jesus died neither in bed nor by accident but was sentenced and executed as an insurrectionist. Therefore, his death is a crisis for the history of Jesus, and it is no less a crisis for the God he expected. To this theme we must now turn.

C. *The Death of Jesus and the Crisis of God.* As we have noted repeatedly, Jesus' death is not the surprise ending but the capstone of a career. But not just any career! Just as we do not build our theological reflection on Jesus' ideas of the kingdom, so we do not require now to know his thoughts about his death. We reckon, rather, with the theological implications of what Jesus *did* with regard to his destiny.

We know that he was neither tricked into going to Jerusalem nor summoned to appear there; rather, he went deliberately. While we cannot know his motives or his aims,[45] we are not completely bereft of data with which to work. Sufficient guidance for our observations is provided by the saying, "I have a baptism with which to be baptised, and how I wish it were already accomplished!" (Lk. 12:50).[46] So imprecise an *interpretation* of his death would scarcely have been invented by the church, since the "Passion predictions" show that the

228

trend was to have Jesus speak explicitly about his death. Consequently, we may say that Jesus regarded suffering, with the attendant possibility of death, not as a surprise or a breakdown of his work but as somehow inevitably part of it, and that he did not evade it. It is enough to know this.[47]

If Jesus' work was set in motion by the grasp of the kingdom and of the God whose "godhood" was about to be effectuated, then he apparently faced his destiny expecting vindication by the One in whom he trusted. Yet he died without vindication. Unlike Socrates, who vindicated himself in his death-scene at which he presided, Jesus was not manifest victor but manifest victim. He died without a single sign from the God whose kingly rule he sought to effectuate in advance. His death was no less ambiguous than his life had been, though it was consistent: the God whose fidelity cannot be calculated on the basis of man's attainments lifted not a finger on behalf of the one who trusted him utterly. By sundown, all three men on their crosses were equally dead. The God who, according to Jesus, sends sun and rain on just and unjust alike did not give Jesus preferential treatment either. Jesus died without a word or a wink from God to reassure him that, whatever the gawking crowd might think, he knew that Jesus was not only innocent but valid where it mattered. When we speak of Jesus clarifying and correcting our understanding of the character of God, we mean precisely this Jesus and no other.

But how does this man with this death break open a new way of understanding God? Jesus' death is a crisis for our understanding of God because the man who not only pledged his life on God's kingdom but pledged God's rule to those whom he called to follow expired with no ratification whatever. It needs to be emphasized that we are arguing not that this execution was a crisis in the mind of Jesus, though this may have been the case as well, but that it was (and is) a crisis for those with whom he shared his trust. But the truly important thing for our theologizing is that it evokes a decision also from us with respect to the character of God. For Jesus' death forces the question: If one's pre-understanding of God is valid, then Jesus appears not to be; conversely, if Jesus is valid in this career climaxed by this cross, then what we assumed to be the character of God is disclosed to have been off base. But why is this the case? Because apart from Jesus the religious think of God as their patron. On the other hand, despite the fact that we cannot reconstruct the trials of Jesus, and hence the character and the complicity of the Sanhedrin in Jesus' death, it is likely that the interpreters of God also viewed Jesus as an unreliable spokesman for the kingdom, if not as an imposter. Theologically, this means that Jesus was rejected in the name of the God of the law and the prophets. Hence for Jews, no less than for gentiles, Jesus' execution is a crisis for the understanding of God.

Consequently, it was either Jesus' perception of God which was put to death with him or our pre-understanding of God by which we judge Jesus to be guilty of misplacing his trust (whatever benefits it may have brought to the halt and the lame), of misunderstanding the kingdom, and of misconstruing God. On the other hand, if one looks into the character of God through precisely this Jesus, then "God" refers to the one who cannot be required to interfere on behalf of those who trust him, to the one whose integrity and presence are not to be inferred from experiences alone, who keeps his freedom vis-a-vis all men just as he remained free even with respect to Jesus.[48] In light of this disclosure, one need not give up this God in the midst of human agony, for if Jesus is as valid on the cross as he was when he spoke of lilies in Galilee, then God is trustworthy precisely as Jesus said and showed. The model for thinking of God which is not exhausted by our experience or exposed as dead by our dying is none other than the historical Jesus destined for the cross.

In light of this Jesus and his dying, we can see that the character of God here disclosed was not a new development at all, but has been the character of the God of Israel all along —though not that of the gentiles. This is the same God who did not intervene to prevent Solomon's or Herod's temple from being destroyed, who did not underwrite permanently even the victory of the Maccabean liberation front or save the holy Akiba from his tormentors. Nor did he stretch out his hand against the Crusaders who, while en route to battle infidel Turks, paused to slaughter so-called unbelieving Jews in the valley of the Rhine. Nor did he rescue Bonhoeffer or quench the furnaces in Poland. The integrity of this God does not express itself primarily in patronage. He has always sent sun and rain on just and unjust alike, though by our canons he ought to give the sinner either a drought or a flood. Still, after Verdun, Auschwitz, Dresden, and Vietnam, can one believe that any other God is trustworthy? The only God who is trustworthy is the One who does not interfere to protect the pious but who is present in the thick of darkness, perhaps even as thick darkness. That, and no other, is the God of Jesus. This does not, of course, eclipse the joyous celebration of God's kingdom which marked Jesus' work in Galilee. But it is to insist that if "Jesus" is restricted to the convivial guest at suppers with sinners, he will readily be abandoned as untrustworthy when one's life comes apart, when one's child dies of leukemia, when one is hosed down by the police, or dies a death utterly meaningless within an absurd history. In short, because the whole event called "Jesus" is marked by both joy and tragedy, whoever perceives God through this lens is redeemed from a simplistic theology that is repeatedly shattered by life's bittersweet compounds. Furthermore, just as Jesus' perception of the kingdom has both judgment and grace (an eminently Jewish paradox!) so the understanding of God, forged and tempered by the whole event of Jesus come to a head in the cross, shows that God is present in wrath no less than in grace and salvation. (Could it be that one reason Christian theology often appears so bumblingly helpless today is that it has no real place for the wrath of God—precisely when we live in the midst of God's wrath and judgment?)

But are we shifting from hard theological work to soaring rhetoric? Why, in light of Jesus, continue to speak of God at all? Why be careful to say that what died out was only a misconceived God—say the God of the miracle stories or the "God who acts"? [49] Why not say that Jesus' death revealed categorically that there is no God and never was? Christian faith must always remain open to such a counter-charge, as

231

must Judaism, for as soon as one tries to adduce demonstrations to the contrary he had already exchanged the God of the Bible and of Jesus for the inferred God (especially if one infers "God" from positive and fulfilling experiences only!). The New Testament is not merely rhetorical when it speaks of the offense of the cross. This means that Jesus in his dying forces the issue of God in a decisive way precisely because of the career that preceded it. After the cross, one either affirms that God is truly and most profoundly disclosed here in the mysterious alloy of judgment and grace, or turns his back on Jesus and what he stood for (and was hanged for) in his trust.

Now a further step is implicit. Since what matters is not simply a concept "God" but whether God as understood is trustworthy, whoever appropriates the God of Jesus as the One whom he trusts to the uttermost is reconciled to him. One not only has a new concept to contemplate and analyze but stands in right relation to God—that is, he is "rightwised" (=justified).[50] To speak further with Paul, the gospel is the "word of reconciliation" precisely because this word is the story of Jesus through whom God reconciled us to his true character (II Cor. 5:18 ff.). In a word, through the cross, understanding of God and trusting God coalesce, so that it is this God who is trusted or repudiated. In this way, the classical theological point is grounded in the historical Jesus: at the cross, revelation, reconciliation, and faith occur together, or they do not occur at all.

In the New Testament, the pivot of this theology is Jesus' resurrection. Obviously, the theme of the resurrection is a battleground littered with many broken lances and much pierced armor. We will attempt neither to bury the dead honorably nor to restore the wounded to battle fitness nor to rearm the valiant survivors. That is another project. But we must see if we can understand the centrality of the resurrection so that at least the rationale of early Christian thought is intelligible. To do this we concentrate on the *function* of resurrection in the New Testament.[51]

But we do need to disabuse ourselves of presumed meanings of the category "resurrection" in order to hear what the New

Testament says. Suffice it to say that the New Testament never understands it as mere resuscitation (like Lazarus), just as it does not equate resurrection with the rise of faith in the disciples and the emergence of the kerygma (beloved though this is in some circles today), nor as a miracle (a single event interrupting the causal nexus of nature but leaving the observer unchanged—as in defensive orthodoxy). Rather, the New Testament understands by resurrection the eschatological event par excellence. Just as Jesus' mission was a prolepsis of the kingdom, so his destiny is regarded as the prolepsis of the consummation. Just as his life was the paradigm of the "already" in anticipation of the kingdom, so his resurrection is the "already" of what is yet to come. Thus he is the primal End-event and not merely the initial one. As *primus* as well as *prius*, he is made Christ and Lord.[52] To be sure, the New Testament itself shows a rapidly changing and enlarging set of meanings of Jesus' resurrection, but this is one of its earliest meanings. We deal with this not because we assume that only the earliest insights are valid but because it was at that stage that the meaning of resurrection vis-a-vis the historical Jesus was seen most clearly.

But what has the resurrection of Jesus, functioning in this way, to do with the problem of God? Again, only salient and unavoidable points can be noted here.

(a) Characteristically, the New Testament says that God raised Jesus (or that he "was raised").[53] In view of the death of Jesus—whether one has in mind the unrelieved helplessness of Jesus, or the connotations of being crucified, or the view that the interpreters of God's will were implicated in his execution—this is a remarkable statement, for it can only mean that God had not repudiated him but vindicated him. Because the resurrection is commonly discussed generically (What do we mean by resurrection?) we readily overlook the point that resurrection is not simply said to have occurred to someone but that it was Jesus and none other whom God raised (there were three corpses that day). This means that the early Christians understood the resurrection not as an anonymous event manifesting the power of God or the inbreaking of the End in

general (any resurrection might have made this point), but as
an event inseparable from Jesus, precisely the Jesus whose
death was the end result of his way of trusting God. Consequently, to say that God raised *Jesus* is to say that God is
trustworthy as Jesus had claimed, that he had vindicated and
ratified the man who bet his life, and that of others, on the
kingdom. It is important to grasp this in a non-pietistic way,
for it underscores the fact that Jesus' non-validated life of trust
is what God ratified. It is the whole Jesus whom God counter-
signs by resurrection. It is the open-ended Jesus whom God
discloses to be valid and trustworthy.

(b) To perceive what this says about God we need to
recall that it is the God of the kingdom whom Jesus trusted.
The kingdom, we said, was the effectuation of God's fidelity
to himself and to his creation, and we cited Pannenberg's dictum that God's being is his rule. Concretely, the resurrection
therefore does not suggest that on Easter God *became* faithful
to himself but that his fidelity and trustworthiness, which
Jesus had laid hold of, were confirmed. Easter is not simply
the antidote to Good Friday which God administers belatedly
to the victim to show that he is a faithful Father after all. On
that basis, the resurrection could have remained a secret between God and Jesus, so to speak. But then it would only have
been Jesus-in-relation-to-God who would have been vindicated
and not the whole Jesus who pledged God's kingship to men.
In other words, the appearance stories express the conviction
that, by making the risen Jesus manifest to those who had
trusted him before and now trust him anew, God confirmed
the kingdom as effectuated by Jesus[54]—namely that God's
kingly rule has no criteria by which one can prove its presence
or its character from phenomena but rather that God's power
is his freedom to keep faith with himself and with men on his
own terms. The appearance stories report not that the disciples
found the risen Lord where they sought him, but that they
were surprised and startled to be accosted by him, whether
behind locked doors, on the road or by the lake (even in Mt.
28:16 ff. "some doubted" what they saw). It was that way with
the kingly rule of God which had laid hold of Jesus and had

234

sent him to surprise publicans and Pharisees with his presence.

(c) That God will vindicate the faithful was a firmly embedded expectation in Jewish theology. A resurrection, however, asserted that he had done so already, ahead of time. This had a double effect: it announced anew that the End was here proleptically (only Jesus was resurrected and the world did not change) and it made Jesus the effective clue to the sort of life God vindicates as a mark of his own integrity. *Whom God vindicates discloses the character of God.*[55] Whoever affirms the resurrection knows what to do with himself (become a disciple) and where to look for his trustworthy clue to God's integrity (Jesus).

While this mode of thought may be intelligible, it is far from appropriable for many persons. Moreover, the reasoning involved here is grounded in apocalyptic theology.[56] Since this was but one mode of theologizing in the ancient world (we think of philosophical mysticism or cultic initiation theology as alternatives, for instance) the question emerges: must one think in the apocalyptic mode in order to see in Jesus the decisive clue to God's character? As a whole, the New Testament itself answers this negatively, since the Fourth Gospel is intensely concerned with this theme and yet has drastically shifted away from the apocalyptic mode in favor of the incarnational mode in which the death of Jesus marks his return to the Father. In this Gospel, the death of Jesus is not a crisis of God. Consistently, the kingdom of God no longer appears as the burden of Jesus, and in its place stands the eternal life that the Son brings. But even here, the motif of vindication and ratification of Jesus beyond death occurs, for it is implied in the view that Jesus returns to the Father who sent him. Without elaborating further, it is now clear that if the New Testament can adopt and develop various ways of understanding Jesus' relation to God, nothing canonical precludes doing an analogous task today (see also Chapter 3).

Those theologians concerned with the phenomenology of language and of man's linguisticality have undertaken such a task, especially Fuchs and Ebeling. Appropriate to this idiom, then, is their formulation that on Easter the center of Jesus came through in language—in the kerygma. Consistently, Fuchs denies that Jesus' death produced a crisis in the disciples (thus implying the need of Jesus' vindication to restore their faith), and contends instead that what resurrection really means is the emergence into articulate expression of what Jesus had already shared with his disciples. In other words, this theological venture accents the continuity between what the historical Jesus provided and what was perceived after Easter, so that Easter is no longer the overturning of doubt and the validation of Jesus but the flowering of faith because that which Jesus had been about—evoking faith—has now happened under the aegis of his life and word. Instead of the resurrected Jesus being a prolepsis of the End, the situation of Jesus and his circle is a prolepsis of the church. In this way certain of the difficult problems concerning (any) resurrection are avoided, and continuity with Jesus is made viable.

Pursuing a critique of such a program takes us away from our central concern and must be taken up at another time. In the meanwhile, it might repay us to ponder this question: Can any restatement of the resurrection which does not see in the death of Jesus a crisis for our understanding of God actually permit Jesus to reconcile us *to* God? Or, to rephrase it, can an interpretation of Jesus which concentrates so intently on his coming to speech make it possible for a person to entrust himself to the mystery of life beyond the enigma of his own dying? [57] The root problem remains: in what can I trust unto the end? What is sufficiently trustworthy to die for? I still want to know whether this Jesus is valid where it counts—at life's nadir—just as I want to know whether there is a future for the created world. Because these issues are heard and responded to in apocalyptic theology, I am convinced that the apocalyptic mode merits serious attention today.

Instead of rehabilitating apocalyptic theology here, we restrict ourselves to one consideration: whether appropriating the main-line New Testament understanding of Jesus' resurrection (i.e., non-Johannine) commits us to a *deus ex machina* theology in which God intervenes after all. Implicit here is the moral credibility of the God of Jesus' resurrection, for on this turns our reconciliation to him.

The difficulties of thinking of God "out there" need no rehearsal here because that is not what is at issue anyway. What does need to be identified is the real issue—whether that one reality whose ineluctible encompassing we confess and identify by the word "God" is to be conceptualized in ways that allow him to have freedom and integrity vis-a-vis man or whether we shall reduce him to a logarithmic function of our existence. In a day when theology struggles for sheer survival, it is especially important to clarify what sort of God we are impelled to theologize about, lest we lose our case altogether by some anxious settlement out of court which looks good at the moment. Pondering and testing the viability of thinking of God as having sufficient integrity and freedom to recede as well as to reveal himself must not be confused with a return to the shoddy stereotypes so frequently (and cheaply) derided—the cosmic meddler, the heavenly fixer, the unpredictable and arbitrary miser who must be cajoled or flattered into releasing a blessing now and then. It is strange that so many theologians hear a categorical imperative to beat that dead horse repeatedly.

In apocalyptic theology the moral integrity of the reality identified as God is non-negotiable, just as God's indifference to man and the world is not even up for discussion because it is precluded. What is problematic is, *mutatis mutandis*, precisely our problem—whether this moral integrity can be counted on to manifest itself redemptively so that men can rely on it sufficiently to rectify life and the world at great cost, or whether such effort is finally a heroic attempt to spit against the wind. The apocalyptist, moreover, no more expects a series of divine interventions on behalf of the faithful than does so-called modern man. What he counts on is a decisive act that will halt the tide of perversity and restore the whole creation. He does not expect an evolution, cosmic or historical, that will produce this goal, for, like our modern man again, he has been sobered by history. The definitive and rectifying surge of this reality, of the eschatological act of God, has really nothing at all to do with a *deus ex machina* but is a protest against it.

237

The former is grounded in the conviction that the reality termed God is moral, the latter in the idea of a universe closed off by immutable natural laws. Whenever the resurrection is split off from its natural, original theological matrix it is trivialized into a mere miracle that is suspect by natural law. But the resuscitation of a corpse has nothing to do with resurrection, as already noted. Rather, resurrection has to do with creation of a new mode of existence as a response of God to the irradicable perverseness of history. As such, it is as mythological as the creation of the present cosmos (neither the explosion theory nor the condensation theory of the "origin" of the universe deals with creation in the strict sense but only with a radical change in what had already been created). Resurrection, therefore, is grounded in the freedom and power of God to create afresh, out of death, as he originally created absolutely, *ex nihilo*. The re-creation of Jesus by resurrection, then, affirms God's moral integrity with respect to the one who was shaped by his perception of God's integrity, and thereby the vindication of Jesus and the self-vindication of God coincide.

It is Paul who grasped these issues most perceptively. In Rom. 4:17 he speaks of God as the one "who gives life to the dead and calls into existence the things that do not exist" (RSV). Moreover, he saw that the resurrection of Jesus cannot be reduced to a miracle on Jesus' corpse (as the empty tomb stories tend to do) but is an event that must include those who participate in Jesus ("baptized into his death" as he puts it in Rom. 6:3). Therefore, Jesus' resurrection is God's commitment also to those who share in Jesus by trust and sacramental participation. Paul's theology of justification is the soteriological restatement of the same perspective: only the God who is free to resurrect Jesus is free to set right the godless (Rom. 4:5).

Just as Jesus' career does not initiate belief in God, so his resurrection cannot generate it; rather, it serves to designate and clarify the God who is to be trusted and thereby intersects our presumed understanding of God and of what is the last word on human life. The vindication of Jesus includes the vindication of his own unswerving dependence on God expressed in the cry of dereliction spoken *to* God. For God to ratify that life is to disclose that he had been implicated in Jesus all along. This is why Jesus' resurrection is a denial of the *deus ex machina* who remains uninvolved in Jesus but who appears on the scene like Superman out of the blue to resuscitate Jesus from the grave. Jesus' resurrection affirms that God had always been "with" Jesus, even on the cross; indeed, that God's presentness with Jesus can be counted on to be paradigmatic for his presentness with all who trust this Jesus. In this sense, we can agree with Bultmann that the message of the cross and resurrection summons us to a decision about our self-understanding.

If these terse formulations take us in the right direction, then the question, "What really happened?" is as misplaced as asking how creation occurred *ex nihilo* and as speculating on how the end will occur. Furthermore, while the theological issues articulated in the concept "resurrection" must be identified, it is doubtful whether they can be reduced to something else.

The other question that we identified concerns the moral credibility of a God who would allow precisely this Jesus to die unvalidated and unrescued, who then vindicated him out of death, but who thereafter permits the vicissitudes of history to flow unabated over mankind; for this appears to call into question the very vindication of Jesus. Commonly, the rejection of apocalyptic theology rests on the failure of early Christian expectation to materialize. The objection itself implies that Christian hope would be valid if one could show empirically at least its gradual actualization. (Even in Pannenberg's and Moltmann's work one scents traces of a subtle return to using apocalyptic as a map for world history, whatever the avowed, and disavowed, intent may be.) But the validation and invalidation of apocalyptic theological horizons proceeds not simply by checking them against world-historical events in the sense of development, but by the quality and scope of the understanding of God and man which they provide, and by the way the community of faith is enabled to live in the world without fulfillment. The apocalyptic image and pledge of a redeemed world (not simply a consummated world) articulate the gap between history and its *telos* in order to guard against identifying any movement with fulfillment on the one hand, and to provide a model and set of images by which the community perceives the character of God's impingement on the world in order to maintain its repentance and responsible life in the world. (Dorothee Sölle was close to seeing this. See Chapter 4.) This myth too must not be reduced to something else but released to function precisely as myth—an image of redemption which precludes idolizations of the present and keeps the future open.

In this light, the vindication of Jesus—the Jesus whose life does not end with manifest proof of his validity—means that he who restructures his understanding of God and of himself on the basis of Jesus can come to terms with his own incompleteness, with the non-validated character of his own existence. He is freed from the compulsion of vindicating himself or knowing that others do so, and from the demand that God vindicate him now. Instead, on the basis of Jesus he ventures to entrust himself and his vindication to God, and is prepared to receive it where Jesus did—beyond death. Thereby he is reconciled to his own unfinishedness and mortality, and to the One whom he trusts to affirm him beyond the night of death. Such a theological understanding underlies Jesus' own words about the secret righteousness that depends totally on God alone for vindication (Mt. 6:1-18), and lays hold of Paul's insight that on the basis of Jesus one ceases to establish his own righteousness but relies on God's verdict. Further, he who trusts God on this basis is liberated also from the compulsion to prove the Christian hope to be correct by historical progress, but knows that he can live in a world of broken hopes without himself being broken because the event of Jesus has taught him that God's relation to him and the world cannot be inferred directly from man's attainments. Armed with this freedom, he is also free to change the world, for on the one hand, this world does not legitimate him any longer, and, on the other, he knows that whatever happens to him cannot really separate him from God because nothing finally separated Jesus from God either.

D. *The Jesus of God.* Because our entire essay was concerned to sketch the potential role of the historical Jesus for preaching and theology, we largely eschewed speaking of the role of God; indeed, we deliberately began this chapter "from below." Nevertheless, we cannot leave the impression that we regard God to be passive, a transcendent bystander who, with a certain amount of curiosity and self-interest, looks upon the whole event, wistfully seeking a piece of the action for himself. Our remarks about God's having been "with" Jesus should have shown that this is foreign to our intent and contrary to the heart of Christian theology from its inception. Actually a systematic theology might well restate afresh everything we have argued thus far, and do so from the standpoint of God's initiative—at least if one is prepared to think in a Trinitarian way. Clearly such a task exceeds the scope of this essay, and doubtless that of the essayist as well. Nonetheless, it is appropriate to indicate in a rough way the direction in which such a restatement could move in relation to classical questions.

If one begins with God's initiative in the web of events called "Jesus," one would face the question, *How* is Jesus God's instrument for man's salvation? As soon as this question is asked, what comes to mind immediately is the entire history of christological discussion. Whether one looks to the "proto-adoptionist" Christologies of early Christianity according to which God empowered Jesus to be his man for the hour by endowing him with the Spirit, or to the assertion of his Virgin Birth according to which God acted decisively already in the genesis of Jesus (or to the doctrine of the Immaculate Conception according to which he prepared a sinless mother of whom he was to be born), or to the incarnation theology which served notice that in Jesus we deal with the pre-existent Word himself who has always been God's representative—the point is that all these (and other) tracks were laid to help the train of Christian reflection move toward an adequate answer to the

241

question, How is it possible that in dealing with Jesus we are dealing with God's own action? The later christological controversies over the body of Jesus (Was it a human body really born *of* Mary or a specially created body merely born *through* her?), over his person (Can one say that his body was human but his spirit, will, or mind was divine?), over the relation of the Father to the Son (Was he who was incarnated—the Logos —the primal creature or the Creator?), etc., all grapple with this question and are nothing less—and a good deal more—than a sustained and variegated effort to answer precisely and adequately the question: If through Jesus God himself saves man, how shall we understand the Jesus who lived in Nazareth, taught in Capernaum and died in Jerusalem?

If, in the next place, one asks, *Why* was the Jesus-event set in motion in the first place? one is led directly to the theology of God's "attributes," and from there to his "aims." That is, one sets the Jesus-event in the context of God's faithfulness to his people and of his love for his creation. Implicit in such considerations is an understanding of man as estranged from, if not actually hostile to, God. In this light, it soon becomes evident that unless one says God's attributes are for his own enjoyment, they actualize themselves manward. That is, it would be insufficient to assert merely that the Father loves the Son if that love did not impel him to send the Son, for God's love would be a curious love indeed if it did not reach outward to all his creation.[58] Since love without sacrifice is ultimately unthinkable (even eros may require sacrifice in order to gain the beloved object for oneself), one soon coordinates God's love-sacrifice with Jesus' life and death. In other words, pursuing the question "Why?" leads to multiple efforts to articulate what English language theology calls the "atonement." This is characteristically grounded in both the attributes of God (love and justice) and in the aims of God for his creation (redemption).[59]

In similar ways, questions about *persons* reconciled to God through Jesus lead to reflection on the empowering presence of God as Spirit and the relation of this reality to the act of God in Jesus, and ultimately to the Trinitarian understanding

242

of God. They also lead to reflection about the community created by God through Jesus (ecclesiology and sacraments), and to the theme of the mission and destiny of that community. Each of these questions leads back to the historical Jesus, just as correlating Jesus and God leads to these several dogmas. The history of Christian theology shows that its hallmark is the insistence that nothing be said about God or world or man which is unrelated to Jesus; rather, that everything said be thought through and reformulated afresh in light of Jesus. In the process Jesus himself is reconceptualized and reinterpreted.

The upshot of the matter is this: Because in our time historical thinking is as axiomatic a mode of thought as were myth and metaphysics before (though these are not totally superfluous today either), the task is that of rethinking the whole scope of Christian theology in ways that take appropriate account of the historical Jesus. Still, the central theme is the role of Jesus in our understanding of God.

In a word, we may regard Jesus as the parable of God. Taking note of this possibility is our final assignment.

III. Jesus, the Parable of God

Given the intense study of Jesus' parables we need only note briefly the significance of the fact that they were central to it. (a) Characteristically, Jesus used parables to announce the news of the kingdom and to interpret the seriousness of hearing the announcement. (b) The materials and plots of the parables are commonplace: warring kings and shrewd entrepreneurs, or housewives and farmers "doing their thing." Every student of the parables seems constrained to comment on the way they permit one to get the feel of Palestinian life. In a word, the plot of the parables is secular; "God" is not one of their dramatis personae. (c) Jesus assumes that the parables do their work without justification or explanation, though it is not always self-evident to us what that task was seen to be. In any case, the effectiveness of the parables was not a problem

243

for Jesus: he did not struggle to overcome them in order to communicate, but committed himself to communicating through parabolic speech. Why is this the case? In a word, Jesus preferred parables not merely because he found them useful but primarily because there is an inner connection between the parabolic mode of speech and the mode and motive of his work. Jesus concentrated on parabolic speech because he himself was a parabolic event of the kingdom of God.

The import of this will become clearer as we use recent insights into the parables to understand the role of Jesus himself. First, the parables do not explain their subject matter but point to it in such a way that the hearer is required to grasp it in order to understand the parable. The parables point beyond themselves, without being allegories. They are not merely good stories that have no point beyond themselves, but are about something. While allegories are transparent to their referents, parables hint and suggest; they lean toward something not self-evident but which, nonetheless, can be seen if one looks through the parable and with the parable; appropriately, that to which they point becomes visible only through the parable. Funk appropriately begins his recent discussion of the parables with Dodd's observation that the parables "tease" the mind into active thought, and infers rightly that "it is not possible to specify once and for all what the parables mean," [60] for that would make the parable expendable. That is, once the "meaning" would be ascertained, the parable could be discarded like the first stage in a rocket. Consequently, we must say that while God is not a named actor in the stories, they are nonetheless a form of God-talk, because they point to features of God's kingdom and its impingement upon the present. That is what they are about.[61]

This character and role of the parables supports our suggestion that Jesus is himself a parable. Just as the parable has as many points as there are situations into which it is spoken,[62] so Jesus' life has as many disclosure opportunities as there are contexts in which it is used—as the history of Christology clearly shows. Likewise, it should be clear that the nonexpendability of the parable comports with our insistence that Jesus is not expendable for faith but remains its constant point of reference and material for reflection. Above all, Jesus is about God and his kingdom without explaining it analytically or discursively (see below).

Second, in contrast with a simile, which illumines the less known by comparing it with the better known (e.g., He acts like a bear), the parable is a metaphor that presents an imaged action to the hearer in a way sufficiently arresting to require him to rethink the whole in a new way. Grammatically, this distinction is manifest in the difference between saying A *is like* B and A *is* B (He is a bear). As Funk formulates, "If the logic of predication looks *at* phenomena [John's actions are bearlike] the logic of the metaphor looks *through* it" [John is a bear][63] "Bear" summons us to rethink "John" in bear categories, so that by this shocking device we may see him as a whole in a new way. One does not factor "bear" into component elements (fur, claws, etc.) in order to perceive "John," for that would turn the metaphor either into an allegory or into a set of similes (John's fingernails are like bear claws, or he is hairy as a bear); rather, "bear" is a non-factorable window (image) through which John as a whole is set before the hearer.

In the same way, what we have said about the whole Jesus—words, deeds, thrust, career, death—comports with Jesus as a parable. Since the whole Jesus was permeated by the kingdom of God, and since that kingdom is the effectuation of God's reign, it is Jesus as a whole who points to the kingdom in a new way. Just as the parable does not illustrate ideas better stated non-parabolically, and so become dispensable, so Jesus is not merely an illustration for the kingdom which can be more adequately grasped apart from him—say in mystic encounters or in abstract formulations. His task was not to impart correct concepts about the kingdom but to make it possible for men to respond to it; as a parable of the kingly God, he invited men to look through him into the kingdom, with the result that his hearers could not respond to the kingdom without responding to him. That is, they could not entrust themselves to God without entrusting themselves to him; conversely, whoever trusted Jesus trusted the God of whom he was parable.[64] (This is why it is appropriate to speak of Jesus in secondary metaphors as well, such as mediator, priest, sacrifice, etc.)

Third, the parable is really an extended metaphor in the sense that it is a narrative with at least a rudimentary plot; i.e., the parable is a metaphoric life situation with disclosure potential. While some of Jesus' parables depict a typical situation (sower's seed on several soils), thus inviting allegorization because each familiar item invites transposition into another realm of discourse, many of Jesus' parables are characterized by the atypical, the bizarre, the shocking, and the immoral character of their plots. It is hardly typical for a merchant to sell everything to buy a single pearl, nor is it the moral thing for a cashiered manager to tamper with the company books in order to make friends for himself (or to make them indebted to him as well), and so forth. It is important that one not seek ways to circumvent or subvert this offensive quality of the parables, because this is a central feature of them. Precisely their shock value is what makes them effective in accosting the hearer in such a way as to compel him to think afresh not only about his world but about the way he is related to his world.

This is the case with Jesus as well. He not only tells shocking stories but leads a shocking life toward a shocking end. Just as the parables have familiar elements in unfamiliar plots, so Jesus' life has familiar features of Palestinian life in startling juxatposition: he preaches in synagogues but at the beach as well, he consorts with scrupulous Pharisees but ignores ritual washing when he is their guest; he tells his men how to fast, but when others do so his men eat; he understands his healing power as a sign of the kingdom's impinging power but refuses to become a healer, etc. What appear to us to be inconsistencies when measured by presumed norms are for him consistencies with the freedom of the kingdom to be itself and to be other than our expectations. Precisely the offensiveness of the historical Jesus is congruent with his parabolic function, for he arrests the flow of trusts and thoughts and thereby invites us to reorder them, that is, to reorder ourselves (i.e., repent).

246

It is not just the words of Jesus that call men to repent, but the man as a whole; for, as in the case of the parable, one cannot attend to Jesus and still assume that one's knowing and trusting are unchallenged.

Luke tells a story that illustrates Jesus' procedure aptly. A woman in the crowd hailed him, "Blessed is the womb that bore you, and the breasts that you sucked!" Far from being an ode to Mary, this is an oriental way of paying Jesus a compliment. But how does Jesus respond? Not a hint of anything comparable to "Thank you, M'am." Rather, he retorts, "Blessed rather are those who hear the word of God and keep it!" (RSV) On the surface, it appears that he is either irrelevant or impertinent. But here the parabolic Jesus comes through, for his reply puts her in a parable situation in which she can either move forward into a new perception or manifest her bondage to the old. If she is angry with Jesus, she simply inverts her admiration into resentment and remains as she was, outside the kingdom. If she says, "Yes, isn't that true! Jesus certainly knows how to put it!" she also misses the point and remains where she was because she still looks *at* Jesus instead of *through* him. But if she is sufficiently shocked to reflect whether her words come from hearing and doing the Word, if by this encounter she is pried loose from her presuppositions of what a proper response to Jesus is, then the door of the kingdom has opened to her. The point is that the parables function as arresting language-events (to speak with Fuchs) through which something may happen to the hearer. What the parables assert becomes a question to the hearer just as the historical Jesus does (Chapter 3).

Finally, parables are not authenticated by discursive language, nor their vision by the visions of their narrator. (By the latter is meant the "religious experience" as the warrant, as if to say the parables are truth-laden because Jesus was devout or ecstatic.) Their adequacy and their authority are gauged rather by the depth of life which they touch and reconstruct, by the depth of what they overcome. Another way of getting at this is to observe that the parable is legitimated by its subject matter, by that which it portrays and brings

247

near the hearer. An analogy is found in the visual arts, whether sculpture or painting in any of the several nonrepresentational modes. One does not object that because Picasso's faces are not accurate images they are untrue. His faces are "true" to the extent they adequately portray what Picasso sees (true to Picasso) and succeed in reconstructing the viewer's perception sufficiently that he recognizes that it is true also for him because now he sees the way Picasso saw (not what he saw). Both elements are important, because an artist's expressing his vision aptly does not yet assure us that it is profound and not trivial. Nor does an artist confer aesthetic or substantive authority on his work by writing a commentary on it in order to explain or justify what he saw and strove to achieve. To require an artist to explain his work in a critical essay is to require him to admit that he erred in thinking that his perception could be said most aptly in line, color, and texture, and that the relation between medium and subject matter is one of convenience, that painting is a hobby but not a self-constituting career. Because the artist has expressed his point in his work, requiring him to say it all over again in prose discourse is a demand that he cease being an artist. In terms of the Gospels, it is to ask for an unambiguous "sign" to legitimate the parable. But not even the church's explanations of Jesus' parables justify their content, mode, or angle of vision; they justify solely Jesus' use of parables at all.

For our purpose, we can now say that Jesus is affirmed to be trustworthy when those drawn into his orbit discover their deepest distrusts to be healed, that is, when they begin to rely on the God to whom Jesus pointed by parabolic death no less than by parabolic word. Because Jesus' God is the God whose future reconstitutes the present for those who anticipatorily respond to him, the trustworthiness of Jesus is gauged by the depth at which response reorients one's trust and reconstitutes that network of trusts which determines what life actually is like. In a word, he who identifies with Jesus by trust leans into the future, and in his name claims its otherness now; he trusts God to say Yes beyond death for the sake of Jesus. As the vision justifies the painting and the subject matter the parable,

248

so the God of the kingdom justifies Jesus and those who participate with him in expecting vindication only from God. Riveting our expectation there and nowhere else—this is how the parabolic Jesus redeems us from false expectations and releases us to celebrate now the impingement of God. Since his kingdom is present now only as prolepsis and as parable, we live by parable. That is, we trust the historical Jesus.

NOTES TO CHAPTER FIVE

1. That is, not only is Jesus Christ the center of the theological tradition of Christianity but Christians have a Christomorphic way of believing in God. Our concern with the historical Jesus shows how this point can be taken with utter seriousness, for Jesus is no more an addendum to trust in God than he is a presupposition of the kerygma. Precisely because "Jesus" has a describable and perceptible content is the "historical Jesus" able to filter and focus our understanding of God. It is difficult to see how that same can be maintained on a Bultmannian foundation.

2. In his instructive phenomenological analysis of the role of the "historical Jesus question" in Protestant theology, Reinhard Slenczka shows that far-ranging theological questions were never absent from the "quest of the historical Jesus," whether old or new. He shows this by exploring the polarities that marked the entire movement: e.g., accidental truths of history/necessary truths of reason (Lessing); historicity/prototypicality (Schleiermacher); individual/idea (Strauss); ground of faith/content of faith (Herrmann); proclaimer/proclaimed (Bultmann). All attempts to study Jesus historically have had a contemporary theological thrust. *Geschichtlichkeit und Personsein Jesu Christi, FSöT* 18 (Göttingen: Vandenhoeck & Ruprecht, 1967), pp. 303 ff. In taking up explicitly theological issues, then, we are not imposing alien categories onto the subject matter but exposing deliberately what is implicit in it from the start.

3. Slenczka points out that our proposed "Christology from below" is by no means a newborn child but a rather old figure born in the nineteenth century. Useful as his analysis of characteristics of this effort is, it is not clear to me that one makes the historical Jesus the epistemological ground for the divinity of Christ, as he claims. Rather, one should ask whether, in rough analogy to physics (wave and particle theories), one does not face the necessity of different language systems developed in order to deal adequately with different dimensions of reality. *Ibid.*, pp. 309 ff.

4. A convenient sketch of the God problem in recent theology is found in Frederick Herzog, *Understanding God* (New York: Scribner's, 1966), Chap. 1. For a fuller treatment, see Langdon

Gilkey, *Naming the Whirlwind: The Renewal of God-Language* (Indianapolis: Bobbs-Merrill, 1969).

5. H. Richard Niebuhr emphasized repeatedly that revelation, among other things, restructures and revolutionizes what was previously known and trusted. "It is true that revelation is not the communication of new truths and the supplanting of our natural religion by a supernatural one. But it is the fulfillment and the radical reconstruction of our natural knowledge about deity through the revelation of one whom Jesus Christ called 'Father.' All thought about deity now undergoes a metamorphosis. Revelation is not a development of our religious ideas but their continuous conversion." *The Meaning of Revelation* (New York: Macmillan, 1941), p. 182. In *Radical Monotheism and Western Culture* (New York: Harper, 1943), he wrote: "'Revelation does not mean the impartation of certain truths, for propositions do not in themselves establish confidence as a demonstration of loyalty. The event that calls forth faith as confidence is a demonstration of loyalty and the event that calls forth faith as loyalty is some disclosure of a cause." P. 42. Niebuhr, of course, did not focus on the historical Jesus as we have, but his point comports with our argument.

6. This observation is not intended to deny the offense of the incarnation in the ancient world: the Eternal entered time, and so on. Rather, because the rejected alternatives were but variations of the pattern (in Docetism, for instance, God only seemed to take a human body) they attested the same point: this tradition begins with the "First Principle," the Creator, the Eternal, etc. and moves to the event of Jesus. It could do so because atheism as we know it scarcely existed. Consequently, the common observation is not totally true: in ancient times it was the humanity of Jesus which was offensive; today it is his divinity. Actually, his humanity was offensive then because one started with God's utter transcendence; because today the conceptual content of "divinity" is radically eroded, the humanity is offensive because the life history of Jesus appears absurd.

7. It may be necessary to insist explicitly that this dependence is functional; that is, Jesus functions as the basis for our trusting God and for our perception of the God we trust. He is not the "object" of faith in an absolute sense. That would make Jesus a god beside God. Put dogmatically, the Second Person does not compete with the First Person. To the contrary, the First Person is the ground of the Second and of our trust as well. But such formulations are logical reflections on the entire realm of theological discourse, which is itself set in motion by the act of trusting God by trusting Jesus. Because such reflection is concerned with the ontic ground of our possibility of trust in Jesus, it assumes logical priority over the act of trust. But what is logically and ontically prior does not diminish the fact that functionally the Christian depends on Jesus for his understanding of God. One has only to recall that Jewish theology not only proceeds differently but reaches different conclusions.

8. Jürgen Moltmann has called attention to this relatively modern

preoccupation with revelation and has commented on its multiple roots. *Theology of Hope*, trans. from 5th ed. by James W. Leitch (New York: Harper, 1967, 1st German ed., 1964), pp. 44-45.

9. H. Richard Niebuhr therefore speaks of the revelatory event as "a critical point in man's conversation with God" in light of which he interprets the past and present (and implicitly the future as well, though he did not press this). *The Meaning of Revelation*, p. 129. In this book, he repeatedly speaks of the Christian "necessity" of accounting for what one has come to know and trust. E.g., "As we begin with revelation only because we are forced to do so by our limited standpoint in history and faith so we can proceed only by stating in simple, confessional form what has happened to us in our community, how we came to believe, how we reason about things and what we see from our point of view." (Pp. 40-41) This concern with the constraint on the Christian is worlds apart from the concern to "legitimate" or to reject anything that might legitimate.

10. Wolfhart Pannenberg has taken a similar line. *Jesus—God and Man*, trans. W. Wilkens and D. Priebe (Philadelphia: Westminster Press, 1968), pp. 33-34.

11. *The Secular Meaning of the Gospel*, p. 133.

12. H. Richard Niebuhr constantly reasoned against a rigidly Christocentric form of Christianity, for just this reason. See, e.g., *Radical Monotheism*, pp. 58 ff.

13. One is reminded of the dictum of Kirsopp Lake: "I see no reason for believing about Jesus what he did not himself believe." *Paul* (London: Christopher, 1934), p. 126.

14. *A New Quest of the Historical Jesus*, pp. 67-68. In the German edition of 1960 (*Kerygma und historischer Jesus* [Zürich: Zwingli-Verlag]) he speaks of the "Akt des Engagements," p. 85.

15. "How New Is the 'New Quest' of the Historical Jesus?" in *The Historical Jesus and the Kerygmatic Christ*, ed. Carl Braaten and Roy Harrisville (Nashville: Abingdon Press, 1964), pp. 236 ff.

16. This is not the place to explore the relation of revelation to understanding, except to note that I fail to see what the word "revelation" refers to if it does not include understanding (inclusion and equation are not identical, of course). Revelation occurs when one's understanding is restructured and one's response to God is reordered. Moreover, precisely because revelation of God is indirect it evokes reflection and includes perception and understanding. Pannenberg expressed sharply his criticism of the Word of God theology, which appeared at times to talk of immediate revelation of God through the Word. See his Introduction in *Revelation as History*, trans. David Granskou (New York: Macmillan, 1968; German ed., 1961), pp. 33 ff. Accordingly, Pannenberg, and his associates, insisted that the full, direct self-disclosure of God is yet to come and that in Jesus we have a proleptic form of it.

17. In accord with his emphasis on the importance of tradition-matrix for theological understanding, Pannenberg has stressed this also.

See *Jesus—God and Man*, p. 36. See also "The Revelation of God in Jesus of Nazareth" in *Theology as History* (New Frontiers in Theology III), ed. James M. Robinson and John B. Cobb, Jr. (New York: Harper, 1967), pp. 104 ff.

18. If one begins with God and moves to Jesus, one should ponder the point that the incarnation did not occur in a Roman senator or a Greek philosopher. That is, even when beginning with God, it is apparent that incarnation in a Jew was an act of fidelity to Israel—something not yet visible in the common formulation: God became man (any man would have served as well if humanity is the sole criterion). Karl Barth has seen this clearly. *Church Dogmatics: IV.1 The Doctrine of Reconciliation* (New York: Scribner's, 1956), p. 166: "The Word did not simply become any 'flesh.' . . . It became Jewish flesh."

19. For an interesting survey of the understanding of the kingdom of God in Kant, Fichte, Hegel, Schleiermacher, Rothe, and Ritschl (i.e., the pre-apocalyptic understanding), see Christian Walther, *Typen des Reich-Gottes-Verständnisse* "Forschungen zur Geschichte und Lehre des Protestantismus, 10th series, vol. 20" (Munich: Chr. Kaiser Verlag, 1961).

20. See Robinson, *A New Quest of the Historical Jesus*, p. 34.

21. This way of putting it reflects the conviction that the old formulations are not adequate: kingship, not kingdom; reign, not realm. Their inadequacy centers in the latent trend toward abstraction and away from God's reign over the world. It is difficult to conceive of a reign without a realm, just as it is to argue for generalship without an army. Surely God's reign is not a paper kingship analogous to the episcopal sees of certain of the Roman curia! The argument as developed here is largely parallel to (and independent of) Jürgen Moltmann, *Theology of Hope*, pp. 216 ff.

22. *Theology and the Kingdom of God* (Philadelphia: Fortress Press, 1969), p. 55.

23. Both fulfillment and revolution must be seen, lest the kingdom be understood in a Marcionitic sense—as if it were not the Creator's sovereignty with which one must reckon. This view is consonant with that of H. Richard Niebuhr (see n. 4) and with Pannenberg as well. *Jesus—God and Man*, pp. 229 ff.

24. This is forcefully and suggestively outlined by John Maguire in *The Dance of the Pilgrim* (New York: Association Press, 1968), Chap. 1.

25. Seemingly Genesis reflects concern with this theme as well. According to the younger creation story in Gen. 1, Yahweh gives animals *plants* to eat, flesh not being mentioned at all. The older story does not mention the creation of animals and hence ignores their diet as well.

26. This generalization must not obscure the complex development of motifs and images. The problem of death became especially pressing in the time of Daniel (165 B.C.E.) because of martyrdom. The theme of the transformation of nature is much older, perhaps older even than what is commonly designated as "apocalyptic." (Here one must reckon not only with the difference between the

age of the tradition and that of the text in which it now stands but with a still wanting precise definition of "apocalyptic.") Thus, the phrase quoted is from Isa. 11, but the same motif appears in Isa. 35 and 65 where it also is part of the overall transformation of the natural world. At what point these understandings were taken up into the idea of the two Aeons (this world and the world to come) is not readily ascertained. In its fuller form, this view asserts that the curse on the earth which resulted from Adamic disobedience would be lifted; indeed, paradise would be not only "restored" but surpassed. Implicit here is what also Paul takes for granted—that nature was affected by man's disobedience (Rom. 5:12 ff.). Therefore all creation is involved in redemption as well (Rom. 8:18-23). This entire theological syndrome merits sensitive re-examination. While Gordon Kaufman has undertaken to relate nature to redemption as well as to history, he has neglected coming to terms with this dimension of the motif. *Systematic Theology* (New York: Scribner's, 1968), Chap. 22.

27. In addition to the foregoing note, we also recall that the Seer on Patmos "saw" a new heaven and a new earth—an even more radical view (Rev. 21). Yet this is stated already in Isa. 65:17.

28. E.g., the pain of childbirth, which was traced to the curse (Gen. 3:16) is to be no more, and the arduous task of wresting a living from the soil (understood as a curse on the ground in Gen. 3:17 in contrast with the garden) will be replaced with fantastic productivity, and so forth. One should not be misled into a too hasty judgment that such views of the future were crass and materialistic, thereby denying that persons who used such images understood them as metaphors, on the one hand, or into overlooking the theological issue expressed in such language, on the other. One such motif is the conviction that no unaffected residue of paradise remains; that is, this theology thinks tragically of the whole creation not simply as an objectification of sensed guilt but as an expression of the conviction that nothing known to man is without need of redemption if God is truly to be God.

29. The allusion, of course, is to Paul (I Cor. 15:26), who deals with this as he reflects on the implications of Jesus' resurrection in a controversial situation. That death is an enemy was an ancient view already in Paul's time. It was not, of course, the only view, even in the Bible. The Epicureans, for example, saw it much as many do today—as simply the dissolution of that complex of atoms which temporarily constitutes the self. The older Hebrew view was that God created man mortal and that immortality was reserved for the divine, as Gen. 3 also implies. For a somewhat more extensive discussion, though far from adequate, see the contributions by Lou H. Silberman and myself to *Perspectives on Death*, L. O. Mills, ed. (Nashville: Abingdon Press, 1969).

30. Luke 17:21. This saying, whether one translates it as the kingdom is "among you" or "within you," is commonly used to buttress the claim that Jesus' view of the kingdom must be clearly differentiated from, if not contrasted with, apocalyptic. A thorough

treatment of this web of issues exceeds the requirements of this essay. Moreover, we have already indicated that our reflections do not require us to repristinate Jesus' actual thoughts and that it is sufficient to perceive the network in which it is at home and the direction of its thrust. Nevertheless, certain observations are in order and can be made generally. (1) One must not simply equate "apocalyptic theology" with the content of those documents known as "apocalypses," for apocalyptic horizons, assumptions, questions were found in writings far removed from apocalypses such as Enoch. Therefore the argument that Jesus was not apocalyptic because he did not, so far as we know, impart secrets about the future and its schedule, falls to the ground, for that is not what constitutes apocalyptic theology. (2) While the terminology "this age and the age to come" was not common on Jesus' lips, if it crossed them at all, he nevertheless assumes what apocalyptic theology assumes—that the coming of the kingdom means radical reversal (as in certain parables such as Mt. 20:1-6). (3) He understood his exorcistic work as a frontal, decisive attack on Satan and his hosts, the demons (e.g., Mk. 3:27), and associated this with the kingdom; such deeds were not simply acts of mercy. The power of Satan was a central obstacle to the kingdom of God in apocalyptic thought.

31. For a useful survey of this debate, see Victor Paul Furnish, "The Jesus-Paul Debate: From Baur to Bultmann," *BJRL* 47 (1965), 342-81.

32. "The Quest of the Historical Jesus," in *Studies of the Historical Jesus*, p. 23. Fuchs presses an existential reading of this observation so that, by exposing the essentially timeless structure of his response, it can become accessible to us today.

33. Zealots are not mentioned in Mt. 5:41, to be sure. But if the allusion is to the detested practice, then the anti-Zealot edge on the saying would not have been missed by those who were vulnerable to both Roman practice and to Zealotic pressure. Refusal to take a Zealot attitude is manifest also in Lk. 13:1-5, whether or not one should understand "Galileans" here as Zealots. S. G. F. Brandon does not really come to terms with these texts. Against the former he balances sayings such as "I did not come to bring peace but the sword"; the latter he glosses over with the observation that it is not clear that both incidents mentioned by Jesus were political. Certainly, the latter incident (the collapse of the tower) is not, but can this be used to obscure the political overtones of the statement that Pilate mingled the blood of Galileans with the blood of their sacrifices? *Jesus and the Zealots* (Manchester: Manchester University Press, 1967), p. 202, n. 5; p. 316, n. 6. One does not need to construe this reference as meaning a Zealotic insurrection in order to see that the Procurator's police action in the temple precincts, for whatever reason, was precisely the sort of thing which inflamed Zealotic passions. Unfortunately, Martin Hengel does not see this either. *Die Zeloten, AGSU* I (Leiden: Brill, 1961), pp. 57 ff., 344.

34. *Otherworldliness and the New Testament* (New York: Harper, 1954), pp. 83-93.
35. We cannot, and need not, explore here the several ways in which the two seemingly independent sides of Jesus' teaching have been treated. It will be sufficient to refer to Hans Windisch's work as a symptom of a clear analysis combined with unsatisfactory solutions. (*The Meaning of the Sermon on the Mount*, trans. S. Maclean Gilmour [Philadelphia: Westminster Press, 1951; German ed., 1937]). Windisch sees that the Sermon on the Mount as a whole is "conditioned in its entirety by eschatology" (p. 27), and that it includes at the same time sayings that are non-eschatological (e.g., the saying about salt and light or the Golden Rule). He also sees that this is true of the whole of Jesus' teaching (p. 39). Yet he is unable to show what this actually means theologically for the God of the kingdom. Amos Wilder presented a somewhat more adequate solution. He treats the eschatological factor as the ultimate sanction for moral renewal, and the wisdom factor as the fundamental sanction (the nature of God). It turns out, however, that the former is only a formal sanction and the latter the essential one. *Eschatology and Ethics in the Teachings of Jesus*, 2nd ed. (New York: Harper, 1950). Here it appears that the eschatological element functions mainly to impress upon hearers the seriousness of the demand for moral reform. Neither scholar succeeds in thinking theologically about the juxtaposition of the two motifs.
36. Recently, Helmut Flender has undertaken precisely this goal, arguing that given the tension between a this-worldly kingdom and the apocalyptist's view of the New Aeon in which present circumstances will be reversed, Jesus could have held but one view—the former. The latter, he thinks, has been assigned to him by the church. Characteristically, the case for the non-genuineness rests largely on logical "inconsistency" and above all is predicated on an untenable view of apocalyptic—as if apocalyptic had no concern for God the Creator of this world. *Die Botschaft Jesu von der Herrschaft Gottes* (Munich: Chr. Kaiser Verlag, 1968), Chap. 2.
37. The use of the terms "wisdom" and "apocalyptic" here is not to be pressed. They serve, rather, as convenient ways of contrasting those sayings which explicitly refer to eschatological motifs with those from which they are absent. The thesis that apocalyptic is itself a form of wisdom has been rejuvenated by von Rad. The adjudication of that intricate question does not affect our point here, except that if it should prove to be a valid hypothesis one could say not that Jesus brought the motifs together but that he exposed their interrelatedness in a way consistent with his mission. Gerhard von Rad, *Old Testament Theology*, trans. D. M. G. Stalker (New York: Harper, 1965), II, 301 ff. von Rad's hypothesis has been sharpened and carried forward by Peter von der Osten-Sacken, *Die Apokalyptik in ihrem Verhältnis zu Prophetie und Weisheit*, "Theologische Existenz Heute 157" (Munich: Chr. Kaiser Verlag, 1969).

255

38. I am pleased to find that Pannenberg has argued in a parallel way. *Jesus—God and Man*, pp. 229 ff. See also Hans Conzelmann's article, "Jesus Christus" in *RGG* [3] *III*, cols. 637 ff. for somewhat similar views.

39. Pannenberg points in the same direction when he writes, "God is the ultimate good not in isolated transcendency but in the future of his Kingdom. This means that the striving for God as the ultimate good beyond the world is turned into concern for the world." *Theology and the Kingdom of God*, p. 111.

40. This statement should not be read in a Brunnerian way, as if it assumed the "orders of creation." Rather, it simply calls attention to the fact that "creation" does not refer only to things but includes natural relationships and institutions as well, for "creation" is not only a way of speaking of absolute origination but includes the preservation of what has been made.

41. It is Bultmann who, more than anyone else, has emphasized separation from the world as a fundamental hallmark of salvation. In *Theology of the New Testament*, I, he says Jesus' preaching is directed not to the people (nation) but to individuals. Moreover, for Jesus "man is de-secularized [Entweltlicht] by God's direct pronouncement to him, which tears him out of all security of any kind and places him at the brink of the End. And God is 'de-secularized' by understanding His dealing eschatologically: He lifts man out of his worldly ties and places him directly before His own eyes." (P. 25) Even though this paragraph ends by saying that thereby man is "guided into his concrete encounter with his neighbor, in which he finds his true history," Bultmann never succeeds in understanding in a positive way one's relation to society and to cultural ties. They seem always in need of being overcome. (Jürgen Moltmann has stated sharply and analyzed critically the sociology of this mode of salvation. *Theology of Hope*, pp. 311 ff., 329.) Strangely Bultmann asserts that "whether or not we designate him [Jesus] as a Jew is a quibbling about words; at all events we cannot call him a Christian. As a historical figure he stands within Judaism; . . . not only his language and conceptuality are Jewish, but his eschatological proclamation as well as his ethical teaching are, by the very nature of the case, related to Jewish eschatology and legality, appropriate their problematic and are not at all conceivable apart from them." "The Primitive Christian Kerygma and the Historical Jesus," p. 19. But to assert all this is precisely *not* to quibble over words!

42. This point does not require us to show that Jesus regarded himself as personified Israel, etc.

43. Dorothee Sölle, speaking of the "provisional Christ," said that he "enables non-Jews to become Jews; that is to say, he enables them to live in postponement." *Christ the Representative*, p. 112.

44. This argument is loosely parallel to Pannenberg's contention that "only when all occurrence is ended can the divinity of God be known on the basis of the connection with history." *Theology as History*, p. 122.

45. Günther Bornkamm is content to say that Jesus went to carry his

mission to the center of Judaism in order to confront it with his summons to the kingdom. *Jesus of Nazareth*, p. 154. While he says Jesus' intent cannot be doubted, he does not say what the final decision he sought was, or how it was related to the course of events which must have transpired.

46. Lk. 12:50 presents intricate problems, partly because of its position in Luke, partly because of its relation to Mk. 10:38-39, partly because of its presumed content. The Nag Hammadi Gospel of Thomas (Log. 10, 16) suggests a complex transmission of this tradition, for only in Luke is the saying about the "baptism" joined to that about casting fire (and probably in the Lukan tradition). Scholarly observations about this saying turn out to be of remarkably little help. One thing is clear, however: Oscar Cullmann's view—here Jesus interpreted his own death as vicarious suffering, symbolized it in the saying about his baptism (pointing backward to the rite in the Jordan and forward to the impending end), and thereby laid the foundation for the Pauline doctrine of baptism in Rom. 6—is too ingenious to be persuasive. *Baptism in the New Testament*, SBT 1 (1950), 19-20; also *The Christology of the New Testament*, trans. S. C. Guthrie and C. A. M. Hall (Philadelphia: Westminster Press, 1959), p. 67. R. H. Fuller generally followed Cullmann in *The Mission and Achievement of Jesus*, SBT 12 (1959), 59 ff. Much more sound is George Beaseley-Murray, *Baptism in the New Testament* (London: Macmillan, 1963), pp. 72-77.

The most serious objection to the authenticity of Lk. 12:50 is whether the expression "to be baptized with a baptism" is possible in Hebrew or Aramaic (no parallels exist, to my knowledge), though this "internal accusative" is found in Hebrew and Aramaic. On this problem, see A. Oepke, *"Bapto"* in Kittel, ThWB I. The *Greek* papyrological data adduced by Moulton and Milligan should not be used to say, as they do, that the data show that Jesus spoke of his passion as a baptism (*The Vocabulary of the Greek Testament*, p. 102), though it is not proven that Jesus never used Greek. Since lexical and grammatical arguments have not been decisive, it may be wise to follow Jeremias, who regards it as a typical double metaphor (fire and water), and expresses no doubts about its genuineness. *The Parables of Jesus*, trans. S. H. Hook (New York: Scribner's, 1963, based on 6th German ed., 1962), pp. 163-64. See also Gerhard Delling, *"Baptisma baptisthenai,"* NovTest 2 (1958), 92-115.

47. In formulating the matter so cautiously, we take account of the problems in the foregoing note, and at the same time insist that we are not permitted to infer that Jesus interpreted his death as taking upon himself the role of the Suffering Servant. We are modestly concluding that the saying has good claims to being authentic Jesus-material and that we can use it to infer the fact that Jesus faced the likelihood of suffering and did not evade it. For our purpose, that is what matters. We are also rejecting Bultmann's view that "the greatest embarrassment to the attempts to reconstruct a portrait of Jesus is the fact that we cannot know

how Jesus understood his end, his death." "The Primitive Christian Kerygma and the Historical Jesus," p. 23. Led by the new quest, he assumes that the issue turns on grounding Christian theology in the mind of Jesus. This is precisely what is not as necessary as commonly asserted.

48. Pannenberg reminds us that in the Old Testament, repeatedly fulfillment of the prophetic word was not exactly what had been foretold. *Theology as History*, p. 122.

49. Is it coincidence that the theology of the "mighty acts of God" had its heyday precisely in the time when American power was at its zenith, when we could confidently point to the rescue at Dunkirk and Hitler's failure to invade England as confirmation in our own time? Is it accidental that it was the victors who celebrated this theology?

50. The use of "rightwising" to translate Paul's "justification" comes from my late colleague, Kendrick Grobel, who appropriated this old English term in his translation of Bultmann's *Theology of the New Testament*, vol. I.

51. A convenient place to survey the exegetical and theological issues as they have developed recently is the volume of essays edited by C. F. D. Moule, *The Significance of the Message of the Resurrection for Faith in Jesus Christ*, SBT 8 (2nd series) (Napierville, Ill.: Allenson, 1968).

52. Slenczka, moving along a different track of thought, points out that in the New Testament, Jesus' resurrection not only validates his previous earthly life but accents his ongoing role as acting subject. *Geschichtlichkeit und Personsein Jesu Christi*, pp. 328 ff.

53. The expression "he will rise" is virtually unique to Mark; the Matthean and Lukan parallels to Mk. 8:31; 9:31; 10:34 have "will be raised" (except the Lukan parallel to the last). So also I Cor. 15:4. Consonant with this emphasis on God's action is the form ὤφθη usually paraphrased "appeared," but which means literally "was made [by God] to be seen." So I Cor. 15:5 ff. For a recent examination of exegetical questions concerning the term ὤφθη see Gerhard Delling's contribution to the volume of essays edited by C. F. D. Moule, *The Significance of the Message of the Resurrection*, pp. 78 ff.

54. Pannenberg, *Jesus—God and Man*, pp. 225-26.

55. *Ibid.*, pp. 127-28; *Theology as History*, p. 114, where Pannenberg comments on the emphasis on the *self*-disclosure of God, emphasized in recent theology. Willi Marxsen objects to the interpretation of resurrection as the vindication of Jesus, largely, it seems, because he introduces a time factor into an essentially theological issue; that is, he misreads the argument so as to accuse it of making the life of Jesus a mere "prelude." See his essay in the volume edited by C. F. D. Moule, *The Significance of the Message of the Resurrection*, pp. 45-46.

56. I fail to see the basis for Moltmann's saying that because Jesus is called "the first fruits of those that slept" the understanding of his resurrection is no longer in an apocalyptic framework. Precisely

the opposite is the case. *Theology of Hope*, p. 193. The same observation holds true for his remarks on pp. 82-83.
57. Moltmann rightly distinguishes "word event" from promise. *Theology of Hope*, p. 85.
58. Karl Barth put it well: "To put it in the simplest way, what unites God and us men is that He does not will to be God without us, that He creates us rather to share with us . . . His own incomparable being and life and act, that He does not allow His history to be His and ours ours, but causes them to take place as a common history. That is the special truth which the Christian message has to proclaim at its very heart." *Church Dogmatics* IV, 1: *The Doctrine of Reconciliation* (New York: Scribner's, 1956), p. 7. This theme is developed in his popular *The Humanity of God* (Richmond: John Knox Press, 1960), Chap. 2.
59. E.g., Barth: "It is not that He first wills and works the being of the world and man, and then ordains it to salvation. But God creates, preserves and over-rules man for this prior end and with this prior purpose, that there may be a being distinct from Himself ordained for salvation." *Church Dogmatics* IV, 1, p. 9.
60. Robert W. Funk, *Language, Hermeneutic and Word of God* (New York: Harper, 1966), pp. 133, 135, resp. A somewhat parallel and highly suggestive book on the parables was published by Dan O. Via, *The Parables* (Philadelphia: Fortress Press, 1967).
61. By speaking of the parables as pointing to God and as the lens by which one looks Godward, I distance myself from Fuchs's view that as a language-event the kingdom of God comes with the parables. This emphasis is picked up also by James M. Robinson, who titles his brief essay "Jesus' Parables as God Happening," in *Jesus and the Historian* (Colwell Festschrift), ed. T. F. Trotter (Philadelphia: Westminster Press, 1968), pp. 134 ff. Hence he speaks of "the material role of the language itself in the actualizing of God's reign" (p. 143) and of "the event of Jesus' language in which God's reign happens as reality's true possibility" (p. 145). This claims too much for language. We recall, furthermore, Pannenberg's observation that "only in gnostic thought does Word appear as the bearer of a direct divine self-revelation." *Revelation as History*, p. 12. This natural capacity of language to make God present (or absent) has its roots in Heidegger, as is well known. But for precisely this reason, one should ponder the warnings sounded by Hans Jonas, "Heidegger and Theology" in *The Phenomenon of Life* (New York: Harper, 1966), pp. 235 ff.
62. Funk, *Language, Hermeneutic and Word of God*, p. 151.
63. *Ibid.*, p. 145.
64. Ernst Fuchs once formulated it well: "The special thing in Jesus' teaching proclamation is the analogical power with which Jesus makes himself, his obedience, the norm for his disciples' reflection without saying so." *Hermeneutik* 3rd ed. (Bad Cannstatt: R. Müllerschön Verlag, 1963), p. 228.

EPILOGUE

We may now reformulate the argument and suggest what appears to be part of the task ahead.

We engaged in conversations on so wide a front because emancipation required it. Concretely, one constant motif has been our concern to show that the way Lessing posed the question has proved to be a cul-de-sac because once the wedge was driven between the historically reconstructed Jesus and absolute faith, it was inevitable that either the historical study of Jesus be under pressure to show how Christian faith is indeed anchored in Jesus in a demonstrable way, or the results of stingent critical work be declared irrelevant to the Christian faith. Therefore the Word of God theology that dominated the middle years of this century appealed to the immediately self-attesting Word. Despite its much criticized Christomonism

261

in content, when viewed in terms of our question this response is to be seen as the most massive theology of the Spirit yet evolved, for everything rests on the immediately known Word, which excludes everything but acquiescence. British-based theology, on the other hand, continued to ground Christian theology in "the life of our Lord" largely by refusing to engage in thoroughgoing criticism of the Gospels. We have proposed a way of redirecting the discussion so as to avoid these alternatives. This is why we have not been in the least concerned to argue the authenticity of this or that saying in order to be able to salvage the tradition by anchoring it in the mind of Jesus, but have been concerned, on the other hand, to insist that thorough criticism of the Gospels does provide us with sufficient data about Jesus that the contour of his life as a whole can come into view, and that this can be the core of Christian preaching and the dominant datum with which theology works. By emphasizing the non–self-validation of the historical Jesus and, conversely, his capacity to concentrate decisive questions about God and man, we have sought to allow the past event of Jesus to retain its own integrity while making him central to the preaching and reflection of the Christian community.

Ours is not the only proposal attempted, for the new hermeneutic has also undertaken to work out an alternative to the inherited problem. Without in the least being ungrateful for its initiative in moving beyond Bultmann, we must nonetheless find an alternative to the new hermeneutic as well. First, because the new hermeneutic is set in motion by the concern to ground Christian self-understanding in Jesus' own understanding of the self, it is unable to let Jesus be truly independent of the church and sovereign of it; that is, it is too vulnerable to making Jesus its ideological construct. Second, and more important, by restricting the significance of Jesus to what came to expression in his words and deeds, the new hermeneutic has not yet been able to accord Jesus' execution the place it always enjoyed in Christian theology. Yet, this is the climax of the historical Jesus, and therefore the point from which point to the celebrative response to Jesus, or the way we have sought a way to rehabilitate the use of the whole Jesus in preaching and reflection. It would repay one amply to investigate the history of theology to ascertain who the bedfellows turn out to be who concentrate on the words of Jesus!

In proposing our alternative, we have not only worked toward a fuller understanding of the content of the name "Jesus" but have also attempted to recast the categories by which we speak appropriately of our religious relation to him. Accordingly, we have spoken of trust as the proper way to respond to Jesus, claiming that trusting Jesus launches a salvific process and a clarification of our understanding of God. As was pointed out at the outset, no claim is being entered to the effect that this is the sole way of speaking about one's relation to Jesus. Nor has the full potential of trust been explored here. Important motifs could (and should) be developed in ways consistent with the motif of trust. Among them are the place of the church as the community in which trust is sustained and nurtured, and the sacraments as the acts by which one declares his identification with Jesus and pledges his fidelity. I would also insist that "trust" as a fundamental category can and must be supplemented by other modes of discourse, such as hope or love. After all, a word or a motif is but a window through which one looks into reality and sees some things clearly; no word or category allows one to see everything. It would also repay one to consider carefully a range of words and categories which point to the celebrative response to Jesus, or the way in which trust releases one's initiative and freedom to act responsibly in the world. Trust, as here developed, is not to be understood as passivity, as sheer steadfastness in adversity; actually, when grounded in trust in God, man's activity is also part of the glory of God. Hence one could explore with profit how repentance is an activity set in motion by appropriating Jesus as the paradigm. The development of these themes could not be included in this book, already long and complex. It must simply be noted that they can be developed out of what has been said here.

Another motif that has undergirded the entire argument is my conviction that today the chief theological questions are more moral than ontic and epistemological. Put tersely, given the gross exploitation of man by man, the massacre of children, and the growing impoverishment of the poor of the earth, the Christian message and its theology forfeit the right to be heard if they become so preoccupied with the problems of being, of knowing being, and of right ways of speaking of being that they assume that believing in God at all is self-evidently a moral act. The chief question today is whether God can be counted on to keep faith with his creation, whether in the last instance that reality to which the word "God" points has the kind of integrity on which men can rely. Actually this is the form that the ontological and epistemological question of God should take. If God's freedom and integrity cannot be affirmed, then what reason remains—other than the momentum of scholastic inquiry—to be theologians at all? In working out a theological stance oriented toward the moral integrity of God, moreover, faith and ethics become two sides of the same coin. If the integrity of God is affirmed on the basis of Jesus, then the fundamental mode of Christian existence is not fulfillment of frustrated potential so much as discipleship or participation in rectification. In this way, perhaps, the massive and pervasive internalization of faith can be overcome. To make these somewhat strident observations is not to declare the ontological side of theology out of bounds, just as returning to the Old Testament angle of vision is not to be declared a Rechabite move by those who enjoy the Greek academy. As I have tried to indicate, albeit briefly, the ontic question emerges inescapably, and legitimately, as soon as one insists on ascertaining the ground in Jesus and in man for the salvific relationship. The fact that biblical theologians did not think in ontic terms does make it illegitimate to do so. Still, given today's preoccupation with this mode of doing theology, the paramount need is to rejuvenate the possibility of pressing the moral dimension. In our time, it is the moral enigma which raises the theological question in our culture as a whole; to leave it unaddressed, or to subsume it as a sub-category of the problems of being is, in my judgment, no longer justifiable.

Finally, one thing has become increasingly clear in the development of this book: both New Testament students and systematic theologians would do well to attend seriously the work done in Chicago decades ago. I have no interest in re-pristinating the work of Shailer Mathews and Shirley Jackson Case, for example; but it is ever more clear that in their own way they addressed the theological problems that they detected in the American experience, and did so with a clarity and conviction sadly lacking in the derivative theology in vogue since World War II. For them the paramount task was not restating the catechisms of the Reformation but of making the historical-critical enterprise in theology fruitful so that the whole life of man might be healed. To put it in dogmatic terms, they were interested not only in justification but also in sanctification—the tokens of life healed by God. They surmised, I believe, that a self deciding always and repeatedly against the world was no real self but an abstracted self turned inward. They perceived that man is social and that he lives his life in structures and institutions that cannot simply be designated "world" to be overcome by deciding selves. In any case, whatever their limitations—and they are real, especially their inability to appreciate the bastardy of man—they yet have something to teach us. Furthermore, perhaps because they were more concerned to address their culture than to squabble with other theologians they also had something to say and the capacity to say it clearly. They were alert to the interplay of faith and culture, and so did not regard historicity as a dragon to be slain. In short, a further task is to make the sociology of knowledge fruitful in theology, not as a reductionist procedure but as a way of ascertaining the folk religion, in and out of the university environment, against which Christian trust in Jesus struggles because of its fidelity to Jesus, who is the paradigm for man and the parable of God.

INDEX

Achtemeier, P., 45 *n* 37; 98 *n* 95

Adam, K., 90 *n* 36

Albright, W. F., 94 *n* 61

Althaus, P., 151 *n* 78; 201 *n* 46

Aner, K., 83 *n* 3

Barth, K., 53; 89 *n* 31; 90 *n* 36; 92 *n* 48; 169; 195 *n* 12; 198 *n* 21; 200 *n* 37; 220; 252 *n* 18; 259 *n* 58, *n* 59

Bartsch, H. W., 94 *n* 61

Bauer, W., 43 *n* 23

Beaseley-Murray, G., 257 *n* 46

Bell, D., 136 *n* 9

Berger, P., 93 *n* 51; 94 *n* 60

Betz, H. D., 43 *n* 26; 151 *n* 75; 205 *n* 64

Blackham, H. J., 93 *n* 51

Boers, H. W., 139 *n* 24

Bolewski, H., 58

Bornkamm, G., 34; 42 *nn* 16-17; 43 *n* 18; 46 *n* 43; 90 *n* 36; 93 *n* 54; 94 *n* 61; 98 *n* 96, *n* 99; 142 *n* 39; 256 *n* 45

Bousset, W., 65; 98 *n* 100; 143 *n* 40

Bowman, J., 140 *n* 27

Bowman, J. W., 140 *n* 29

Braaten, C., 41 *n* 8; 90 *n* 36

267

Brandon, S. G. F., 41 n 5; 254 n 33
Braun, H., 42 n 12
Brown, J., 84 n 7
Brown, R. E., 44 n 28
Bruce, F. F., 140 n 28
Bultmann, R., 19; 30-31; 34; 41 n 12; 45 n 34; 46 n 43; 48; 50-58; 60-62; 65; 67; 70; 86 n 11, nn 13-15; 87 n 18, n 21; 88 n 23, n 26, n 28; 89 n 29, n 31, n 32; 90 nn 36-38; 91 nn 43-45, n 47; 92 n 49; 93 n 52, n 59; 94 nn 60-63, n 66; 96 n 81; 99 n 104; 108-9; 126-29; 135 n 3; 141 n 33; 143 n 40; 144 n 43; 151 n 78; 164; 174; 185; 239; 249 n 2; 256 n 41; 257 n 47
Burton, E. D., 148 n 54

Cadbury, H. J., 42 n 16
Caird, G., 145 n 46
Cairns, D., 87 n 18; 91 n 44
Campbell, R., 85 n 10
Chadwick, H., 83 n 2; 143 n 39
Colpe, C., 145 n 43
Conzelmann, H., 42 n 16; 137 n 17; 256 n 38
Cox, H., 104
Cullmann, O., 138 n 19; 257 n 46
Cushman, R., 201 n 45

Danielou, J., 141 n 31
Daube, D., 140 n 27
de Faye, E., 149 n 62
Delekat, F., 200 n 35
Delling, G., 257 n 46; 258 n 53
Dibelius, M., 92 n 46; 137 n 15, n 16; 139 n 25; 140 n 28; 142 n 38; 145 n 46
Diem, H., 85 n 8, n 10; 88 n 24

Dodd, C. H., 44 n 29, n 31; 109; 137 n 15; 141 n 31; 142 n 36; 143 n 39; 205 n 67; 220; 244
Dovring, K., 135 n 4; 136 n 8
Drijvers, J. W., 145 n 45

Ebeling, G., 9; 60-62; 64-67; 71; 78; 94 n 64; 95 n 72, n 73, n 76; 96 n 77, n 79, n 82; 97 n 87, n 88, n 90, n 91; 98 n 99, n 100, n 103; 116; 121; 167; 194 n 5, n 10; 205 n 66; 220-21; 235
Eisler, R., 40 n 5
Ellul, J., 104; 135 n 5, n 6; 136 n 9, n 10, n 12, n 14

Farley, E., 135 n 3
Farmer, W., 29; 44 n 30
Farrer, A., 45 n 32
Ferré, N., 148 n 55
Fischer-Appelt, P., 195 n 13
Flender, H., 255 n 36
Frank, E., 51
Fuchs, E., 25; 31; 62-65; 67; 70; 96 n 80, n 81; 97 n 88, n 95; 98 n 99, n 100; 99 n 104; 100; 121; 152 n 80; 163-64; 167; 205 n 69; 220-21; 223; 235; 254 n 32; 259 n 61, n 64
Fuller, R. H., 31; 138 n 18, n 23; 140 n 29; 147 n 48, n 51; 257 n 46
Funk, R. W., 97 n 88; 244-45; 259 n 60, n 62, n 63
Furnish, V., 254 n 31

Gärtner, B., 142 n 38
Georgi, D., 43 n 26
Gese, H., 206 n 74
Gilkey, L., 193 n 1; 199 n 29, n 30; 249 n 4

Gollwitzer, H., 193 *n* 2; 199 *n* 33, *n* 35; 200 *n* 36; 201 *n* 40, *n* 41

Grant, R. M., 149 *n* 62

Grässer, E., 149 *n* 59

Grobel, K., 43 *n* 24; 149 *n* 61; 258 *n* 50

Gustafson, J., 206 *n* 70

Haenchen, E., 43 *n* 21; 45 *n* 40; 87 *n* 18

Hahn, F., 138 *n* 18, *n* 23

Hamilton, W., 135 *n* 2

Harnack, A., 41 *n* 6; 53; 92 *n* 47, *n* 49; 95 *n* 72

Harris, R., 141 *n* 31

Hartmann, W., 206 *n* 71

Harvey, V., 21; 41 *n* 11; 86 *n* 12; 127; 204 *n* 60, *n* 61; 217

Hasenhüttl, G., 89 *n* 32; 90 *n* 36

Heidegger, M., 86 *n* 12; 90 *n* 36; 93 *n* 51; 97 *n* 88; 259 *n* 61

Heitmüller, W., 143 *n* 40

Henderson, I., 90 *n* 36

Hengel, M., 254 *n* 33

Herrmann, W., 52-53; 65; 98 *n* 100; 162-69; 171-72; 175; 181; 194 *n* 11; 195 *nn* 12-14; 196 *nn* 15-18; 198 *nn* 20-22; 249 *n* 2

Herzog, F., 249 *n* 4

Hodgson, P., 46 *n* 45

Holcomb, H., 198 *nn* 24-27; 199 *n* 29, *n* 31

Holloway, J., 136 *n* 13

Hooker, M., 140 *n* 29

Jeremias, J., 25; 40 *n* 1; 43 *n* 23; 45 *n* 32, *n* 38; 58-60; 65; 67; 95 *n* 69, *n* 70; 96 *n* 82; 137 *n* 17; 140 *n* 29; 257 *n* 46

Jonas, H., 149 *n* 63; 259 *n* 61

Kähler, M., 19; 24; 41 *n* 7, *n* 8; 46 *n* 47; 47; 180; 202 *n* 50

Käsemann, E., 40 *n* 1; 45 *n* 41; 46 *n* 44; 88 *n* 21; 89 *n* 32; 95 *n* 70, *n* 71; 100; 146 *n* 48

Kaufman, G., 153 *n* 84; 193 *n* 4; 206 *n* 72; 253 *n* 26

Kaufman, W., 99 *n* 107

Keck, L. E., 40 *n* 3; 43 *n* 17; 98 *n* 96; 151 *n* 75; 253 *n* 29

Kelsey, D., 175; 202 *n* 53; 203 *n* 54; 204 *n* 62

Kierkegaard, S., 49; 52-53; 57; 64; 83 *nn* 6-10; 87 *n* 14; 94 *n* 65; 109

Knox, J., 32; 205 *n* 65

Knox, W., 148 *n* 54

Koester, H., 45 *n* 33; 151 *n* 71

Körner, J., 93 *n* 52

Kumazawa, Y., 90 *n* 36

Laeuchli, S., 151 *n* 72

Lake, K., 251 *n* 13

Larson, A., 136 *n* 7

Lessing, G., 18; 40 *n* 4; 48; 49; 57; 64; 83 *n* 2, *n* 5; 84 *n* 7; 94 *n* 63; 164; 177; 181; 198 *n* 20; 202 *n* 52; 249 *n* 2

Lindars, B., 141 *n* 30, *n* 31; 142 *n* 37; 149 *n* 58

Luz, U., 151 *n* 75

McKenzie, J., 89 *n* 31

MacQuarrie, J., 93 *n* 51

Maguire, J., 252 *n* 24

Manson, T. W., 44 *n* 31

Marcel, G., 47; 99 *n* 105

Marcus, H., 194 *n* 8

Marle, R., 86 *n* 12; 90 *n* 36

Martin, R. P., 146 *n* 48

Martyn, J. L., 141 *n* 32; 152 *n* 82

Marxsen, W., 42 *n 16*; 152 *n 80*; 258 *n 55*
Michel, O., 149 *n 59*
Mollegen, A. T., 202 *n 51*
Moltmann, J., 220; 239; 250 *n 8*; 252 *n 21*; 256 *n 41*; 258 *n 56*; 259 *n 57*
Montefiore, H., 148 *n 57*
Moule, C. F. D., 139 *n 24*; 258 *n 51*

Niebuhr, H. R., 47; 70; 154; 184; 207 *n 76*; 208; 250 *n 5*; 251 *n 9*, *n 12*; 252 *n 23*
Niebuhr, Reinhold, 193 *n 2*, *n 4*; 220
Niebuhr, R. R., 204 *n 63*; 205 *n 65*
Nineham, D. E., 45 *n 31*
Nock, A. D., 145 *n 45*; 147 *n 48*
Norden, E., 142 *n 38*
Norris, R. A., 150 *n 64*; 193 *n 1*

Oepke, A., 257 *n 46*
Ogden, S., 41 *n 11*; 86 *n 12*; 90 *n 36*; 91 *n 40*, *n 41*; 166; 217
Ogletree, T., 92 *n 48*
Opocensky, M., 194 *n 10*

Pannenberg, W., 46 *n 45*; 93 *n 54*; 98 *n 101*; 208; 220-21; 239; 251 *n 10*, *n 16*, *n 17*; 252 *n 23*; 256 *n 38*, *n 39*, *n 44*; 258 *n 48*, *n 55*; 259 *n 61*
Pelikan, J., 150 *n 70*
Perrin, N., 42 *n 16*; 43 *n 20*; 45 *n 41*; 94 *n 60*; 197 *n 18*; 205 *n 67*
Pesch, R., 43 *n 18*
Petrie, C. S., 45 *n 32*

Quispel, G., 145 *n 44*; 149 *n 62*

Reidinger, O., 200 *n 35*
Reimarus, H. S., 18-19; 27; 40 *n 4*, *n 5*; 127; 138 *n 19*
Rese, M., 140 *n 29*
Rhode, J., 42 *n 16*
Ricoeur, P., 160; 194 *n 9*
Ritschl, D., 94 *n 67*; 154
Roberts, T. A., 84 *n 5*
Robinson, J. M., Jr., 41 *n 11*; 42 *n 12*, *n 13*; 43 *n 19*, *n 21*; 46 *n 45*; 86 *n 12*; 92 *n 49*; 95 *n 70*; 109; 134; 138 *n 22*; 142 *n 36*; 149 *n 60*; 152 *n 80*; 163; 197 *n 19*; 216; 251 *n 14*; 259 *n 61*
Rordorf, W., 87 *n 18*

Sanders, E., 43 *n 25*
Sawyerr, H., 45 *n 31*
Schleiermacher, F., 18; 32; 40 *n 2*; 65; 89 *n 32*; 169; 175; 201 *n 47*; 217; 249 *n 2*
Schlier, H., 145 *n 46*
Schmithals, W., 86 *n 12*; 90 *n 40*; 91 *n 42*; 144 *n 43*
Schnackenburg, R., 147 *n 50*, *n 52*
Schneemelcher, W., 43 *n 22*
Schniewind, J., 93 *n 54*, *n 58*
Schottroff, L., 150 *n 70*
Schulz, S., 88 *n 21*; 151 *n 74*
Schweitzer, A., 17; 19; 41 *n 7*; 143 *n 39*; 220
Schweizer, E., 42 *n 16*; 137 *n 16*; 148 *n 56*
Scroggs, R., 194 *n 7*
Silberman, L., 141 *n 30*; 253 *n 29*
Slenczka, R., 249 *n 2*, *n 3*; 258 *n 52*
Smith, D. M., Jr., 202 *n 48*; 203 *n 56*
Sölle, D., 170-73; 176; 199 *n 35*; 200 *n 36*, *n 37*, *n 38*; 201 *n 39*; 240; 256 *n 43*

Stauffer, E., 90 *n* 36
Stendahl, K., 141 *n* 30
Strauss, D. F., 18; 84 *n* 7; 201
    n 47; 249 *n* 2
Strecker, G., 152 *n* 81
Stuhlmacher, P., 144 *n* 40

Talbert, C., 40 *n* 4
Tasker, R. V. G., 139 *n* 27
Tillich, P., 101; 150 *n* 64; 151
    n 77; 152 *n* 78; 173-76; 180;
    201 *nn* 42-45, *n* 47; 202
    nn 49-53; 203 *nn* 54-56;
    204 *n* 58; 211; 216
Troeltsch, E., 53; 92 *n* 48

van Buren, P., 166-70; 172; 198
    n 23, *n* 25; 199 *n* 28, *n* 30,
    n 32, *n* 34; 206 *n* 72; 212;
    213

Verheyden, J. C., 40 *n* 2
Via, D. O., 86 *n* 12; 259 *n* 60
Vielhauer, P., 46 *n* 42
Voelkel, R., 98 *n* 100; 195 *n* 13
von der Osten-Sacken, P., 255
    n 37
von Rad, G., 255 *n* 37

Walther, Chr., 252 *n* 19
Weiss, J., 41 *n* 7; 196 *n* 18; 220
Whitton, J., 136 *n* 7
Wilckens, U., 137 *n* 16; 153
    n 83
Wilder, A., 197 *n* 18; 224; 255
    n 35
Williams, N. P., 193 *n* 3
Windisch, H., 255 *n* 35
Winter, P., 41 *n* 5
Wrede, W., 22; 41 *n* 7; 143
    n 40